MW01070926

SENDEROS 1A

Spanish for a Connected World

Boston, Massachusetts

On the cover: Viejo San Juan, Puerto Rico.

Publisher: José A. Blanco
Editorial Development: Armando Brito, Jhonny Alexander Calle, Deborah Coffey, María Victoria Echeverri, Jo Hanna Kurth, Megan Moran, Jaime Patiño, Raquel Rodríguez, Verónica Tejeda, Sharla Zwirek
Project Management: Sally Giangrande, Tiffany Kayes
Rights Management: Ashley Poreda, Annie Pickert Fuller
Technology Production: Egle Gutiérrez, Jamie Kostecki, Reginald Millington, Fabián Montoya, Paola Ríos Schaaf
Design: Radoslav Mateev, Gabriel Noreña, Andrés Vanegas
Production: Oscar Díez, Adriana Jaramillo

Student Text (Casebound-SIMRA) ISBN: 978-1-68005-628-0

Teacher's Edition ISBN: 978-1-68005-630-3

Library of Congress Control Number: 2017949931

1 2 3 4 5 6 7 8 9 TC 22 21 20 19 18 17

Printed in Canada.

SENDEROS 1A

Spanish for a Connected World

Table of Contents

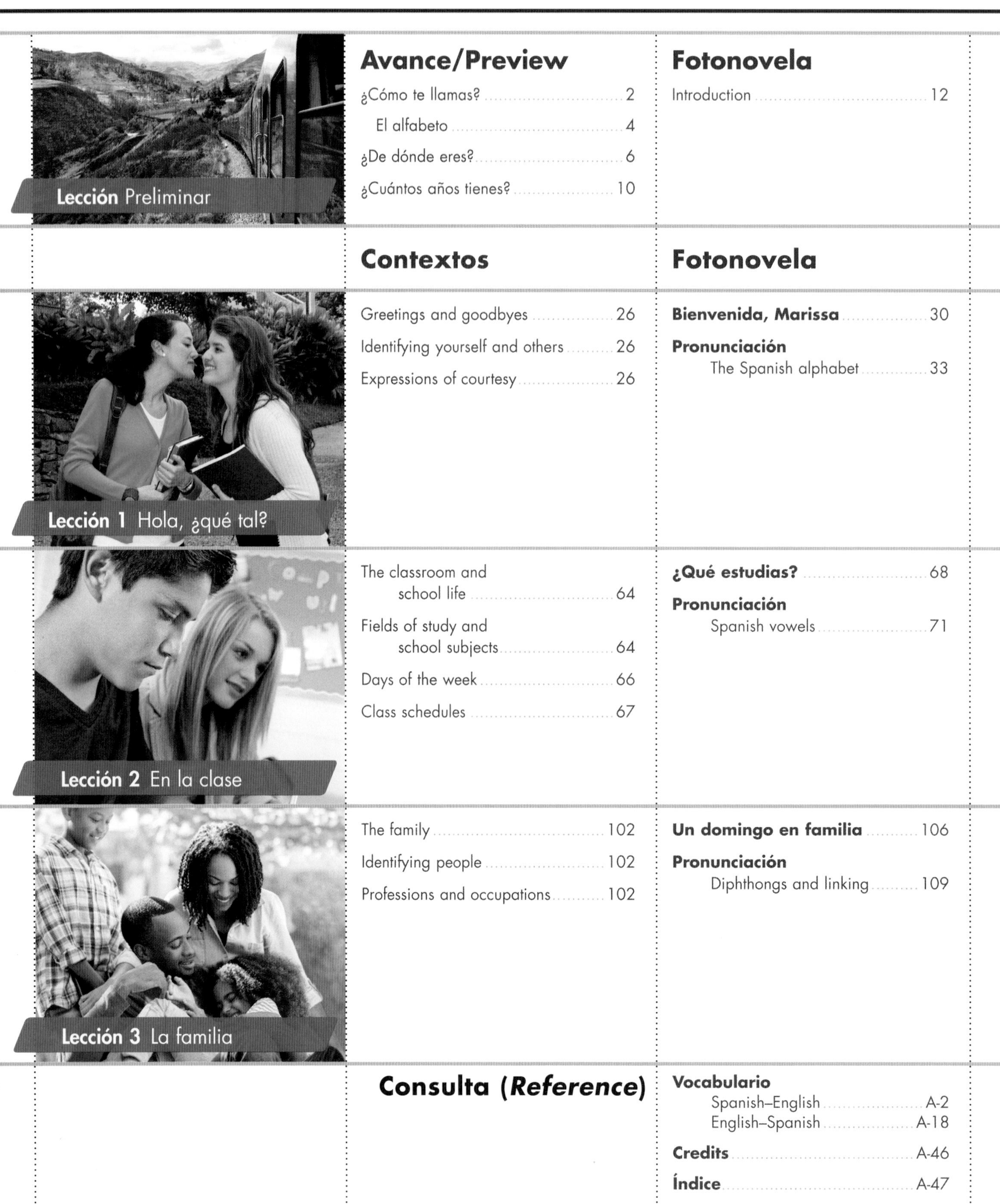

Cultura

Avance/Preview

Síntesis

Cultura

Estructura

Adelante

Icons

Familiarize yourself with these icons that appear throughout **Senderos**.

- Listening activity/section
- Pair activity
- Group activity

The Spanish-Speaking World

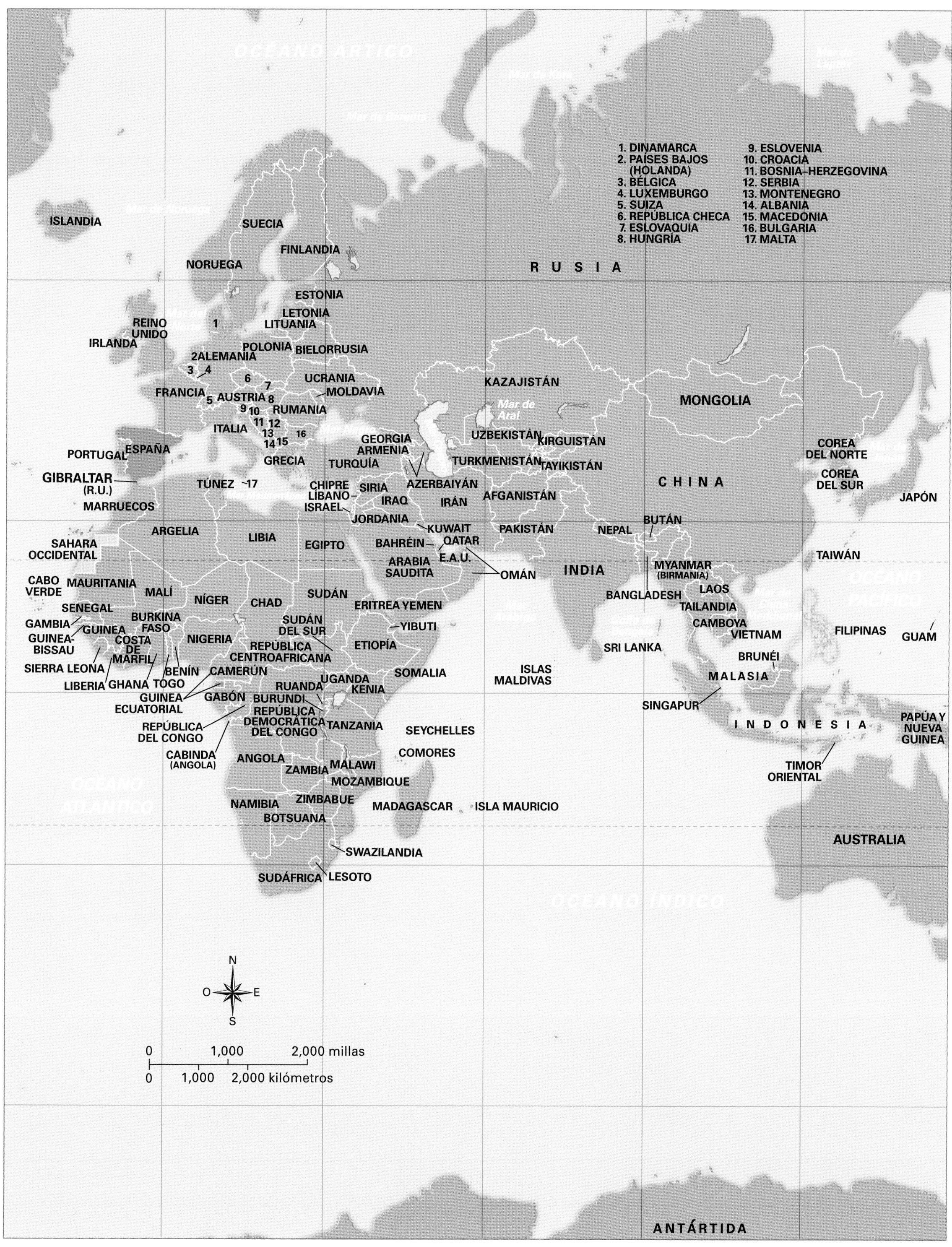

OCÉANO ÁRTICO
Mar de Kara
Mar de Laptev
Mar de Barents
Mar de Noruega
ISLANDIA
SUECIA
FINLANDIA
NORUEGA
RUSIA
1. DINAMARCA
2. PAÍSES BAJOS (HOLANDA)
3. BÉLGICA
4. LUXEMBURGO
5. SUIZA
6. REPÚBLICA CHECA
7. ESLOVAQUIA
8. HUNGRÍA
9. ESLOVENIA
10. CROACIA
11. BOSNIA-HERZEGOVINA
12. SERBIA
13. MONTENEGRO
14. ALBANIA
15. MACEDONIA
16. BULGARIA
17. MALTA
ESTONIA
LETONIA
LITUANIA
REINO UNIDO
Mar del Norte
IRLANDA
POLONIA
BIELORRUSIA
ALEMANIA
UCRANIA
MOLDAVIA
FRANCIA
AUSTRIA
RUMANIA
ITALIA
Mar Negro
KAZAJISTÁN
Mar de Aral
MONGOLIA
UZBEKISTÁN
KIRGUISTÁN
GEORGIA
ARMENIA
PORTUGAL
ESPAÑA
GRECIA
TURQUÍA
TURKMENISTÁN
TAYIKISTÁN
COREA DEL NORTE
Mar del Japón
COREA DEL SUR
GIBRALTAR (R.U.)
TÚNEZ
CHIPRE
SIRIA
AZERBAIYÁN
CHINA
JAPÓN
LÍBANO
ISRAEL
Mar Mediterráneo
IRAQ
IRÁN
AFGANISTÁN
MARRUECOS
JORDANIA
KUWAIT
BUTÁN
ARGELIA
LIBIA
EGIPTO
BAHRÉIN
QATAR
PAKISTÁN
NEPAL
SAHARA OCCIDENTAL
E.A.U.
TAIWÁN
ARABIA SAUDITA
MYANMAR (BIRMANIA)
CABO VERDE
MAURITANIA
MALÍ
OMÁN
INDIA
OCÉANO PACÍFICO
NÍGER
CHAD
SUDÁN
BANGLADESH
LAOS
SENEGAL
ERITREA
YEMEN
TAILANDIA
Mar de China Meridional
GAMBIA
BURKINA FASO
Mar Arábigo
Golfo de Bengala
GUINEA
SUDÁN DEL SUR
YIBUTI
CAMBOYA
GUINEA-BISSAU
COSTA DE MARFIL
NIGERIA
VIETNAM
FILIPINAS
GUAM
REPÚBLICA CENTROAFRICANA
ETIOPÍA
SRI LANKA
BRUNÉI
SIERRA LEONA
BENÍN
CAMERÚN
SOMALIA
ISLAS MALDIVAS
MALASIA
LIBERIA
GHANA
TOGO
UGANDA
RUANDA
KENIA
GUINEA ECUATORIAL
GABÓN
BURUNDI
SINGAPUR
REPÚBLICA DEMOCRÁTICA DEL CONGO
TANZANIA
SEYCHELLES
INDONESIA
PAPÚA Y NUEVA GUINEA
REPÚBLICA DEL CONGO
COMORES
CABINDA (ANGOLA)
ANGOLA
MALAWI
ZAMBIA
TIMOR ORIENTAL
MOZAMBIQUE
OCÉANO ATLÁNTICO
NAMIBIA
ZIMBABUE
MADAGASCAR
ISLA MAURICIO
BOTSUANA
AUSTRALIA
SWAZILANDIA
SUDÁFRICA
LESOTO
OCÉANO ÍNDICO
N
O
E
S
0 1,000 2,000 millas
0 1,000 2,000 kilómetros
ANTÁRTIDA

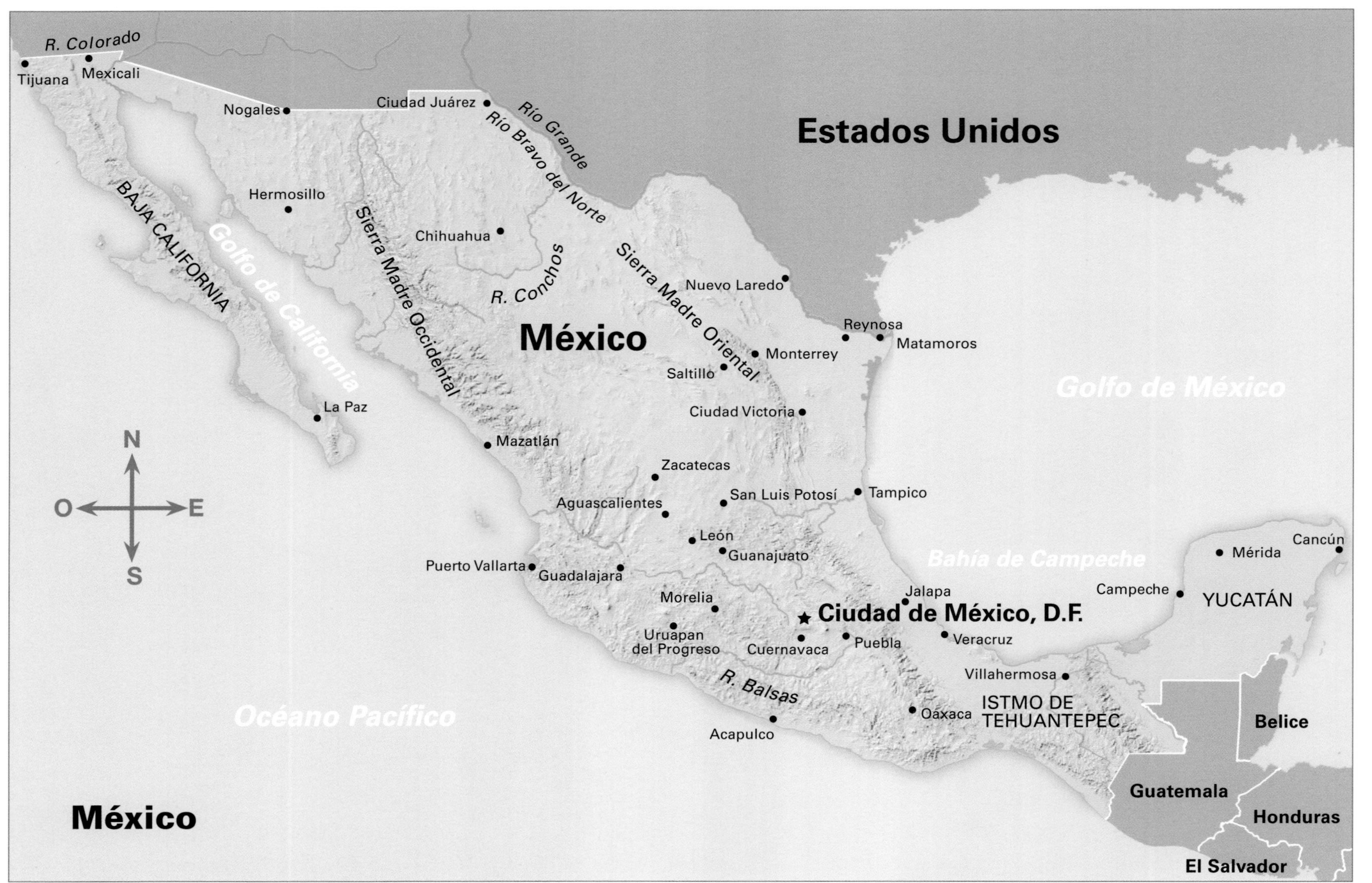
R. Colorado
Tijuana
Mexicali
Nogales
Ciudad Juárez
Río Grande
Río Bravo del Norte
Estados Unidos
Hermosillo
BAJA CALIFORNIA
Golfo de California
Sierra Madre Occidental
Chihuahua
R. Conchos
Sierra Madre Oriental
Nuevo Laredo
México
Reynosa
Matamoros
Monterrey
Saltillo
Golfo de México
La Paz
Ciudad Victoria
N
Mazatlán
Zacatecas
O
E
San Luis Potosí
Tampico
Aguascalientes
León
Guanajuato
Bahía de Campeche
Mérida
Cancún
Puerto Vallarta
Guadalajara
Jalapa
Campeche
YUCATÁN
S
Morelia
Ciudad de México, D.F.
Uruapan del Progreso
Cuernavaca
Puebla
Veracruz
Villahermosa
R. Balsas
Océano Pacífico
Oaxaca
ISTMO DE TEHUANTEPEC
Belice
Acapulco
Guatemala
Honduras
México
El Salvador

Central America and the Caribbean

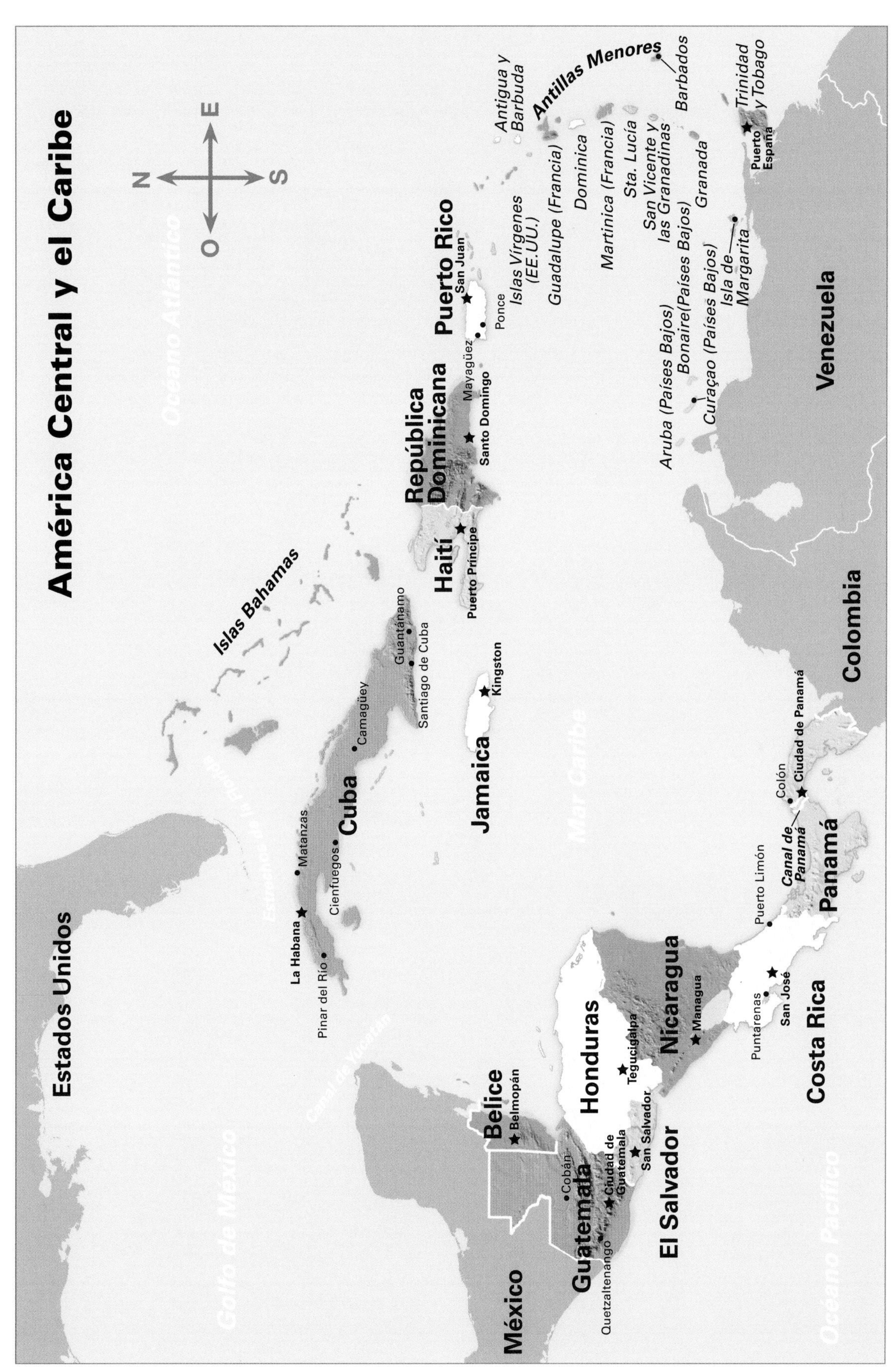

Mar Caribe
Barranquilla
Maracaibo
Caracas
Puerto España
Trinidad y Tobago
Venezuela
R. Orinoco
Georgetown
Paramaribo
Guyana
Cayena
Surinam
Guayana Francesa
Medellín
Colombia
Bogotá
Cali
Pasto
Quito
Ecuador
Guayaquil
R. Negro
R. Amazonas
Belém
Manaus
Iquitos
Perú
R. Madeira
Cordillera de los Andes
Recife
Lima
Cuzco
Lago Titicaca
Salvador
Brasil
Brasilia
Arequipa
La Paz
Bolivia
R. Paraguay
Arica
Sucre
Iquique
Océano Pacífico
R. Paraná
Belo Horizonte
São Paulo
Rio de Janeiro
Santos
Antofagasta
Salta
Paraguay
Asunción
Chile
R. Uruguay
Córdoba
Pôrto Alegre
Mendoza
Valparaíso
Rosario
Santiago
Uruguay
Buenos Aires
Montevideo
Argentina
Concepción
Bahía Blanca
Océano Atlántico
Puerto Montt
N
O
E
S
Estrecho de Magallanes
Islas Malvinas
Punta Arenas
Tierra del Fuego
América del Sur
Islas Galápagos
Océano Pacífico
Isla Pinta
Isla Marchena
Isla Genovesa
Isla Isabela
Línea ecuatorial
Volcán Darwin
Isla Santiago
(San Salvador)
Isla Fernandina
Puerto Ayora
Isla San Cristóbal
Isla Santa Cruz
Santo Tomás
Puerto Baquerizo Moreno
Isla Santa María
Isla Española

Mar Cantábrico
Francia
Pirineos
Andorra
Gijón
Avilés
Santander
San Sebastián
La Coruña
Oviedo
CANTABRIA
Bilbao
GALICIA
ASTURIAS
PAÍS VASCO
Pamplona
NAVARRA
Pontevedra
Burgos
LA RIOJA
CATALUÑA
Gerona
Vigo
Palencia
Océano Atlántico
Zamora
Valladolid
Lérida
Zaragoza
Braga
CASTILLA-LEÓN
Barcelona
Oporto
Tarragona
Salamanca
Segovia
España
ARAGÓN
Ávila
Madrid
Coimbra
COMUNIDAD VALENCIANA
Serra da Estrela
Toledo
Islas Baleares
Menorca
Cáceres
Valencia
Palma de Mallorca
Portugal
EXTREMADURA
CASTILLA-LA MANCHA
Mallorca
Mérida
Ibiza
Lisboa
Badajoz
Albacete
Setúbal
Formentera
Sierra Morena
Alicante
Mar Mediterráneo
Córdoba
Jaén
Murcia
ANDALUCÍA
Cartagena
Huelva
Sevilla
Granada
Sierra Nevada
Almería
Málaga
Cádiz
Algeciras
Gibraltar (R.U.)
Estrecho de Gibraltar
Ceuta (Esp.)
Melilla (Esp.)
Marruecos
N
O
E
S
Islas Canarias
La Palma
Santa Cruz de la Palma
Lanzarote
Tenerife
Santa Cruz de Tenerife
Arrecife
Gomera
Puerto del Rosario
Hierro
Las Palmas de Gran Canaria
Fuerteventura
Gran Canaria
Marruecos
Océano Atlántico

The Spanish-Speaking World

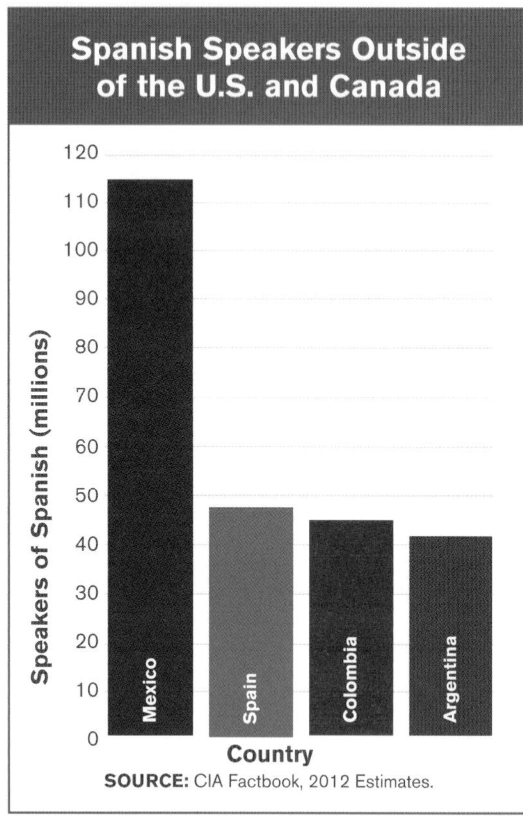

Do you know someone whose first language is Spanish? Chances are you do! More than approximately forty million people living in the U.S. speak Spanish; after English, it is the second most commonly spoken language in this country. It is the official language of twenty-two countries and an official language of the European Union and United Nations.

The Growth of Spanish

Have you ever heard of a language called Castilian? It's Spanish! The Spanish language as we know it today has its origins in a dialect called Castilian (castellano in Spanish). Castilian developed in the 9th century in north-central Spain, in a historic provincial region known as Old Castile. Castilian gradually spread towards the central region of New Castile, where it was adopted as the main language of commerce. By the 16th century, Spanish had become the official language of Spain and eventually, the country's role in exploration, colonization, and overseas trade led to its spread across Central and South America, North America, the Caribbean, parts of North Africa, the Canary Islands, and the Philippines.

Spanish in the United States

1500 — 1600 — 1700

16th Century
Spanish is the official language of Spain.

1565
The Spanish arrive in Florida and found St. Augustine.

1610
The Spanish found Santa Fe, today's capital of New Mexico, the state with the most Spanish speakers in the U.S.

Spanish in the United States

Spanish came to North America in the 16th century with the Spanish who settled in St. Augustine, Florida. Spanish-speaking communities flourished in several parts of the continent over the next few centuries. Then, in 1848, in the aftermath of the Mexican-American War, Mexico lost almost half its land to the United States, including portions of modern-day Texas, New Mexico, Arizona, Colorado, California, Wyoming, Nevada, and Utah. Overnight, hundreds of thousands of Mexicans became citizens of the United States, bringing with them their rich history, language, and traditions.

This heritage, combined with that of the other Hispanic populations that have immigrated to the United States over the years, has led to the remarkable growth of Spanish around the country. After English, it is the most commonly spoken language in 43 states. More than 12 million people in California alone claim Spanish as their first or "home" language.

You've made a popular choice by choosing to take Spanish in school. Not only is Spanish found and heard almost everywhere in the United States, but it is the most commonly taught foreign language in classrooms throughout the country! Have you heard people speaking Spanish in your community? Chances are that you've come across an advertisement, menu, or magazine that is in Spanish. If you look around, you'll find that Spanish can be found in some pretty common places. For example, most ATMs respond to users in both English and Spanish. News agencies and television stations such as CNN and Telemundo provide Spanish-language broadcasts. When you listen to the radio or download music from the Internet, some of the most popular choices are Latino artists who perform in Spanish. Federal government agencies such as the Internal Revenue Service and the Department of State provide services in both languages. Even the White House has an official Spanish-language webpage! Learning Spanish can create opportunities within your everyday life.

1800 | 1900 | 2015

1848
Mexicans who choose to stay in the U.S. after the Mexican-American War become U.S. citizens.

1959
After the Cuban Revolution, thousands of Cubans emigrate to the U.S.

2015
Spanish is the 2nd most commonly spoken language in the U.S., with more than approximately 52.5 million speakers.

Why Study Spanish?

Learn an International Language

There are many reasons to learn Spanish, a language that has spread to many parts of the world and has along the way embraced words and sounds of languages as diverse as Latin, Arabic, and Nahuatl. Spanish has evolved from a medieval dialect of north-central Spain into the fourth most commonly spoken language in the world. It is the second language of choice among the majority of people in North America.

Understand the World Around You

Knowing Spanish can also open doors to communities within the United States, and it can broaden your understanding of the nation's history and geography. The very names Colorado, Montana, Nevada, and Florida are Spanish in origin. Just knowing their meanings can give you some insight into the landscapes for which the states are renowned. Colorado means "colored red;" Montana means "mountain;" Nevada is derived from "snow-capped mountain;" and Florida means "flowered." You've already been speaking Spanish whenever you talk about some of these states!

State Name	Meaning in Spanish
Colorado	"colored red"
Florida	"flowered"
Montana	"mountain"
Nevada	"snow-capped mountain"

Connect with the World

Learning Spanish can change how you view the world. While you learn Spanish, you will also explore and learn about the origins, customs, art, music, and literature of people in close to two dozen countries. When you travel to a Spanish-speaking country, you'll be able to converse freely with the people you meet. And whether in the U.S., Canada, or abroad, you'll find that speaking to people in their native language is the best way to bridge any culture gap.

Why Study Spanish?

Explore Your Future

How many of you are already planning your future careers? Employers in today's global economy look for workers who know different languages and understand other cultures. Your knowledge of Spanish will make you a valuable candidate for careers abroad as well as in the United States or Canada. Doctors, nurses, social workers, hotel managers, journalists, businessmen, pilots, flight attendants, and many other professionals need to know Spanish or another foreign language to do their jobs well.

Expand Your Skills

Studying a foreign language can improve your ability to analyze and interpret information and help you succeed in many other subject areas. When you first begin learning Spanish, your studies will focus mainly on reading, writing, grammar, listening, and speaking skills. You'll be amazed at how the skills involved with learning how a language works can help you succeed in other areas of study. Many people who study a foreign language claim that they gained a better understanding of English. Spanish can even help you understand the origins of many English words and expand your own vocabulary in English. Knowing Spanish can also help you pick up other related languages, such as Italian, Portuguese, and French. Spanish can really open doors for learning many other skills in your school career.

How to Learn Spanish

Start with the Basics!

As with anything you want to learn, start with the basics and remember that learning takes time! The basics are vocabulary, grammar, and culture.

Vocabulary | Every new word you learn in Spanish will expand your vocabulary and ability to communicate. The more words you know, the better you can express yourself. Focus on sounds and think about ways to remember words. Use your knowledge of English and other languages to figure out the meaning of and memorize words like **conversación, teléfono, oficina, clase,** and **música**.

Grammar | Grammar helps you put your new vocabulary together. By learning the rules of grammar, you can use new words correctly and speak in complete sentences. As you learn verbs and tenses, you will be able to speak about the past, present, or future, express yourself with clarity, and be able to persuade others with your opinions. Pay attention to structures and use your knowledge of English grammar to make connections with Spanish grammar.

Culture | Culture provides you with a framework for what you may say or do. As you learn about the culture of Spanish-speaking communities, you'll improve your knowledge of Spanish. Think about a word like **salsa**, and how it connects to both food and music. Think about and explore customs observed on **Nochevieja** (New Year's Eve) or at a **fiesta de quince años** (a girl's fifteenth birthday party). Watch people greet each other or say good-bye. Listen for idioms and sayings that capture the spirit of what you want to communicate!

Teenagers celebrating at a **fiesta de quince años**.

Listen, Speak, Read, and Write

Listening | Listen for sounds and for words you can recognize. Listen for inflections and watch for key words that signal a question such as **cómo** (*how*), **dónde** (*where*), or **qué** (*what)*. Get used to the sound of Spanish. Play Spanish pop songs or watch Spanish movies. Borrow audiobooks from your local library, or try to visit places in your community where Spanish is spoken. Don't worry if you don't understand every single word. If you focus on key words and phrases, you'll get the main idea. The more you listen, the more you'll understand!

Speaking | Practice speaking Spanish as often as you can. As you talk, work on your pronunciation, and read aloud texts so that words and sentences flow more easily. Don't worry if you don't sound like a native speaker, or if you make some mistakes. Time and practice will help you get there. Participate actively in Spanish class. Try to speak Spanish with classmates, especially native speakers (if you know any), as often as you can.

Reading | Pick up a Spanish-language newspaper or a pamphlet on your way to school, read the lyrics of a song as you listen to it, or read books you've already read in English translated into Spanish. Use reading strategies that you know to understand the meaning of a text that looks unfamiliar. Look for cognates, or words that are related in English and Spanish, to guess the meaning of some words. Read as often as you can, and remember to read for fun!

Writing | It's easy to write in Spanish if you put your mind to it. And remember that Spanish spelling is phonetic, which means that once you learn the basic rules of how letters and sounds are related, you can probably become an expert speller in Spanish! Write for fun—make up poems or songs, write e-mails or instant messages to friends, or start a journal or blog in Spanish.

Tips for Learning Spanish

Practice, practice, practice!

Seize every opportunity you find to listen, speak, read, or write Spanish. Think of it like a sport or learning a musical instrument—the more you practice, the more you will become comfortable with the language and how it works. You'll marvel at how quickly you can begin speaking Spanish and how the world that it transports you to can change your life forever!

- Listen to Spanish radio shows and podcasts. Write down words that you can't recognize or don't know and look up the meaning.
- Watch Spanish TV shows, movies, or YouTube clips. Read subtitles to help you grasp the content.
- Read Spanish-language newspapers, magazines, or blogs.
- Listen to Spanish songs that you like —anything from Shakira to a traditional mariachi melody. Sing along and concentrate on your pronunciation.

- Seek out Spanish speakers. Look for neighborhoods, markets, or cultural centers where Spanish might be spoken in your community. Greet people, ask for directions, or order from a menu at a Mexican restaurant in Spanish.
- Pursue language exchange opportunities (**intercambio cultural**) in your school or community. Try to join language clubs or cultural societies, and explore opportunities for studying abroad or hosting a student from a Spanish-speaking country in your home or school.
- Connect your learning to everyday experiences. Think about naming the ingredients of your favorite dish in Spanish. Think about the origins of Spanish place names in the U.S., like Cape Canaveral and Sacramento, or of common English words like *adobe, chocolate, mustang, tornado,* and *patio*.
- Use mnemonics, or a memorizing device, to help you remember words. Make up a saying in English to remember the order of the days of the week in Spanish (L, M, M, J, V, S, D).
- Visualize words. Try to associate words with images to help you remember meanings. For example, think of a **paella** as you learn the names of different types of seafood or meat. Imagine a national park and create mental pictures of the landscape as you learn names of animals, plants, and habitats.
- Enjoy yourself! Try to have as much fun as you can learning Spanish. Take your knowledge beyond the classroom and make the learning experience your own.

Lección preliminar

Communicative Goals

I will be able to:

- **Identify myself and say where I am from**
- **Say how old I am**
- **Identify objects in the classroom**
- **Count from 1 to 30**

Conversaciones

Vocabulario

Hola.	*Hello., Hi.*
¿Cómo se llama usted?	*What is your name? (formal)*
¿Cómo te llamas?	*What is your name? (informal)*
Me llamo…	*My name is…*
¿Y usted?	*And you? (formal)*
¿Y tú?	*And you? (informal)*
Mucho gusto.	*It's a pleasure.*
El gusto es mío.	*The pleasure is all mine.*
Igualmente.	*Likewise.*
Encantado/a.	*Charmed. Delighted.*
el nombre	*name*
el señor (Sr.)	*Mr.*
la señora (Sra.)	*Ms., Mrs.*

—Hola. Me llamo Tomás.
—Me llamo Victoria. Mucho gusto, Tomás.

—Me llamo Antonia Guzmán. ¿Y usted?
—Daniel Soto. Encantado, señora Guzmán.
—Igualmente, señor Soto.

—Hola, señor. ¿Cómo se llama usted?
—Mateo Pérez. ¿Y tú? ¿Cómo te llamas?
—Me llamo Eduardo Salinas.
—Mucho gusto, Eduardo.
—El gusto es mío, señor Pérez.

Common Names

Get started learning Spanish by using a Spanish name in class. You can choose from the lists on these pages, or you can find one yourself. How about learning the Spanish equivalent of your name? The most popular Spanish girl's names are Lucía, María, Paula, Sofía, and Valentina. The most popular boy's names in Spanish are Alejandro, Daniel, David, Mateo, and Santiago. Is your name, or that of someone you know, in the Spanish top five?

Los 5 nombres más populares

Chicos	Chicas
Alejandro	Lucía
Daniel	María
David	Paula
Mateo	Sofía
Santiago	Valentina

Más nombres de chicos	Más nombres de chicas
Antonio (Toni)	Alicia
Camilo	Beatriz (Bea, Beti, Biata)
Carlos	Blanca
César	Catalina
Diego	Carolina (Carol)
Ernesto	Claudia
Felipe	Diana
Francisco (Paco)	Emilia
Guillermo	Irene
Ignacio (Nacho)	Julia
Javier (Javi)	Laura
Juan	Liliana
Leonardo	Lourdes
Luis	Margarita (Marga)
Marcos	Marta
Oscar (Óscar)	Natalia
Rafael (Rafa)	Patricia
Sergio	Rocío
Vicente	Verónica

Práctica

1 **Completa el diálogo** Select the answer that completes each mini-dialogue.

1. ¿Cómo se llama?
   a. Igualmente. b. Eduardo Vargas.
2. Mucho gusto, señor.
   a. El gusto es mío. b. ¿Y tú?
3. Me llamo Sofía. ¿Y tú?
   a. Jaime. b. Encantada.
4. Encantado, señora.
   a. Alicia Núñez. b. Igualmente.
5. ¿Cómo te llamas?
   a. Señor Rivas. b. Enrique. ¿Y tú?

2 **¿Cómo te llamas? ¿Cómo se llama usted?** How would you ask the following people their names? Write down the right question according to the situation.

1. a substitute teacher
2. a student who just transferred to your school
3. the child who moved in across the street
4. the new school librarian
5. your parent's coworker who comes to dinner

El alfabeto

el artista (a)

el bebé (be)

el calendario (ce)

el dinosaurio (de)

el elefante (e)

el karate (ka)

el limón (ele)

el mapa (eme)

el norte (ene)

la lasaña (eñe)

el teléfono (te)

el universo (u)

el volcán (ve)

el sándwich (doble ve)

el saxofón (equis)

Las vocales del español *Spanish vowels*

The Spanish alphabet has five vowels. Note that some vowels need an accent. When you are spelling out a word that has an accent on it, use the expression **con acento**.
—¿Cómo se escribe teléfono?
—Se escribe t - e - l - e con acento - f - o - n - o.

Repite, por favor

Listen to and repeat each word. Pay attention to how each vowel is pronounced.

a	llama	Encantada.	Alejandro
e	español	elefante	Elena
i	insecto	Igualmente.	Iván
o	cómo	Hola.	Óscar
u	tú	Mucho gusto.	Úrsula

la flor (efe)

la guitarra (ge)

el hospital (hache)

el insecto (i)

la jirafa (jota)

el océano (o)

la pirata (pe)

la química (cu)

la rata (ere)

el sofá (ese)

el yogur
(i griega, ye)

el zoológico (zeta)

¿Cómo se escribe...? *How do you write . . . ? (How do you spell . . . ?)*

PROFESORA (*TEACHER*) Elena, ¿cómo se escribe *dinosaurio*?

ELENA Se escribe d - i - n - o - s - a - u- r - i - o.

PROFESORA Y Víctor, ¿cómo se escribe *mapa*?

VÍCTOR Se escribe m - a - p - a.

PROFESORA Muy bien.

3 **¿Cómo se escribe tu nombre?** Listen as each student spells his or her name. Then write down the name you hear spelled.

1. Me llamo...
2. Me llamo...
3. Me llamo...
4. Me llamo...
5. Me llamo...

Soy de los Estados Unidos

Ser *To be*

yo soy	*I am*
tú eres	*you are (familiar)*
él es	*he is*
ella es	*she is*
usted es	*you are (formal)*
nosotros somos	*we are*
nosotras somos	*we are (all-female group)*
ellos son	*they are*
ellas son	*they are (all-female group)*
ustedes son	*you are (plural)*

Vocabulario

la bandera	*flag*
la capital	*capital (city)*
la chica	*girl*
el chico	*boy*
la nacionalidad	*nationality*
el país	*country*

—Hola. Me llamo Justin. Yo soy de los Estados Unidos.
—Y yo soy Valentina. Soy de España.

—Marcos, ¿de dónde eres?
—Soy de San Juan, Puerto Rico.
—¿Y tú, Natalia?
—Yo soy de Costa Rica.

—Señora Paz, ¿de dónde es usted?
—De la República Dominicana. ¿Y usted, señor Hernández?
—Soy de México.

—¿De dónde es Elena Gaetano?
—Ella es de Buenos Aires, Argentina.
—¿Y de dónde son Mateo y Lucas Moreno?
—Ellos son de Bogotá, Colombia.

Los países y las banderas

Las capitales

Argentina	**Buenos Aires**
Colombia	**Bogotá**
Costa Rica	**San José**
El Salvador	**San Salvador**
España	**Madrid**
Estados Unidos	**Washington, D.C.**
México	**la Ciudad de México**
Panamá	**la Ciudad de Panamá**
Perú	**Lima**
Puerto Rico	**San Juan**
República Dominicana	**Santo Domingo**
Venezuela	**Caracas**

Práctica

1 

Concentración In groups of four, create a set of 24 cards to play a matching game. Your teacher will give each group blank cards. Each student takes six cards. On one side of a card, write the name of a country. On a second card, write the capital city of that country. When you're finished, you will have 12 different country cards and 12 different capital city cards.

Argentina | Buenos Aires

To play:

1. Have one member of the group shuffle or mix up the cards well. Then deal them face down on the desk in four rows of six cards.
2. The first player turns over two cards. The object of the game is to match countries with their capitals. If the cards match, that player gets to keep them. If not, turn the cards face down again.
3. The next player turns over two cards, and play continues until all 24 cards have been matched up.
4. The player with the most cards wins.

2 **¿De dónde son?** The following people are from the capital city of their countries. Say where they are from. Follow the model.

modelo

Cristina: Colombia
Ella es de Bogotá. or Es de Bogotá.

Sergio y Pablo: Estados Unidos
Ellos son de Washington, D.C. or Son de Washington, D.C.

1. Vicente: Costa Rica
2. Lisa y Ana María: Panamá
3. Beatriz: Perú
4. el señor Ortiz: Argentina
5. Antonio y Enrique: República Dominicana
6. Javier Fernández: España
7. la señora Flores: El Salvador
8. Rosario y Lourdes: Puerto Rico
9. Matías Muñoz: Venezuela
10. Lupe Sandoval: México

Comunicación

3 **Lee el párrafo** Read the following short paragraph about the members of the Spanish Club (**los miembros del Club de Español**). Then indicate whether each statement about it is **cierto** (true) or **falso** (false). Correct the false statements.

¿De dónde son los miembros del Club de Español? Zack y Carmen son de los Estados Unidos. Zack es de San Diego y Carmen es de Miami. Anita, Rebeca y Antonio son de la capital de México. Jorge es de Bogotá y Linda es de Lima. Ricky es de Puerto Rico y Sandra, la presidenta del Club, es de Madrid.

1. Carmen es de los Estados Unidos.
2. Linda es de Argentina.
3. Jorge es de Venezuela.
4. Zack es de California.
5. Ricky es de Costa Rica.
6. Tres (*three*) miembros son de la Ciudad de México.
7. La presidenta del Club se llama Rebeca.
8. Nadie (*No one*) es de El Salvador.

4  **Turnos** With a partner, take turns asking and answering the following questions. Follow the model.

modelo

Estudiante 1: *¿Tú eres de Argentina?*
Estudiante 2: *Sí, soy de Argentina. / No. Soy de Perú.*

1. ¿Tú eres de Venezuela?
2. ¿Tú eres de los Estados Unidos?
3. ¿Cómo se escribe tu (*your*) nombre?
4. ¿De dónde eres? (*Answer with a state name.*)
5. ¿De dónde eres? (*Answer with a city or town name.*)

5  **Preguntas** In groups of three, take turns asking each other your own questions about countries and capitals. Follow the model.

modelo

Estudiante 1: *Jackie, ¿de dónde eres?*
Estudiante 2: *Soy de Chicago.*
Estudiante 3: *¿Cómo se escribe Chicago?*
Estudiante 4: *Se escribe c - h - i - c - a - g - o.*

Los números

Los números 1 a 30

1	uno
2	dos
3	tres
4	cuatro
5	cinco
6	seis
7	siete
8	ocho
9	nueve
10	diez
11	once
12	doce
13	trece
14	catorce
15	quince
16	dieciséis
17	diecisiete
18	dieciocho
19	diecinueve
20	veinte
21	veintiuno
22	veintidós
23	veintitrés
24	veinticuatro
25	veinticinco
26	veintiséis
27	veintisiete
28	veintiocho
29	veintinueve
30	treinta

—Hola. Me llamo Carlos.
Yo tengo siete años.

—Hola. Soy Mariana.
Tengo doce años. ¿Y tú?

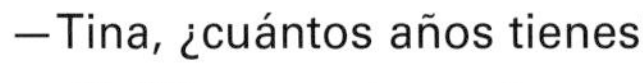

—Tina, ¿cuántos años tienes?
—¿Yo? Tengo quince años.
—¿Y tú, Miguel?
—Tengo dieciséis.

Vocabulario

el año / los años	*year / years*
¿Cuántos años tienes?	*How old are you? (familiar)*
¿Cuántos años tiene usted?	*How old are you? (formal)*
(Yo) tengo [número] años.	*I am [number] years old.*

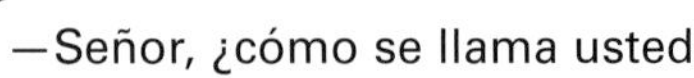

—Señor, ¿cómo se llama usted?
—Me llamo Santiago García.
—¿Y cuántos años tiene usted?
—Tengo veintisiete años.

Práctica

1 **Asociaciones** Say the number associated with the following items.

1. Number of hours in a day
2. Number of inches in a foot
3. Number of eggs in half a dozen
4. Number of days in April, June, September, and November
5. Number of days in February in a regular year
6. Number of stripes on the American flag
7. Number of dwarfs that lived with Snow White
8. Number of hours you attend school each day
9. Number of socks or gloves in a pair

2 **¡Suerte!** On a separate piece of paper, draw a game grid like a tic-tac-toe board with nine spaces. In each space, write a different number from 1 to 30. Your teacher will then say a series of numbers. When you hear a number on your game grid, mark an **X** through it. When you have three in a row, call out **¡Suerte!** (*Luck!*).

~~6~~	17	22
28	4	8
19	~~11~~	13

3	24	~~8~~
~~16~~	22	30
7	15	1

3 **En parejas** With a partner write out the following numbers in Spanish, and then spell them out loud.

1. 23	3. 11	5. 9	7. 15	9. 22
2. 17	4. 29	6. 30	8. 4	10. 16

Comunicación

4  **Entrevista** Interview a classmate. Ask for the following information.

- his/her name
- how you spell his/her first or last name
- where he/she is from
- how old he/she is

El comienzo de esta historia

Throughout this course, you will follow a group of students while they live and travel in Mexico. You will meet the Díaz family, whose household includes their son Felipe and daughter Jimena, and a visiting student, Marissa, from the U.S. Over the course of the series, Jimena, Felipe, Marissa, and their friends explore el D.F. and other parts of Mexico. Their adventures take them through some of the greatest natural and cultural treasures of Mexico, as well as the highs and lows of everyday life. Here are the main characters you will meet in Fotonovela, starting in Lección 1.

netbook amigos fotos más ▾

Acerca de mí

Nombre: Marissa Wagner

Ciudad: Appleton, Wisconsin

Edad: 19

Intereses:
- Cultura mexicana
- Arqueología
- Latinoamérica
- Esquí acuático

netbook amigos fotos más ▾

Acerca de mí

Nombre: Felipe Díaz

Ciudad: México, D.F.

Edad: 21

Intereses:
- Música
- Fútbol
- Vóleibol
- Televisión

netbook amigos fotos más ▾

Acerca de mí

Nombre: Jimena Díaz

Ciudad: México, D.F.

Edad: 17

Intereses:
- Documentales
- Medicina
- Cine de acción
- Libros de ciencias

netbook amigos fotos más ▾

Acerca de mí

Nombre: Miguel Ángel Lagasca

Ciudad: Bilbao (España)

Edad: 26

Intereses:
- Pintura y dibujo
- Historia del arte
- Arte latinoamericano
- Arte moderno
- Arte español

netbook amigos fotos más ▾

Acerca de mí

Nombre: Juan Carlos Rossi

Ciudad: Buenos Aires

Edad: 19

Intereses:
- Ciencias ambientales
- Computadoras
- Fútbol
- Cine de ficción y terror

netbook amigos fotos más ▾

Acerca de mí

Nombre: Carolina Velázquez de Díaz

Ciudad: La Habana (Cuba)

Edad: 45

Intereses:
- Arte
- Danza
- Ópera
- Cine mexicano

Práctica

1 **¿Cierto o falso?** Indicate whether each statement is **cierto** or **falso**. Then, correct the false statements.

1. Felipe tiene 15 años.
2. Miguel es de México D.F.
3. Marissa tiene 19 años.
4. Jimena es de Buenos Aires.
5. Carolina es de Cuba.
6. Juan Carlos tiene 18 años.

2 **Intereses** Scan the profiles and write down which characters are interested in the following topics:

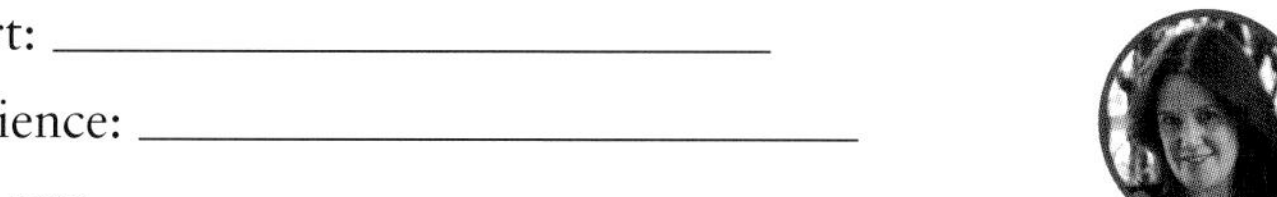

1. Art: ______________________
2. Science: ______________________
3. Sports: ______________________
4. Latin America: ______________________
5. Archeology: ______________________
6. Film: ______________________
7. Computers: ______________________
8. Spain: ______________________

CAROLINA

FELIPE

MARISSA

JUAN CARLOS

JIMENA

MIGUEL

3 **Preguntas** With a classmate, take turns asking questions about the **Fotonovela** characters. Follow the model.

modelo

Estudiante 1: ¿Cuáles son los intereses de Marissa?
Estudiante 2: La cultura mexicana, la arqueología, Latinoamérica y el esquí acuático.
Estudiante 1: ¿De dónde es Felipe?
Estudiante 2: Felipe es de México.
Estudiante 1: ¿Cuántos años tiene Miguel?
Estudiante 2: Miguel tiene 26 años.

EN DETALLE

Aquí se habla español

Spanish is spoken here

Spanish has been spoken in the territory that became the United States since the sixteenth century, when explorers from Spain began settling areas in Florida, California, and the American Southwest. Later, when neighboring Mexico gained its independence from Spain, most of Spain's western settlements became part of that country. After the Mexican-American War, these same areas became part of the United States. And in 1898, Puerto Rico also became a U.S. territory.

Throughout the twentieth century, people from Spanish-speaking countries came to America for a variety of reasons. Of course, they brought the Spanish language with them. Many families have now lived in the United States for three or more generations. For that reason, Spanish is the main language of 40 million Americans. Plus, there are another six million students who are learning Spanish just as you are.

There are more Spanish speakers in the United States than all the speakers of French, Chinese, German, Italian, Korean, Vietnamese, and Native American languages combined. Clearly, **¡aquí se habla español!**

"Young" Cities and the Next Generation

Currently, the ten U.S. cities with the largest Hispanic populations are:

1. New York (NY)
2. Los Angeles (CA)
3. Houston (TX)
4. San Antonio (TX)
5. Chicago (IL)
6. Phoenix (AZ)
7. Dallas (TX)
8. El Paso (TX)
9. San Diego (CA)
10. San Jose (CA)

While these cities already have a large Hispanic population, others might move into the top ten within the next 15 to 25 years. They include Seattle, Denver, Atlanta, Washington, D.C., Boston, Las Vegas, and Charlotte (NC), where one third of the "under 18" population is comprised of young people of Hispanic heritage.

ACTIVIDADES

1 **¿Cierto o falso?** Indicate whether these statements are true (**cierto**) or false (**falso**). Correct the false statements.

1. No one in the United States spoke Spanish until the twentieth century.
2. The Spanish-speaking population grew because of immigration.
3. Puerto Rico became a U.S. territory in 1989.
4. Spanish explorers first brought the language to North America.
5. Mexico acquired a large territory after the Mexican-American War.
6. Most of the cities with large Hispanic populations are in New York and Arizona.
7. Cities with young Hispanic populations are all in the West.
8. In the United States, there are more people who speak Spanish than speak Asian languages.

ASÍ SE DICE

Comidas hispanas (*Hispanic foods*)

las empanadas	*small pastries filled with meat, cheese, or vegetables*
los tamales	*cornmeal dough with different fillings wrapped in a corn husk and steamed*
el ceviche	*fresh fish and seafood cured in lemon or lime juice*
los maduros fritos	*thinly sliced plantains fried with garlic*
la ropa vieja	*shredded beef, onions, and tomatoes, served with rice, black beans, and plantains*

EL MUNDO HISPANO

La televisión

In the United States, there are hundreds of Spanish-language and bilingual television channels. Some of the best-known Spanish-language networks are:

- **Univisión:** ranks as the fifth highest rated network in the U.S. in number of viewers
- **Telemundo:** broadcasts news programs, reality shows, soap operas, and movies from Spanish-speaking countries
- **Estrella:** broadcasts entertainment television and movies from the Spanish-speaking world
- **VeMe:** offers many lifestyle programs about health, fitness, cooking, home repair, decorating, and so on.

Watching a Spanish-language TV show can help you with your ability to *listen to* and *speak* the language. You will also *see* aspects of various cultures that are different from your own.

PERFIL

Los salvadoreños de Washington, D.C.

As in many large cities, the Hispanic population of Washington, D.C. includes people from many different national origins, each with its own distinct culture. A large Salvadoran community, many of whom left El Salvador for political and economic reasons, now call the District of Columbia home.

Whether you visit or live in Washington, you can taste the rich culture of El Salvador in the many Salvadoran restaurants and cafes that serve a traditional dish called **pupusas**. Pupusas are thick tortillas prepared with corn **masa** (*dough*) and cooked on a flat griddle called a **comal.** They are delicious plain, but many fans of the dish prefer filling them with pork or other meat, refried beans, and cheese. A fermented cabbage and chile salad called **curtido** often accompanies a serving of pupusas. And don't forget the hot sauce! **¡Buen provecho!** (*Enjoy your meal!*)

Conexión Internet

What other Hispanic dishes are popular in the U.S.? What countries did they come from originally?

Use the Web to find more cultural information related to this **Cultura** section.

ACTIVIDADES

2 **Completa la oración** Complete each sentence with the correct missing word or phrase.

1. ____________ is a dish of marinated fish and shellfish.
2. In the United States, there are many ____________ television channels.
3. One of the most popular networks in the U.S. that broadcasts in Spanish is ____________.
4. If you watch a TV show in Spanish it can help you ____________ and speak better.
5. In a Salvadoran restaurant, you can order ____________ that can be served plain or with various fillings.
6. Several Latin American dishes are prepared with a cornmeal dough called ____________.
7. Many Salvadorans who came to the U.S. settled in ____________.
8. To say you hope someone enjoys his/her meal, you would use the expression ____________.

En mi salón de clases hay...

Vocabulario

¿Cuál es...?	*Which is . . .?*
¿cuántos/cuántas?	*how many?*
el profesor	*(male) teacher*
la profesora	*(female) teacher*
hay	*there is; there are*
mi	*my*
su	*your*

el libro
la pluma
el cuaderno
la tarea
el lápiz
la computadora
el reloj
la profesora
la pizarra
los estudiantes
el escritorio
la mochila
el pupitre
la silla

Hay

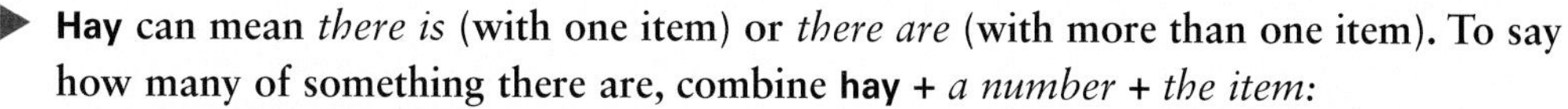

- **Hay** can mean *there is* (with one item) or *there are* (with more than one item). To say how many of something there are, combine **hay** + *a number* + *the item:*

  Hay diez lápices.
  There are ten pencils.

  Hay tres relojes.
  There are three clocks.

  ¿Cuántos libros **hay**?
  How many books are there?

- When saying there is one of something, the number **uno** changes to **un** before masculine nouns and **una** before feminine nouns.

  Hay **un** cuaderno.
  There is one notebook.

el cuaderno

  Hay **una** silla.
  There is one chair.

la silla

Práctica

1 **El nuevo salón de clases** Mrs. Martínez asks a school administrator, Mrs. Álvarez, about her new Spanish class and classroom. Listen to their conversation and indicate whether the statements below are true (**cierto**) or false (**falso**). Correct the false statements.

1. El salón de clases de la señora Martínez es el número dos.
2. Hay dos pizarras en el salón de clases.
3. La señora Martínez tiene 30 estudiantes.
4. Hay 25 sillas y 25 escritorios.

Comunicación

2 **En la clase** Take turns asking each other how many of each item there are in your classroom. Follow the model.

modelo

Estudiante 1: ¿Cuántas mochilas hay en la clase?
Estudiante 2: Hay quince mochilas.

1. sillas
2. profesores/profesoras
3. relojes
4. escritorios
5. pizarras
6. estudiantes
7. chicas
8. chicos

Las materias

Vocabulario

las materias	*subjects*
el arte	*art*
las ciencias	*science*
el español	*Spanish*
la geografía	*geography*
la historia	*history*
el inglés	*English*
las matemáticas	*math*
la música	*music*
estudio	*I study*
estudias	*you study*

Expresiones útiles

¿Cómo se dice ___ en español?	*How do you say ___ in Spanish?*
Con permiso.	*Excuse me.*
De nada.	*You're welcome.*
¿De veras?	*Really?*
¿En qué página estamos?	*What page are we on?*
Más despacio, por favor.	*Slower, please.*
Muchas gracias.	*Thanks a lot.*
No entiendo.	*I don't understand.*
No sé.	*I don't know.*
Por favor.	*Please.*
¿Qué significa ___?	*What does ___ mean?*
Tengo una pregunta.	*I have a question.*

ALINA Señor Morales, ¿cómo se dice *history* en español?
SEÑOR MORALES Se dice **historia**.
ALINA Ah... ¿y cómo se escribe, por favor?
SEÑOR MORALES Se escribe h - i - s - t - o - r - i - a.
ALINA Muchas gracias.

HÉCTOR Pablo, ¿estudias inglés?
PABLO No. Estudio español. ¿Y tú?
HÉCTOR ¡Estudio inglés y español!

VALERIA Hola. ¿Cómo te llamas?
DIANA Soy Diana. ¿Y tú?
VALERIA Me llamo Valeria. ¿Estudias matemáticas?
DIANA Sí, estudio álgebra.

Práctica

3 **¿Qué estudias?** Match the subjects with the topics below.

la historia

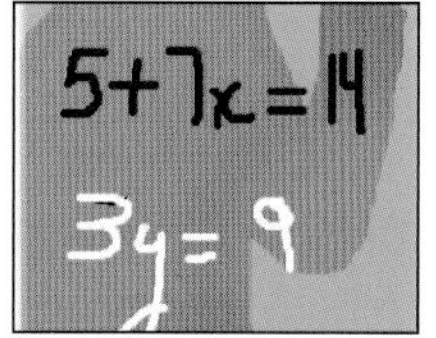

las matemáticas

la música

el arte

el español

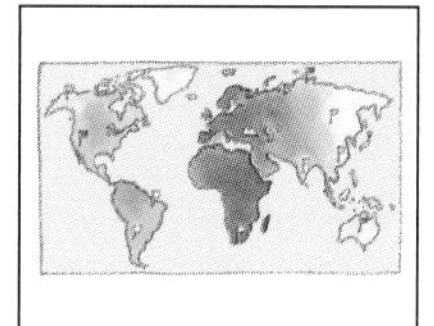
la geografía

1. Picasso, Van Gogh, Henry Moore
2. el vocabulario, América Latina, las conjugaciones
3. los números, las operaciones, las ecuaciones
4. La Constitución, Lincoln, las trece colonias
5. el mapa, los países, los continentes

4 **¿Qué dices?** What would you say in Spanish in the following situations?

modelo

Your teacher asks you to read sentence 5, but you haven't opened your book yet.
¿En qué página estamos?

1. You need to ask your teacher a question.
2. Your teacher is speaking way too fast.
3. Someone says **Gracias** to you.
4. Two people are blocking the door and you need to get by.
5. You don't understand the word **salud.**
6. Someone asks a question you cannot answer.
7. You'd like to know how to say *fish* in Spanish.

¿Qué día es hoy?

Vocabulario

¿Qué día es hoy?	*What day is today?*
Hoy es...	*Today is . . .*
lunes	*Monday*
martes	*Tuesday*
miércoles	*Wednesday*
jueves	*Thursday*
viernes	*Friday*
sábado	*Saturday*
domingo	*Sunday*
el almuerzo	*lunch*
el examen	*test, exam*
el horario (de clases)	*(class) schedule*
la semana	*week*
ayer	*yesterday*
mañana	*tomorrow*

SEÑOR OLIVARES Señora Robles, ¿qué día es hoy?
SEÑORA ROBLES Hoy es miércoles.
SEÑOR OLIVARES Gracias.

PROFESORA Benjamín, ¿cuáles son los días de la semana?
BENJAMÍN Lunes, martes... jueves...
PROFESORA ¡Ah, ah, ah!
BENJAMÍN No, no. Lunes, martes, miércoles, jueves, viernes, sábado y domingo.
PROFESORA Muy bien.

PAPÁ Sarita, ¿qué día es hoy?
SARITA Hoy es... sábado.
PAPÁ Sí, hoy es sábado. Y ayer fue (*was*)...
SARITA Viernes.
PAPÁ Bien. Y mañana será (*will be*)...
SARITA Mañana será domingo.
PAPÁ Muy bien.

CARLOS Ah, ¡hoy es viernes!
MANUELA No, mañana será viernes. Hoy es jueves. Tengo examen en la clase de matemáticas.
CARLOS ¿Hoy no es viernes? ¿De veras?
PABLO Sí, amigo. Hoy es jueves de veras.

AYER	HOY	MAÑANA
viernes	sábado	domingo

lunes	martes	miércoles	jueves	viernes	sábado	domingo
7	8	9	10	11	12	13

Práctica

1 **Los horarios** Read about David's and Alina's class schedules. Then, using the information they give about their classes, create their daily schedules on a separate sheet of paper. Use the following grid as a model.

El horario de ____________________

7:30	8:30	9:30	10:30	11:30	12:00	1:00
				almuerzo		

1. Hola. Me llamo David. En mi escuela tengo cuatro clases antes del almuerzo (*before lunch*): álgebra, historia, inglés y biología. Después del (*After*) almuerzo, estudio música y español.
2. Hola. Soy Alina. Hoy tengo dos exámenes. Tengo un examen en la primera (*first*) clase del día, ciencias, y después del almuerzo tengo un examen en la clase de matemáticas. Después de ciencias, tengo las clases de inglés, de español y de arte. Y la última (*last*) clase del día es historia americana.

2 **El horario de Mariana** This week, Mariana has only half-days at school. Listen to her schedule for this week. Then indicate whether the statements below are **cierto** (*true*) or **falso** (*false*). Correct the false statements.

Vocabulario útil

cada día *each day*
mi clase favorita *my favorite class*
tiene *(she) has*
estudia *(she) studies, takes*

1. Mariana tiene dos clases cada día.
2. El martes tiene la clase de inglés.
3. Mariana no estudia geografía.
4. Mariana estudia arte y música.
5. Mariana tiene su (*her*) clase favorita el miércoles.

Comunicación

3 **En parejas** Working with a partner, take turns asking each other questions about your schedules. Follow the model.

modelo

Estudiante 1: ¿Estudias historia?
Estudiante 2: Sí, estudio historia.
Estudiante 1: ¿Cómo se llama la profesora?
Estudiante 2: Se llama señora Watkins.

Recapitulación

1 **¿Cómo se escribe?** You will hear several words spelled out that you have learned in this chapter. Write each word as you hear them.

El alfabeto *pp. 4–5*

El alfabeto

a	a	j	jota	r	ere
b	be	k	ka	s	ese
c	ce	l	ele	t	te
d	de	m	eme	u	u
e	e	n	ene	v	ve (*or* uve)
f	efe	ñ	eñe	w	doble ve (*or* doble u)
g	ge	o	o	x	equis
h	hache	p	pe	y	i griega (*or* ye)
i	i	q	cu	z	zeta

2 **¿De dónde son?** Say where these people are from. If a country is mentioned, say that they are from the capital of that country. If a capital is given, say what country they are from. Follow the model.

¿De dónde eres? *pp. 6–7*

modelo

Elena / Washington, D.C. — Elena es de los Estados Unidos.

Enrique / Estados Unidos — Enrique es de Washington, D.C.

1. el señor Gómez / Madrid
2. Verónica y Beatriz / Costa Rica
3. tú / El Salvador
4. nosotros / San Juan
5. Rebeca / Buenos Aires
6. los chicos / República Dominicana
7. yo / Colombia
8. Marcel y Roberto / Lima

ser ***to be***

yo soy	*I am*
tú eres	*you are (familiar)*
él es	*he is*
ella es	*she is*
usted es	*you are (formal)*
nosotros somos	*we are*
nosotras somos	*we are (all-female group)*
ellos son	*they are*
ellas son	*they are (all-female group)*
ustedes son	*you are (plural)*

3 **¿Cuántos años tiene...?** Write how old each person is. Spell out their ages in words. Follow the model.

¿Cuántos años tienes? *pp. 10–11*

modelo

Miguel (15) — Miguel tiene quince años.

1. tú (11)
2. Mónica (19)
3. usted (28)
4. Rafael (7)
5. Amanda (16)
6. yo (*state your age*)

Miguel

Expresiones

(Yo) tengo [número] años.	*I am [number] years old.*
(Tú) tienes [número] años.	*You are [number] years old.*
Usted tiene [número] años.	*You are [number] years old.*
Él/Ella tiene [número] años.	*He/She is [number] years old.*

4 **¿Cuántos hay?** Say how many of each thing there are either in the classroom (**en el salón de clases**) or in the backpack (**en la mochila**) depending on the size of each object. Use the verb **hay** and follow the model.

modelo

2

Hay dos pizarras en el salón de clases. ***or***
En el salón de clases hay dos pizarras.

1. 24
2. 1
3. 30
4. 15
5. 5
6. 8
7. 3
8. 12

5 **Tu horario de clases ideal** Create your ideal class schedule. Using a grid, write in the five school days of the week, and plan for five classes per day plus a period for lunch (**el almuerzo**). Once you have completed your grid, write five sentences about your schedule. **Note:** To say you do something on a certain day, use **los** + the day.

modelo

Los lunes tengo geografía, …

Lunes				
geografía				
álgebra				

Mi información personal Your teacher will give you a student information form to fill in. Complete the information under the heading **MI INFORMACIÓN**. Use real information or pretend to be someone else! Fill in all the categories on your form. Then, in pairs, you and a partner will take turns asking and answering questions about each other's information. Fill in the **LA INFORMACIÓN DE MI COMPAÑERO/A** section of your form with his or her information. You will need to ask questions about the following:

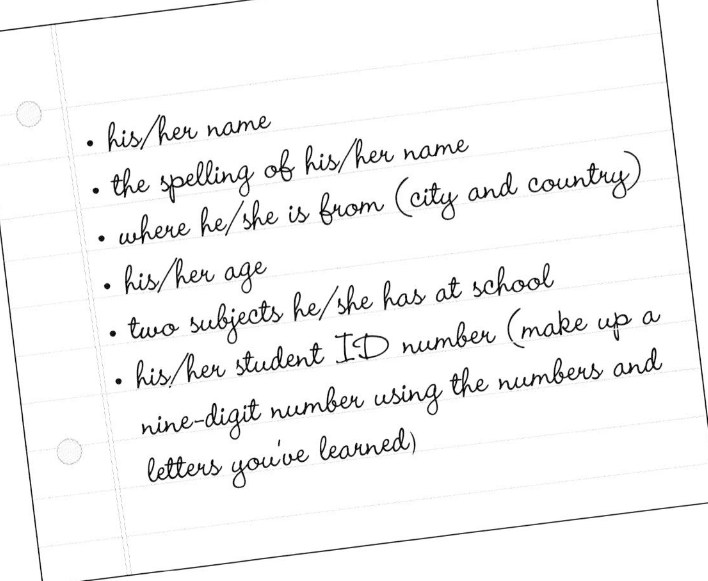

You may ask for your partner's information in any order. When you have finished filling out the form, compare what you wrote to the information on your partner's form.

modelo

Estudiante 1: ¿Cuál es tu número de identidad?
Estudiante 2: Es 14 - B 8 3 - Q 22 7.
Estudiante 1: Repite, por favor...

Estudiante 2: ¿Estudias historia?
Estudiante 1: Sí, estudio historia. ¿Y tú?
Estudiante 2: No.

Hola, ¿qué tal?

1

Communicative Goals

You will learn how to:

- **Greet people in Spanish**
- **Say goodbye**
- **Identify yourself and others**
- **Talk about the time of day**

A PRIMERA VISTA

- **Guess what the people on the photo are saying:**
  a. Adiós. b. Hola. c. salsa
- **Most likely they would also say:**
  a. Gracias. b. fiesta c. Buenos días.
- **The women are:**
  a. amigas b. chicos c. señores

Hola, ¿qué tal?

Más vocabulario

Buenos días.	*Good morning.*
Buenas noches.	*Good evening; Good night.*
Hasta la vista.	*See you later.*
Hasta pronto.	*See you soon.*
¿Cómo se llama usted?	*What's your name? (form.)*
Le presento a...	*I would like to introduce you to (name). (form.)*
Te presento a...	*I would like to introduce you to (name). (fam.)*
el nombre	*name*
¿Cómo estás?	*How are you? (fam.)*
No muy bien.	*Not very well.*
¿Qué pasa?	*What's happening?; What's going on?*
por favor	*please*
De nada.	*You're welcome.*
No hay de qué.	*You're welcome.*
Lo siento.	*I'm sorry.*
Gracias.	*Thank you; Thanks.*
Muchas gracias.	*Thank you very much; Thanks a lot.*

Variación léxica

Items are presented for recognition purposes only.

Buenos días. ⟷ Buenas.
De nada. ⟷ A la orden.
Lo siento. ⟷ Perdón.
¿Qué tal? ⟷ ¿Qué hubo? (*Col.*)
Chau ⟷ Ciao; Chao

1

ELENA Patricia, le presento a Jorge Perales.
PATRICIA Encantada.
SEÑOR PERALES Igualmente. ¿De dónde es usted, señorita?
PATRICIA Soy de México. ¿Y usted?
SEÑOR PERALES De Puerto Rico.

2

TOMÁS ¿Qué tal, Alberto?
ALBERTO Regular. ¿Y tú?
TOMÁS Bien. ¿Qué hay de nuevo?
ALBERTO Nada.

3

SEÑOR VARGAS Buenas tardes, señora Wong. ¿Cómo está usted?
SEÑORA WONG Muy bien, gracias. ¿Y usted, señor Vargas?
SEÑOR VARGAS Bien, gracias.
SEÑORA WONG Hasta mañana, señor Vargas. Saludos a la señora Vargas.
SEÑOR VARGAS Adiós.

Práctica

1 Escuchar Listen to each question or statement, then choose the correct response.

1. a. Muy bien, gracias. b. Me llamo Graciela.
2. a. Lo siento. b. Mucho gusto.
3. a. Soy de Puerto Rico. b. No muy bien.
4. a. No hay de qué. b. Regular.
5. a. Mucho gusto. b. Hasta pronto.
6. a. Nada. b. Igualmente.
7. a. Me llamo Guillermo Montero. b. Muy bien, gracias.
8. a. Buenas tardes. ¿Cómo estás? b. El gusto es mío.
9. a. Saludos a la Sra. Ramírez. b. Encantada.
10. a. Adiós. b. Regular.

2 Identificar You will hear a series of expressions. Identify the expression (**a**, **b**, **c**, or **d**) that does not belong in each series.

1. ___
2. ___
3. ___
4. ___

3 Escoger For each expression, write another word or phrase that expresses a similar idea.

modelo
¿Cómo estás? *¿Qué tal?*

1. De nada.
2. Encantado.
3. Adiós.
4. Hasta la vista.
5. Mucho gusto.

4 Ordenar Put this scrambled conversation in order.

—Muy bien, gracias. Soy Rosabel.
—Soy de México. ¿Y tú?
—Mucho gusto, Rosabel.
—Hola. Me llamo Carlos. ¿Cómo estás?
—Soy de Argentina.
—Igualmente. ¿De dónde eres, Carlos?

CARLOS ______________________
ROSABEL ______________________
CARLOS ______________________
ROSABEL ______________________
CARLOS ______________________
ROSABEL ______________________

5 **Completar** Complete these dialogues.

modelo

¿Cómo estás?
Muy bien, gracias.

1. — ______________
   — Buenos días. ¿Qué tal?
2. — ______________
   — Me llamo Carmen Sánchez.
3. — ______________
   — De Canadá.
4. — Te presento a Marisol.
   — ______________
5. — Gracias.
   — ______________
6. — ______________
   — Regular.
7. — ______________
   — Nada.
8. — ¡Hasta la vista!
   — ______________

6 **Cambiar** Correct the second part of each conversation to make it logical.

modelo

¿Qué tal?
~~No hay de qué.~~ Bien. ¿Y tú?

1. — Hasta mañana, señora Ramírez. Saludos al señor Ramírez.
   — *Muy bien, gracias.*
2. — ¿Qué hay de nuevo, Alberto?
   — *Sí, me llamo Alberto. ¿Cómo te llamas tú?*
3. — Gracias, Tomás.
   — *Regular. ¿Y tú?*
4. — Miguel, te presento a la señorita Perales.
   — *No hay de qué, señorita.*
5. — ¿De dónde eres, Antonio?
   — *Muy bien, gracias. ¿Y tú?*
6. — ¿Cómo se llama usted?
   — *El gusto es mío.*
7. — ¿Qué pasa?
   — *Hasta luego, Alicia.*
8. — Buenas tardes, señor. ¿Cómo está usted?
   — *Soy de Puerto Rico.*

¡LENGUA VIVA!

The titles **señor, señora**, and **señorita** are abbreviated **Sr., Sra.**, and **Srta.** Note that these abbreviations are capitalized, while the titles themselves are not.

•••

There is no Spanish equivalent for the English title *Ms.;* women are addressed as **señora** or **señorita.**

Comunicación

7 **Diálogos** With a partner, complete and role-play these conversations.

Conversación 1

—Hola. Me llamo Teresa. ¿Cómo te llamas tú?

—____

—Soy de Puerto Rico. ¿Y tú?

—____

Conversación 2

—____

—Muy bien, gracias. ¿Y usted, señora López?

—____

—Hasta luego, señora. Saludos al señor López.

—____

Conversación 3

—____

—Regular. ¿Y tú?

—____

—Nada.

8 **Conversaciones** This is the first day of class. Write four short conversations based on what the people in this scene would say.

9 **Situaciones** With a partner, role-play these situations.

1. On your way to the library, you strike up a conversation with another student. You find out the student's name and where he or she is from before you say goodbye.
2. At the library you meet up with a friend and find out how he or she is doing.
3. As you're leaving the library, you see your friend's father, Mr. Sánchez. You say hello and send greetings to Mrs. Sánchez.
4. Make up a real-life situation that you and your partner can role-play with the language you've learned.

Bienvenida, Marissa

Marissa llega a México para pasar un año con la familia Díaz.

PERSONAJES

MARISSA

SRA. DÍAZ

1

MARISSA ¿Usted es de Cuba?

SRA. DÍAZ Sí, de La Habana. Y Roberto es de Mérida. Tú eres de Wisconsin, ¿verdad?

MARISSA Sí, de Appleton, Wisconsin.

2

MARISSA ¿Quiénes son los dos chicos de las fotos? ¿Jimena y Felipe?

SRA. DÍAZ Sí. Ellos son estudiantes.

3

DON DIEGO Buenas tardes, señora. Señorita, bienvenida a la Ciudad de México.

MARISSA ¡Muchas gracias!

4

MARISSA ¿Cómo se llama usted?

DON DIEGO Yo soy Diego. Mucho gusto.

MARISSA El gusto es mío, don Diego.

5

DON DIEGO ¿Cómo está usted hoy, señora Carolina?

SRA. DÍAZ Muy bien, gracias. ¿Y usted?

DON DIEGO Bien, gracias.

6

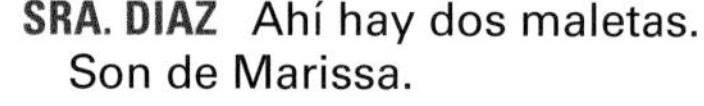

SRA. DÍAZ Ahí hay dos maletas. Son de Marissa.

DON DIEGO Con permiso.

DON DIEGO

SR. DÍAZ

FELIPE

JIMENA

SR. DÍAZ ¿Qué hora es?

FELIPE Son las cuatro y veinticinco.

SRA. DÍAZ Marissa, te presento a Roberto, mi esposo.

SR. DÍAZ Bienvenida, Marissa.

MARISSA Gracias, señor Díaz.

JIMENA ¿Qué hay en esta cosa?

MARISSA Bueno, a ver, hay tres cuadernos, un mapa... ¡Y un diccionario!

JIMENA ¿Cómo se dice mediodía en inglés?

FELIPE "*Noon*".

FELIPE Estás en México, ¿verdad?

MARISSA ¿Sí?

FELIPE Nosotros somos tu diccionario.

Expresiones útiles

Identifying yourself and others

¿Cómo se llama usted?
What's your name?
Yo soy Diego, el portero. Mucho gusto.
I'm Diego, the doorman. Nice to meet you.
¿Cómo te llamas?
What's your name?
Me llamo Marissa.
My name is Marissa.
¿Quién es...? / ¿Quiénes son...?
Who is...? / Who are...?
Es mi esposo.
He's my husband.
Tú eres..., ¿verdad?/¿cierto?/¿no?
You are..., right?

Identifying objects

¿Qué hay en esta cosa?
What's in this thing?
Bueno, a ver, aquí hay tres cuadernos...
Well, let's see, here are three notebooks...
Oye/Oiga, ¿cómo se dice *suitcase* en español?
Hey, how do you say suitcase *in Spanish?*
Se dice *maleta*.
You say maleta.

Saying what time it is

¿Qué hora es?
What time is it?
Es la una. / Son las dos.
It's one o'clock. / It's two o'clock.
Son las cuatro y veinticinco.
It's four twenty-five.

Polite expressions

Con permiso.
Pardon me; Excuse me. (to request permission)
Perdón.
Pardon me; Excuse me. (to get someone's attention or excuse yourself)
¡Bienvenido/a! *Welcome!*

¿Qué pasó?

1 **¿Cierto o falso?** Indicate if each statement is **cierto** or **falso**. Then correct the false statements.

	Cierto	Falso
1. La Sra. Díaz es de Caracas.	❍	❍
2. El Sr. Díaz es de Mérida.	❍	❍
3. Marissa es de Los Ángeles, California.	❍	❍
4. Jimena y Felipe son profesores.	❍	❍
5. Las dos maletas son de Jimena.	❍	❍
6. El Sr. Díaz pregunta "¿qué hora es?".	❍	❍
7. Hay un diccionario en la mochila (*backpack*) de Marissa.	❍	❍

2 **Identificar** Indicate which person would make each statement. One name will be used twice.

1. Son las cuatro y veinticinco, papá.
2. Roberto es mi esposo.
3. Yo soy de Wisconsin, ¿de dónde es usted?
4. ¿Qué hay de nuevo, doña Carolina?
5. Yo soy de Cuba.
6. ¿Qué hay en la mochila, Marissa?

MARISSA FELIPE SRA. DÍAZ DON DIEGO JIMENA

¡LENGUA VIVA!

In Spanish-speaking countries, **don** and **doña** are used with first names to show respect: **don Diego**, **doña Carolina**. Note that these titles, like **señor** and **señora**, are not capitalized.

3 **Completar** Complete the conversation between Don Diego and Marissa.

DON DIEGO Hola, (1)__________.
MARISSA Hola, señor. ¿Cómo se (2)__________ usted?
DON DIEGO Yo me llamo Diego, ¿y (3)__________?
MARISSA Yo me llamo Marissa. (4)__________.
DON DIEGO (5)__________, señorita Marissa.
MARISSA Nos (6)__________, don Diego.
DON DIEGO Hasta (7)__________, señorita Marissa.

4 **Conversar** Imagine that you are chatting with a traveler you just met at the airport. With a partner, prepare a conversation using these cues.

Estudiante 1		Estudiante 2
Say "good afternoon" to your partner and ask for his or her name.	→	Say hello and what your name is. Then ask what your partner's name is.
Say what your name is and that you are glad to meet your partner.	→	Say that the pleasure is yours.
Ask how your partner is.	→	Say that you're doing well, thank you.
Ask where your partner is from.	→	Say where you're from.
Say it's one o'clock and say goodbye.	→	Say goodbye.

Pronunciación

The Spanish alphabet

The Spanish and English alphabets are almost identical, with a few exceptions. For example, the Spanish letter **ñ (eñe)** doesn't occur in the English alphabet. Furthermore, the letters **k (ka)** and **w (doble ve)** are used only in words of foreign origin. Examine the chart below to find other differences.

¡LENGUA VIVA!

Note that **ch** and **ll** are digraphs, or two letters that together produce one sound. Conventionally they have been considered part of the alphabet, but **ch** and **ll** do not have their own entries when placing words in alphabetical order, as in a glossary.

Letra	Nombre(s)	Ejemplos	Letra	Nombre(s)	Ejemplos
a	a	adiós	m	eme	mapa
b	be	bien, problema	n	ene	nacionalidad
c	ce	cosa, cero	ñ	eñe	mañana
ch	che	chico	o	o	once
d	de	diario, nada	p	pe	profesor
e	e	estudiante	q	cu	qué
f	efe	foto	r	ere	regular, señora
g	ge	gracias, Gerardo, regular	s	ese	señor
h	hache	hola	t	te	tú
i	i	igualmente	u	u	usted
j	jota	Javier	v	ve	vista, nuevo
k	ka, ca	kilómetro	w	doble ve	*walkman*
l	ele	lápiz	x	equis	existir, México
ll	elle	llave	y	i griega, ye	yo
			z	zeta, ceta	zona

AYUDA

The letter combination **rr** produces a strong trilled sound which does not have an English equivalent. English speakers commonly make this sound when imitating the sound of a motor. This sound occurs with the **rr** between vowels and with the **r** at the beginning of a word: **puertorriqueño, terrible, Roberto,** etc.

El alfabeto Repeat the Spanish alphabet and example words after your teacher.

Práctica Spell these words aloud in Spanish.

1. nada
2. maleta
3. quince
4. muy
5. hombre
6. por favor
7. San Fernando
8. Estados Unidos
9. Puerto Rico
10. España
11. Javier
12. Ecuador
13. Maite
14. gracias
15. Nueva York

Refranes Read these sayings aloud

1 Seeing is believing.
2 Silence is golden.

EN DETALLE

Saludos y besos en los países hispanos

In Spanish-speaking countries, kissing on the cheek is a customary way to greet friends and family members. Even when people are introduced for the first time, it is common for them to kiss, particularly in non-business settings. Whereas North Americans maintain considerable personal space when greeting, Spaniards and Latin Americans tend to decrease their personal space and give one or two kisses (**besos**) on the cheek, sometimes accompanied by a handshake or a hug. In formal business settings, where associates do not know one another on a personal level, a simple handshake is appropriate.

Greeting someone with a **beso** varies according to gender and region. Men generally greet each other with a hug or warm handshake, with the exception of Argentina, where male friends and relatives lightly kiss on the cheek. Greetings between men and women, and between women, generally include kissing, but can differ depending on the country and context. In Spain, it is customary to give **dos besos**, starting with the right cheek first. In Latin American countries, including Mexico, Costa Rica, Colombia, and Chile, a greeting consists of a single "air kiss" on the right cheek. Peruvians also "air kiss," but strangers will simply shake hands. In Colombia, female acquaintances tend to simply pat each other on the right forearm or shoulder.

Tendencias

País	Beso	País	Beso
Argentina	💋	**España**	💋💋
Bolivia	💋	**México**	💋
Chile	💋	**Paraguay**	💋💋
Colombia	💋	**Puerto Rico**	💋
El Salvador	💋	**Venezuela**	💋/💋💋

ACTIVIDADES

1 **¿Cierto o falso?** Indicate whether these statements are true (**cierto**) or false (**falso**). Correct the false statements.

1. In Spanish-speaking countries, people use less personal space when greeting than in the U.S.
2. Men never greet with a kiss in Spanish-speaking countries.
3. Shaking hands is not appropriate for a business setting in Latin America.
4. Spaniards greet with one kiss on the right cheek.
5. In Mexico, people greet with an "air kiss."
6. Gender can play a role in the type of greeting given.
7. If two women acquaintances meet in Colombia, they should exchange two kisses on the cheek.
8. In Peru, a man and a woman meeting for the first time would probably greet each other with an "air kiss."

ASÍ SE DICE

Saludos y despedidas

¿Cómo te/le va?	*How are things going (for you)?*
¡Cuánto tiempo!	*It's been a long time!*
Hasta ahora.	*See you soon.*
¿Qué hay?	*What's new?*
¿Qué onda? (Méx., Arg., Chi.); ¿Qué más? (Ven., Col.)	*What's going on?*

EL MUNDO HISPANO

Parejas y amigos famosos

Here are some famous couples and friends from the Spanish-speaking world.

- **Penélope Cruz** (España) y **Javier Bardem** (España) Both Oscar-winning actors, the couple married in 2010. They starred together in ***Vicky Cristina Barcelona*** (2008).
- **Gael García Bernal** (México) y **Diego Luna** (México) These lifelong friends became famous when they starred in the 2001 Mexican film ***Y tu mamá también***. They continue to work together on projects, such as the 2012 film ***Casa de mi padre.***

- **Salma Hayek** (México) y **Penélope Cruz** (España) These two close friends developed their acting skills in their home countries before meeting in Hollywood.

PERFIL

La plaza principal

In the Spanish-speaking world, public space is treasured. Small city and town life revolves around the **plaza principal**. Often surrounded by cathedrals or municipal buildings like the **ayuntamiento** (*city hall*), the pedestrian **plaza** is designated as a central meeting place for family and friends. During warmer months, when outdoor cafés usually line the **plaza**, it is a popular spot to have a leisurely cup of coffee, chat, and people watch. Many town festivals, or **ferias**, also take place in this space. One of the most famous town squares is the **Plaza Mayor** in the university town of Salamanca, Spain. Students gather underneath its famous clock tower to meet up with friends or simply take a coffee break.

La Plaza Mayor de Salamanca

La Plaza de Armas, Lima, Perú

Conexión Internet

What are the plazas principales in large cities such as Mexico City and Caracas?

Use the Web to find more cultural information related to this **Cultura** section.

ACTIVIDADES

2 **Comprensión** Answer these questions.

1. What are two types of buildings found on the **plaza principal?**
2. What two types of events or activities are common at a **plaza principal?**
3. How would Diego Luna greet his friends?
4. Would Salma Hayek and Gael García Bernal greet each other with one kiss or two?

3 **Saludos** Role-play these greetings with a partner.

1. friends in Mexico
2. business associates at a conference in Chile
3. friends meeting in Madrid's Plaza Mayor
4. Peruvians meeting for the first time
5. relatives in Argentina

1.1 Nouns and articles

Spanish nouns

ANTE TODO A noun is a word used to identify people, animals, places, things, or ideas. Unlike English, all Spanish nouns, even those that refer to non-living things, have gender; that is, they are considered either masculine or feminine. As in English, nouns in Spanish also have number, meaning that they are either singular or plural.

Nouns that refer to living things

Masculine nouns		Feminine nouns	
el hombre	*the man*	**la mujer**	*the woman*
ending in *–o*		ending in *–a*	
el chico	*the boy*	**la chica**	*the girl*
el pasajero	*the (male) passenger*	**la pasajera**	*the (female) passenger*
ending in *–or*		ending in *–ora*	
el conductor	*the (male) driver*	**la conductora**	*the (female) driver*
el profesor	*the (male) teacher*	**la profesora**	*the (female) teacher*
ending in *–ista*		ending in *–ista*	
el turista	*the (male) tourist*	**la turista**	*the (female) tourist*

- Generally, nouns that refer to males, like **el hombre**, are masculine, while nouns that refer to females, like **la mujer**, are feminine.
- Many nouns that refer to male beings end in **–o** or **–or**. Their corresponding feminine forms end in **–a** and **–ora**, respectively.

el conductor

la profesora

- The masculine and feminine forms of nouns that end in **–ista**, like **turista**, are the same, so gender is indicated by the article **el** (masculine) or **la** (feminine). Some other nouns have identical masculine and feminine forms.

el joven *the young man*	**la** joven *the young woman*
el estudiante *the (male) student*	**la** estudiante *the (female) student*

¡LENGUA VIVA!

Profesor(a) and **turista** are *cognates*— words that share similar spellings and meanings in Spanish and English. Recognizing cognates will help you determine the meaning of many Spanish words. Here are some other cognates: **la administración, el animal, el apartamento, el cálculo, el color, la decisión, la historia, la música, el restaurante, el/la secretario/a.**

AYUDA

Cognates can certainly be very helpful in your study of Spanish. Beware, however, of "false" cognates, those that have similar spellings in Spanish and English, but different meanings:

la carpeta *folder*
el/la conductor(a) *driver*
el éxito *success*
la fábrica *factory*

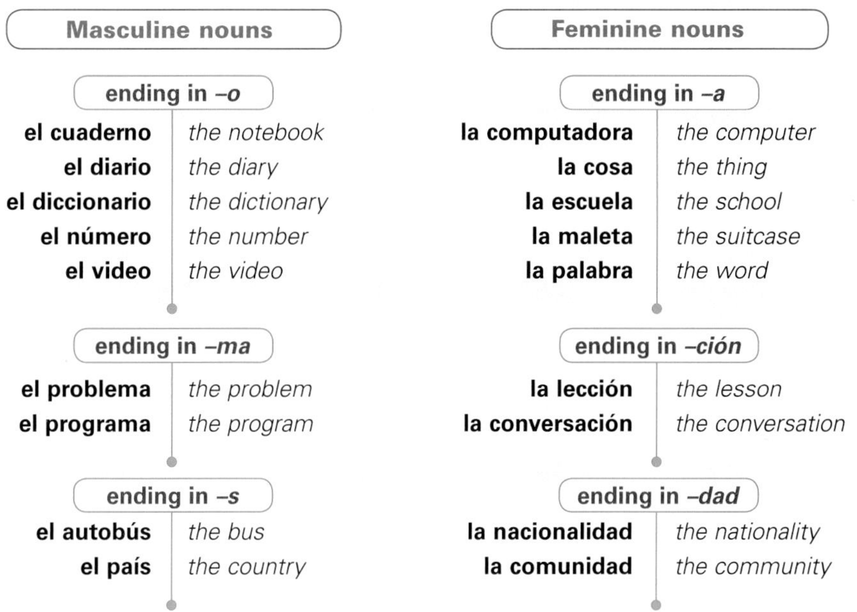

Nouns that refer to non-living things

Masculine nouns		Feminine nouns	
ending in *–o*		**ending in *–a***	
el cuaderno	*the notebook*	**la computadora**	*the computer*
el diario	*the diary*	**la cosa**	*the thing*
el diccionario	*the dictionary*	**la escuela**	*the school*
el número	*the number*	**la maleta**	*the suitcase*
el video	*the video*	**la palabra**	*the word*
ending in *–ma*		**ending in *–ción***	
el problema	*the problem*	**la lección**	*the lesson*
el programa	*the program*	**la conversación**	*the conversation*
ending in *–s*		**ending in *–dad***	
el autobús	*the bus*	**la nacionalidad**	*the nationality*
el país	*the country*	**la comunidad**	*the community*

¡LENGUA VIVA!

The Spanish word for *video* can be pronounced with the stress on the **i** or the **e**. For that reason, you might see the word written with or without an accent: **video** or **vídeo**.

- As shown above, certain noun endings are strongly associated with a specific gender, so you can use them to determine if a noun is masculine or feminine.
- Because the gender of nouns that refer to non-living things cannot be determined by foolproof rules, you should memorize the gender of each noun you learn. It is helpful to learn each noun with its corresponding article, **el** for masculine and **la** for feminine.
- Another reason to memorize the gender of every noun is that there are common exceptions to the rules of gender. For example, **el mapa** (*map*) and **el día** (*day*) end in **–a**, but are masculine. **La mano** (*hand*) ends in **–o**, but is feminine.

Plural of nouns

- To form the plural, add **–s** to nouns that end in a vowel. For nouns that end in a consonant, add **–es**. For nouns that end in **z**, change the **z** to **c**, then add **–es**.

el chic**o** → los chic**os**	la nacionalida**d** → las nacionalida**des**
el diari**o** → los diari**os**	el paí**s** → los paí**ses**
el problem**a** → los problem**as**	el lápi**z** (*pencil*) → los lápi**ces**

- In general, when a singular noun has an accent mark on the last syllable, the accent is dropped from the plural form.

la lecci**ón** → las lecci**ones**   el autob**ús** → los autob**uses**

CONSULTA

You will learn more about accent marks in **Senderos 1B, Lección 4, Pronunciación**, p. 33.

- Use the masculine plural form to refer to a group that includes both males and females.

1 pasajer**o** + 2 pasajer**as** = 3 pasajer**os**   2 chic**os** + 2 chic**as** = 4 chic**os**

Spanish articles

ANTE TODO As you know, English often uses definite articles (*the*) and indefinite articles (*a, an*) before nouns. Spanish also has definite and indefinite articles. Unlike English, Spanish articles vary in form because they agree in gender and number with the nouns they modify.

Definite articles

▶ Spanish has four forms that are equivalent to the English definite article *the*. Use definite articles to refer to specific nouns.

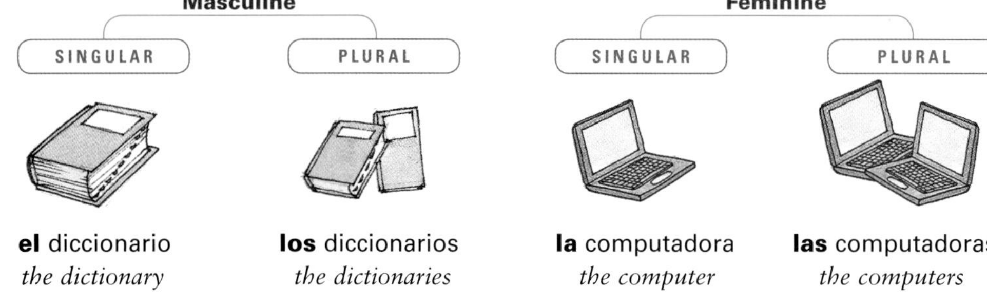

el diccionario *the dictionary* | **los** diccionarios *the dictionaries* | **la** computadora *the computer* | **las** computadoras *the computers*

¡LENGUA VIVA!

Feminine singular nouns that begin with a stressed **a-** or **ha-** require the masculine articles **el** and **un**. This is done in order to avoid repetition of the a sound. The plural forms still use the feminine articles.

el agua *water*
las aguas *waters*
un hacha *ax*
unas hachas *axes*

Indefinite articles

▶ Spanish has four forms that are equivalent to the English indefinite article, which according to context may mean *a*, *an*, or *some*. Use indefinite articles to refer to unspecified persons or things.

un pasajero *a (one) passenger* | **unos** pasajeros *some passengers* | **una** fotografía *a (one) photograph* | **unas** fotografías *some photographs*

¡LENGUA VIVA!

Since **la fotografía** is feminine, so is its shortened form, **la foto**, even though it ends in **–o**.

¡INTÉNTALO! Provide a definite article for each noun in the first column and an indefinite article for each noun in the second column.

¿el, la, los o las?	¿un, una, unos o unas?
1. la chica	1. un autobús
2. ______ chico	2. ______ escuelas
3. ______ maleta	3. ______ computadora
4. ______ cuadernos	4. ______ hombres
5. ______ lápiz	5. ______ señora
6. ______ mujeres	6. ______ lápices

Práctica

1 **¿Singular o plural?** If the word is singular, make it plural. If it is plural, make it singular.

1. el número
2. un diario
3. la estudiante
4. el conductor
5. el país
6. las cosas
7. unos turistas
8. las nacionalidades
9. unas computadoras
10. los problemas
11. una fotografía
12. los profesores
13. unas señoritas
14. el hombre
15. la maleta
16. la señora

2 **Identificar** For each drawing, provide the noun with its corresponding definite and indefinite articles.

las maletas, unas maletas

1. ____________

2. ____________

3. ____________

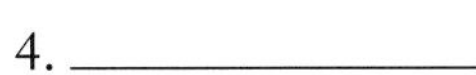

4. ____________

5. ____________

6. ____________

7. ____________

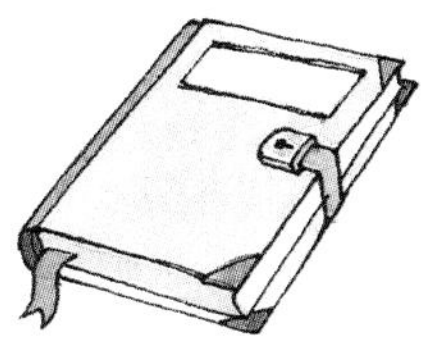

8. ____________

Comunicación

3 **Un juego** With a partner, play a game in which one of you names a noun and the other says a related noun (**un chico; un estudiante**). Keep the chain going until one of you can't think of another noun.

1.2 Numbers 0–30

Los números 0 a 30

0	cero				
1	uno	**11**	once	**21**	veintiuno
2	dos	**12**	doce	**22**	veintidós
3	tres	**13**	trece	**23**	veintitrés
4	cuatro	**14**	catorce	**24**	veinticuatro
5	cinco	**15**	quince	**25**	veinticinco
6	seis	**16**	dieciséis	**26**	veintiséis
7	siete	**17**	diecisiete	**27**	veintisiete
8	ocho	**18**	dieciocho	**28**	veintiocho
9	nueve	**19**	diecinueve	**29**	veintinueve
10	diez	**20**	veinte	**30**	treinta

AYUDA

Though it is less common, the numbers 16 through 29 (except 20) can also be written as three words: **diez y seis, diez y siete...**

- The number **uno** (*one*) and numbers ending in **–uno**, such as **veintiuno**, have more than one form. Before masculine nouns, **uno** shortens to **un**. Before feminine nouns, **uno** changes to **una**.

  un hombre → veinti**ún** hombres   **una** mujer → veinti**una** mujeres

- **¡Atención!** The forms **uno** and **veintiuno** are used when counting (**uno, dos, tres... veinte, veintiuno, veintidós...**). They are also used when the number *follows* a noun, even if the noun is feminine: **la lección uno**.

- To ask *how many people* or *things* there are, use **cuántos** before masculine nouns and **cuántas** before feminine nouns.

- The Spanish equivalent of both *there is* and *there are* is **hay**. Use **¿Hay...?** to ask *Is there...?* or *Are there...?* Use **no hay** to express *there is not* or *there are not*.

—¿**Cuántos** estudiantes **hay**?
How many students are there?

—**Hay** seis estudiantes en la foto.
There are six students in the photo.

—¿**Hay** chicos en la fotografía?
Are there guys in the picture?

—**Hay** tres chicas y **no hay** chicos.
There are three girls, and there are no guys.

¡INTÉNTALO! Provide the Spanish words for these numbers.

1. **7** ________	5. **0** ________	9. **23** ________	13. **12** ________
2. **16** ________	6. **15** ________	10. **11** ________	14. **28** ________
3. **29** ________	7. **21** ________	11. **30** ________	15. **14** ________
4. **1** ________	8. **9** ________	12. **4** ________	16. **10** ________

Práctica

1 **Contar** Following the pattern, write out the missing numbers in Spanish.

1. 1, 3, 5, ..., 29
2. 2, 4, 6, ..., 30
3. 3, 6, 9, ..., 30
4. 30, 28, 26, ..., 0
5. 30, 25, 20, ..., 0
6. 28, 24, 20, ..., 0

2 **Resolver** Solve these math problems.

AYUDA

+ → **más**
– → **menos**
= → **son**

modelo

5 + 3 =

Cinco más tres son ocho.

1. **2 + 15 =**
2. **20 – 1 =**
3. **5 + 7 =**
4. **18 + 12 =**
5. **3 + 22 =**
6. **6 – 3 =**
7. **11 + 12 =**
8. **7 – 2 =**
9. **8 + 5 =**
10. **23 – 14 =**

3 **¿Cuántos hay?** How many persons or things are there in these drawings?

modelo

Hay tres maletas.

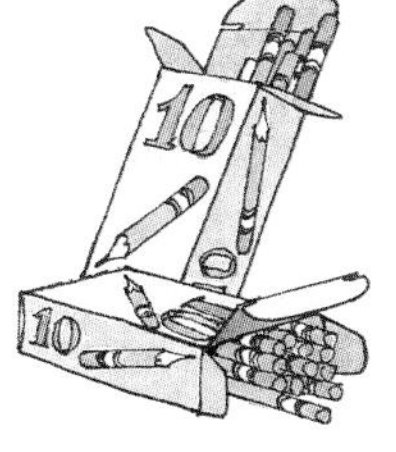

1. ______________

2. ______________

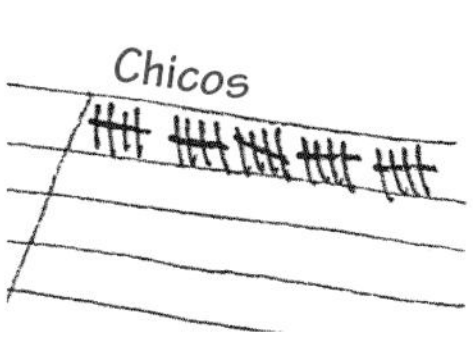

3. ______________

4. ______________

5. ______________

6. ______________

7. ______________

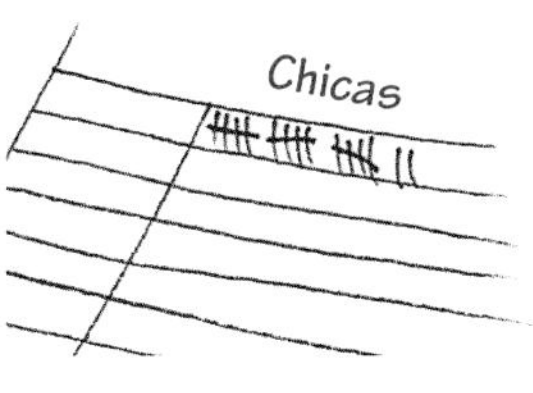

8. ______________

Comunicación

4 **¿Cuántos?** Answer your partner's questions about the place where you study.

1. ¿Cuántos estudiantes hay?
2. ¿Hay un video?
3. ¿Hay una computadora?
4. ¿Hay una maleta?
5. ¿Cuántos mapas hay?
6. ¿Cuántos lápices hay?
7. ¿Hay cuadernos?
8. ¿Cuántos diccionarios hay?
9. ¿Hay un diario?
10. ¿Cuántas fotografías hay?

5 **Preguntas** With a partner, take turns asking and answering questions about the drawing. Talk about:

1. how many children there are
2. how many women there are
3. if there are some photographs
4. if there is a boy
5. how many notebooks there are
6. if there is a bus
7. if there are tourists
8. how many pencils there are
9. if there is a man
10. how many computers there are

1.3 Present tense of ser

Subject pronouns

ANTE TODO In order to use verbs, you will need to learn about subject pronouns. A subject pronoun replaces the name or title of a person and acts as the subject of a verb.

Subject pronouns

SINGULAR		PLURAL	
yo	*I*	**nosotros**	*we* (masculine)
		nosotras	*we* (feminine)
tú	*you* (familiar)	**vosotros**	*you* (masc., fam.)
usted (Ud.)	*you* (formal)	**vosotras**	*you* (fem., fam.)
		ustedes (Uds.)	*you*
él	*he*	**ellos**	*they* (masc.)
ella	*she*	**ellas**	*they* (fem.)

¡LENGUA VIVA!

In Latin America, **ustedes** is used as the plural for both **tú** and **usted**. In Spain, however, **vosotros** and **vosotras** are used as the plural of **tú**, and **ustedes** is used only as the plural of **usted**.

•••

Usted and **ustedes** are abbreviated as **Ud.** and **Uds.**, or occasionally as **Vd.** and **Vds.**

- Spanish has two subject pronouns that mean *you* (singular). Use **tú** when addressing a friend, a family member, or a child you know well. Use **usted** to address a person with whom you have a formal or more distant relationship, such as a superior at work, a teacher, or an older person.

Tú eres de Canadá, ¿verdad, David?
You are from Canada, right, David?

¿**Usted** es la profesora de español?
Are you the Spanish teacher?

- The masculine plural forms **nosotros**, **vosotros**, and **ellos** refer to a group of males or to a group of males and females. The feminine plural forms **nosotras**, **vosotras**, and **ellas** can refer only to groups made up exclusively of females.

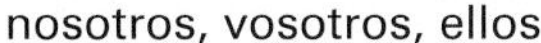
nosotros, vosotros, ellos

nosotros, vosotros, ellos

nosotras, vosotras, ellas

- There is no Spanish equivalent of the English subject pronoun *it*. Generally *it* is not expressed in Spanish.

Es un problema.
It's a problem.

Es una computadora.
It's a computer.

The present tense of ser

ANTE TODO In **Contextos** and **Fotonovela**, you have already used several present-tense forms of **ser** (*to be*) to identify yourself and others, and to talk about where you and others are from. **Ser** is an irregular verb; its forms do not follow the regular patterns that most verbs follow. You need to memorize the forms, which appear in this chart.

The verb ser (*to be*)

SINGULAR FORMS	yo	**soy**	*I am*
	tú	**eres**	*you are* (fam.)
	Ud./él/ella	**es**	*you are* (form.); *he/she is*
PLURAL FORMS	nosotros/as	**somos**	*we are*
	vosotros/as	**sois**	*you are* (fam.)
	Uds./ellos/ellas	**son**	*you are; they are*

Uses of *ser*

- Use **ser** to identify people and things.

—¿Quién **es** él?
Who is he?

—**Es** Felipe Díaz Velázquez.
He's Felipe Díaz Velázquez.

—¿Qué **es**?
What is it?

—**Es** un mapa de España.
It's a map of Spain.

Es Marissa.

Es una maleta.

- **Ser** also expresses possession, with the preposition **de**. There is no Spanish equivalent of the English construction [*noun*] + 's (*Maru's*). In its place, Spanish uses [*noun*] + **de** + [*owner*].

—¿**De** quién **es**?
Whose is it?

—**Es** el diario **de** Maru.
It's Maru's diary.

—¿**De** quién **son**?
Whose are they?

—**Son** los lápices **de** la chica.
They are the girl's pencils.

- When **de** is followed by the article **el**, the two combine to form the contraction **del**. **De** does *not* contract with **la**, **las**, or **los**.

—**Es** la computadora **del** conductor.
It's the driver's computer.

—**Son** las maletas **del** chico.
They are the boy's suitcases.

¡LENGUA VIVA!

Some geographic locations can be referred to either with or without a definite article:

Soy de Estados Unidos./Soy de los Estados Unidos.

• • •

Sometimes a definite article is a part of a proper name, as in **El Salvador, El Paso**, and **Los Ángeles**. In these cases, **de** and **el** do not contract:

Soy de El Salvador.

▶ **Ser** also uses the preposition **de** to express origin.

—¿**De** dónde **es** Juan Carlos?
Where is Juan Carlos from?

—Es **de** Argentina.
He's from Argentina.

—¿**De** dónde **es** Maru?
Where is Maru from?

—**Es de** Costa Rica.
She's from Costa Rica.

▶ Use **ser** to express profession or occupation.

Don Francisco **es conductor**.
Don Francisco is a driver.

Yo **soy estudiante**.
I am a student.

CONSULTA

You will learn more about adjectives in **Estructura 3.1**, pp. 112–114.

▶ Unlike English, Spanish does not use the indefinite article (**un, una**) after **ser** when referring to professions, unless accompanied by an adjective or other description.

Marta **es** profesora.
Marta is a teacher.

Marta **es una** profesora excelente.
Marta is an excellent teacher.

NOTA CULTURAL

Created in 1998, LAN Perú is an affiliate of the Chilean-based LAN Airlines, one of the largest carriers in South America. LAN Perú operates out of Lima, offering domestic flights and international service to select major cities in the Americas and Spain.

¡INTÉNTALO! Provide the correct subject pronouns and the present forms of **ser**.

1. Gabriel _él_ _es_
2. Juan y yo ______ ______
3. Óscar y Flora ______ ______
4. Adriana ______ ______
5. las turistas ______ ______
6. el chico ______ ______
7. los conductores ______ ______
8. los señores Ruiz ______ ______

Práctica

1 **Pronombres** What subject pronouns would you use to (a) talk *to* these people directly and (b) talk *about* them to others?

modelo

un joven *tú, él*

1. una chica
2. el presidente de México
3. tres chicas y un chico
4. un estudiante
5. la señora Ochoa
6. dos profesoras

2 **Identidad y origen** Answer these questions about the people indicated: **¿Quién es?/¿Quiénes son?** and **¿De dónde es?/¿De dónde son?**

modelo

Selena Gomez (Estados Unidos)
¿Quién es? *¿De dónde es?*
Es Selena Gomez. *Es de los Estados Unidos.*

1. Enrique Iglesias (España)
2. Robinson Canó (República Dominicana)
3. Eva Mendes y Marc Anthony (Estados Unidos)
4. Carlos Santana y Salma Hayek (México)
5. Shakira (Colombia)
6. Antonio Banderas y Penélope Cruz (España)
7. Taylor Swift y Demi Lovato (Estados Unidos)
8. Daisy Fuentes (Cuba)

3 **¿Qué es?** Indicate what each object is and to whom it belongs.

modelo

¿Qué es? *¿De quién es?*
Es un diccionario. *Es del profesor Núñez.*

1. 

2. 

3. 

4. 

Comunicación

4 **La clase** Read Stephanie's description of one of her classes. Then indicate whether the following conclusions are **lógico** or **ilógico**, based on what you read.

> Yo soy Stephanie. Soy estudiante de la clase de la señora Rodríguez. Ella es de Uruguay y yo soy de los Estados Unidos. En la clase de la señora Rodríguez hay diez diccionarios de español y una computadora. Los diccionarios son de los estudiantes y la computadora es de la señora Rodríguez.

	Lógico	Ilógico
1. La señora Rodríguez es profesora.	❍	❍
2. Stephanie es de Madrid.	❍	❍
3. Es una clase de español.	❍	❍
4. Hay dos estudiantes en la clase.	❍	❍
5. La señora Rodríguez es de Miami.	❍	❍

5 **Famosos** Describe several famous people using the vocabulary and grammar you have learned. Use the list of professions to think of people from a variety of backgrounds.

NOTA CULTURAL

John Leguizamo was born in Bogotá, Colombia. He is best known for his work as an actor and comedian.

actor *actor*	cantante *singer*	escritor(a) *writer*
actriz *actress*	deportista *athlete*	músico/a *musician*

modelo

▶ *John Leguizamo es actor. Es de Colombia...*

6  **Preguntas** Using the items in the word bank, ask your partner questions about the ad.

¿Cuántas?	¿De dónde?	¿Qué?
¿Cuántos?	¿De quién?	¿Quién?

SOMOS ECOTURISTA, S.A.

Los autobuses oficiales de la Ruta Maya

- 25 autobuses en total
- 30 conductores del área
- pasajeros internacionales
- mapas de la región

¡Todos a bordo!

1.4 Telling time

ANTE TODO In both English and Spanish, the verb *to be* (**ser**) and numbers are used to tell time.

▶ To ask what time it is, use **¿Qué hora es?** When telling time, use **es + la** with **una** and **son + las** with all other hours.

Es la una.

Son las dos.

Son las seis.

▶ As in English, you express time in Spanish from the hour to the half hour by adding minutes.

Son las cuatro **y cinco.**

Son las once **y veinte.**

▶ You may use either **y cuarto** or **y quince** to express fifteen minutes or quarter past the hour. For thirty minutes or half past the hour, you may use either **y media** or **y treinta**.

Es la una **y cuarto.**

Son las nueve **y quince.**

Son las doce **y media.**

Son las siete **y treinta.**

▶ You express time from the half hour to the hour in Spanish by subtracting minutes or a portion of an hour from the next hour.

Es la una **menos cuarto.**

Son las tres **menos quince.**

Son las ocho **menos veinte.**

Son las tres **menos diez.**

¡LENGUA VIVA!

Other useful expressions for telling time:

Son las doce (del día). It is twelve o'clock (p.m.).

Son las doce (de la noche). It is twelve o'clock (a.m.).

▶ To ask at what time a particular event takes place, use the phrase **¿A qué hora (...)?** To state at what time something takes place, use the construction **a la(s)** + *time*.

¿A qué hora es la clase de biología?
(At) what time is biology class?

La clase es **a las dos**.
The class is at two o'clock.

¿A qué hora es la fiesta?
(At) what time is the party?

A las ocho.
At eight.

▶ Here are some useful words and phrases associated with telling time.

Son las ocho **en punto**.
It's 8 o'clock on the dot/sharp.

Son las nueve **de la mañana**.
It's 9 a.m./in the morning.

Es **el mediodía**.
It's noon.

Son las cuatro y cuarto **de la tarde**.
It's 4:15 p.m./in the afternoon.

Es **la medianoche**.
It's midnight.

Son las diez y media **de la noche**.
It's 10:30 p.m./at night.

¡INTÉNTALO! Practice telling time by completing these sentences.

1. (1:00 a.m.) Es la ___una___ de la mañana.
2. (2:50 a.m.) Son las tres ______________ diez de la mañana.
3. (4:15 p.m.) Son las cuatro y ______________ de la tarde.
4. (8:30 p.m.) Son las ocho y ______________ de la noche.
5. (9:15 a.m.) Son las nueve y quince de la ______________.
6. (12:00 p.m.) Es el ______________.
7. (6:00 a.m.) Son las seis de la ______________.
8. (4:05 p.m.) Son las cuatro y cinco de la ______________.
9. (12:00 a.m.) Es la ______________.
10. (3:45 a.m.) Son las cuatro menos ______________ de la mañana.
11. (2:15 a.m.) Son las ______________ y cuarto de la mañana.
12. (1:25 p.m.) Es la una y ______________ de la tarde.
13. (6:50 a.m.) Son las ______________ menos diez de la mañana.
14. (10:40 p.m.) Son las once menos veinte de la ______________.

Práctica

1 **Ordenar** Put these times in order, from the earliest to the latest.

a. Son las dos de la tarde.
b. Son las once de la mañana.
c. Son las siete y media de la noche.
d. Son las seis menos cuarto de la tarde.
e. Son las dos menos diez de la tarde.
f. Son las ocho y veintidós de la mañana.

2 **¿Qué hora es?** Give the times shown on each clock or watch.

modelo

Son las cuatro y cuarto/quince de la tarde.

p.m.

p.m.

p.m.

a.m.

1. __________ 2. __________ 3. __________ 4. __________ 5. __________

a.m.

a.m.

p.m.

6. __________ 7. __________ 8. __________ 9. __________ 10. __________

3 **¿A qué hora?** Indicate at what time these events take place.

modelo

la clase de matemáticas (2:30 p.m.)
La clase de matemáticas es a las dos y media de la tarde.

1. el programa *Las cuatro amigas* (*11:30 a.m.*)
2. el drama *La casa de Bernarda Alba* (*7:00 p.m.*)
3. el programa *Las computadoras* (*8:30 a.m.*)
4. la clase de español (*10:30 a.m.*)
5. la clase de biología (*9:40 a.m.*)
6. la clase de historia (*10:50 a.m.*)
7. el partido (*game*) de béisbol (*5:15 p.m.*)
8. el partido de tenis (*12:45 p.m.*)
9. el partido de baloncesto (*basketball*) (*7:45 p.m.*)

NOTA CULTURAL

Many Spanish-speaking countries use both the 12-hour clock and the 24-hour clock (that is, military time). The 24-hour clock is commonly used in written form on signs and schedules. For example, 1 p.m. is **13h**, 2 p.m. is **14h** and so on. See the photo on p. 57 for a sample schedule.

NOTA CULTURAL

La casa de Bernarda Alba is a famous play by Spanish poet and playwright **Federico García Lorca** (1898–1936). Lorca was one of the most famous writers of the 20th century and a close friend of Spain's most talented artists, including the painter Salvador Dalí and the filmmaker Luis Buñuel.

Comunicación

4 **Escuchar** Laura and David are taking the same courses and are checking to see if they have the same schedule. Listen as they confirm the times of several of their classes.

	Lógico	Ilógico
1. La clase es a las once y media de la mañana.	❍	❍
2. La clase de historia es a las once y cuarto.	❍	❍
3. La fiesta es a las ocho de la noche.	❍	❍
4. Rafael es estudiante.	❍	❍

5 **Preguntas** Answer your partner's questions based on your own knowledge.

1. Son las tres de la tarde en Nueva York. ¿Qué hora es en Los Ángeles?
2. Son las ocho y media en Chicago. ¿Qué hora es en Miami?
3. Son las dos menos cinco en San Francisco. ¿Qué hora es en San Antonio?
4. ¿A qué hora es el programa *Saturday Night Live*?; ¿A qué hora es el programa *American Idol*?

6 **Horas** Write sentences about the times that your favorite TV shows are on. Mention at least three shows.

Síntesis

7 **Situación** With a partner, play the roles of a student reporter interviewing the new Spanish teacher (**profesor(a) de español**) from Venezuela.

Estudiante	Profesor(a) de literatura
Ask the teacher his/her name.	→ Ask the student his/her name.
Ask the teacher what time his/her literature class is.	→ Ask the student where he/she is from.
Ask how many students are in his/her class.	→ Ask to whom the notebook belongs.
Say thank you and goodbye.	→ Say thank you and you are pleased to meet him/her.

Recapitulación

RESUMEN GRAMATICAL

Review the grammar concepts you have learned in this lesson by completing these activities.

1 **Completar** Complete the charts according to the models. 28 pts.

Masculino	Femenino
el chico	*la chica*
	la profesora
	la amiga
el señor	
	la pasajera
el estudiante	
	la turista
el joven	

Singular	Plural
una cosa	*unas cosas*
un libro	
	unas clases
una lección	
un conductor	
	unos países
	unos lápices
un problema	

2 **En la clase** Complete each conversation with the correct word. 22 pts.

César   Beatriz

CÉSAR ¿(1) __________ (Cuántos/Cuántas) chicas hay en la (2) __________ (maleta/clase)?

BEATRIZ Hay (3) __________ (catorce/cuatro) [*14*] chicas.

CÉSAR Y, ¿(4) __________ (cuántos/cuántas) chicos hay?

BEATRIZ Hay (5) __________ (tres/trece) [*13*] chicos.

CÉSAR Entonces (*Then*), en total hay (6) __________ (veintiséis/veintisiete) (7) __________ (estudiantes/chicas) en la clase.

Ariana  Daniel

ARIANA ¿Tienes (*Do you have*) (8) __________ (un/una) diccionario?

DANIEL No, pero (*but*) aquí (9) __________ (es/hay) uno.

ARIANA ¿De quién (10) __________ (son/es)?

DANIEL (11) __________ (Son/Es) de Carlos.

1.1 Nouns and articles *pp. 36–38*

Gender of nouns

Nouns that refer to living things

	Masculine		Feminine
-o	el chico	-a	la chica
-or	el profesor	-ora	la profesora
-ista	el turista	-ista	la turista

Nouns that refer to non-living things

	Masculine		Feminine
-o	el libro	-a	la cosa
-ma	el programa	-ción	la lección
-s	el autobús	-dad	la nacionalidad

Plural of nouns

- ending in vowel + *-s* — la chica → las chicas
- ending in consonant + *-es* — el señor → los señores
  (-z → -ces un lápiz → unos lápices)
- Definite articles: el, la, los, las
- Indefinite articles: un, una, unos, unas

1.2 Numbers 0–30 *p. 40*

0	cero	8	ocho	16	dieciséis
1	uno	9	nueve	17	diecisiete
2	dos	10	diez	18	dieciocho
3	tres	11	once	19	diecinueve
4	cuatro	12	doce	20	veinte
5	cinco	13	trece	21	veintiuno
6	seis	14	catorce	22	veintidós
7	siete	15	quince	30	treinta

1.3 Present tense of *ser* *pp. 43–45*

yo	soy	nosotros/as	somos
tú	eres	vosotros/as	sois
Ud./él/ella	es	Uds./ellos/ellas	son

1.4 Telling time pp. 48–49

Es la una.	*It's 1:00.*
Son las dos.	*It's 2:00.*
Son las tres y diez.	*It's 3:10.*
Es la una y cuarto/ quince.	*It's 1:15.*
Son las siete y media/ treinta.	*It's 7:30.*
Es la una menos cuarto/quince.	*It's 12:45.*
Son las once menos veinte.	*It's 10:40.*
Es el mediodía.	*It's noon.*
Es la medianoche.	*It's midnight.*

3 **Presentaciones** Complete this conversation with the correct form of the verb **ser**. **18 pts.**

JUAN ¡Hola! Me llamo Juan. (1) ________ estudiante en la clase de español.

DANIELA ¡Hola! Mucho gusto. Yo (2) ________ Daniela y ella (3) ________ Mónica. ¿De dónde (4) ________ (tú), Juan?

JUAN De California. Y ustedes, ¿de dónde (5) ________ ?

MÓNICA Nosotras (6) ________ de Florida.

4 **¿Qué hora es?** Write out in words the following times, indicating whether it's morning, noon, afternoon, or night. **28 pts.**

1. It's 12:00 p.m.
____
2. It's 7:05 a.m.
____
3. It's 9:35 p.m.
____
4. It's 5:15 p.m.
____
5. It's 1:30 p.m.
____
6. It's 11:50 a.m.
____
7. It's 3:10 p.m.
____

5 **Canción** Use the two appropriate words from the list to complete this children's song. **4 pts.**

cinco cuántas cuatro media quiénes

"________ patas°
tiene un gato°?
Una, dos, tres y
________."

patas *legs* tiene un gato *does a cat have*

Lectura

Antes de leer

Estrategia

Recognizing cognates

As you learned earlier in this lesson, cognates are words that share similar meanings and spellings in two or more languages. When reading in Spanish, it's helpful to look for cognates and use them to guess the meaning of what you're reading. But watch out for false cognates. For example, **librería** means *bookstore*, not *library*, and **embarazada** means *pregnant*, not *embarrassed*. Look at this list of Spanish words, paying special attention to prefixes and suffixes. Can you guess the meaning of each word?

importante	oportunidad
farmacia	cultura
inteligente	activo
dentista	sociología
decisión	espectacular
televisión	restaurante
médico	policía

Examinar el texto

Glance quickly at the reading selection and guess what type of document it is. Explain your answer.

Cognados

Read the document and make a list of the cognates you find. Guess their English equivalents.

Joaquín Salvador Lavado nació (*was born*) en Argentina en 1932 (mil novecientos treinta y dos). Su nombre profesional es **Quino**. Es muy popular en Latinoamérica, Europa y Canadá por sus tiras cómicas (*comic strips*). *Mafalda* es su serie más famosa. La protagonista, Mafalda, es una chica muy inteligente de seis años (*years*). La tira cómica ilustra las aventuras de ella y su grupo de amigos. Las anécdotas de Mafalda y los chicos también presentan temas (*themes*) importantes como la paz (*peace*) y los derechos humanos (*human rights*).

Después de leer

Preguntas

Answer these questions.

1. What is Joaquín Salvador Lavado's pen name?
2. What is Mafalda like?
3. Where is Mafalda in panel 1? What is she doing?
4. What happens to the sheep in panel 3? Why?
5. Why does Mafalda wake up?
6. What number corresponds to the sheep in panel 5?
7. In panel 6, what is Mafalda doing? How do you know?

Los animales

This comic strip uses a device called onomatopoeia: a word that represents the sound that it stands for. Did you know that many common instances of onomatopoeia are different from language to language? The noise a sheep makes is *baaaah* in English, but in Mafalda's language it is **béeeee**.

Do you think you can match these animals with their Spanish sounds? First, practice saying aloud each animal sound in group B. Then, match each animal with its sound in Spanish. If you need help remembering the sounds the alphabet makes in Spanish, see p. 33.

A

1. ___ **gato**

2. ___ **perro**

3. ___ **vacas**

4. ___ **gallo**

5. ___ **rana**

6. ___ **pato**

7. ___ **cerdo**

B

a. kikirikí b. muuu c. croac d. guau

e. cuac cuac f. miau g. oinc

Escritura

Estrategia

Writing in Spanish

Why do we write? All writing has a purpose. For example, we may write an e-mail to share important information or compose an essay to persuade others to accept a point of view. Proficient writers are not born, however. Writing requires time, thought, effort, and a lot of practice. Here are some tips to help you write more effectively in Spanish.

DO

- Try to write your ideas in Spanish
- Use the grammar and vocabulary that you know
- Use your textbook for examples of style, format, and expression in Spanish
- Use your imagination and creativity
- Put yourself in your reader's place to determine if your writing is interesting

AVOID

- Translating your ideas from English to Spanish
- Simply repeating what is in the textbook or on a web page
- Using a dictionary until you have learned how to use foreign language dictionaries

Tema

Hacer una lista

Create a telephone/address list that includes important names, numbers, and websites that will be helpful to you in your study of Spanish. Make whatever entries you can in Spanish without using a dictionary. You might want to include this information:

- The names, phone numbers, and e-mail addresses of at least four other students
- Your teacher's name, e-mail address, and office hours
- Three phone numbers and e-mail addresses of campus offices or locations related to your study of Spanish
- Five electronic resources for students of Spanish, such as chat rooms and sites dedicated to the study of Spanish as a second language

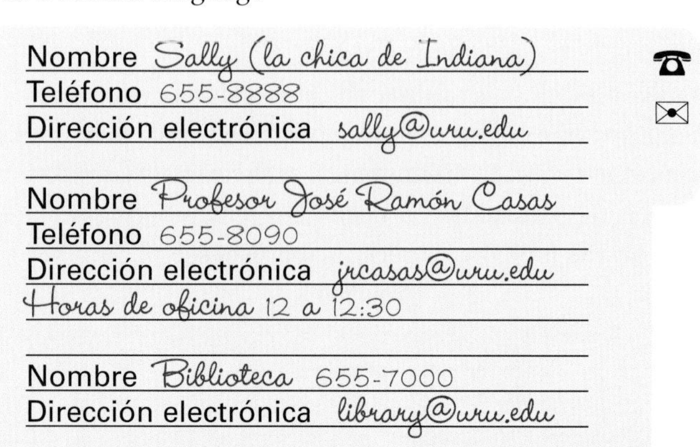

Nombre Sally (la chica de Indiana)
Teléfono 655-8888
Dirección electrónica sally@uru.edu

Nombre Profesor José Ramón Casas
Teléfono 655-8090
Dirección electrónica jrcasas@uru.edu
Horas de oficina 12 a 12:30

Nombre Biblioteca 655-7000
Dirección electrónica library@uru.edu

Escuchar

Estrategia

Listening for words you know

You can get the gist of a conversation by listening for words and phrases you already know.

To help you practice this strategy, listen to the following sentence and make a list of the words you have already learned.

Preparación

Based on the photograph, what do you think Dr. Cavazos and Srta. Martínez are talking about? How would you get the gist of their conversation, based on what you know about Spanish?

Ahora escucha

Now you are going to hear Dr. Cavazos's conversation with Srta. Martínez. List the familiar words and phrases each person says.

Dr. Cavazos	Srta. Martínez
1. ______	9. ______
2. ______	10. ______
3. ______	11. ______
4. ______	12. ______
5. ______	13. ______
6. ______	14. ______
7. ______	15. ______
8. ______	16. ______

Use your lists of familiar words as a guide to come up with a summary of what happened in the conversation..

Comprensión

Identificar

Who would say the following things, Dr. Cavazos or Srta. Martínez?

1. Me llamo...
2. De nada.
3. Gracias. Muchas gracias.
4. Aquí tiene usted los documentos de viaje (*trip*), señor.
5. Usted tiene tres maletas, ¿no?
6. Tengo dos maletas.
7. Hola, señor.
8. ¿Viaja usted a Buenos Aires?

Contestar

1. Does this scene take place in the morning, afternoon, or evening? How do you know?
2. How many suitcases does Dr. Cavazos have?
3. Using the words you already know to determine the context, what might the following words and expressions mean?
   - boleto
   - pasaporte
   - un viaje de ida y vuelta
   - ¡Buen viaje!

Anuncio de MasterCard

Un domingo en familia...

Preparación

Answer these questions in English.

1. Name some foods your family buys at the supermarket.
2. What is something you consider precious that cannot be bought?

Anuncios para los latinos

Latinos form the fastest-growing minority group in the United States; Census Bureau projections show Hispanic populations doubling from 2015–2050, to 106 million. Viewership of the two major Spanish language TV stations, **Univisión** and **Telemundo**, has skyrocketed, sometimes surpassing that of the four major English-language networks. With Latino purchasing power estimated at $1.7 trillion for 2017, many companies have responded by adapting successful marketing campaigns to target a Spanish-speaking audience. Along with the change in language, there often come cultural adaptations important to Latino viewers.

Vocabulario útil

aperitivo	*appetizer*
carne en salsa	*beef with sauce*
copa de helado	*cup of ice cream*
no tiene precio	*priceless*
plato principal	*main dish*
postre	*dessert*
un domingo en familia	*Sunday with the family*

Comprensión

Complete the chart below based on what you see in the video.

	salami	
plato principal		
		$6

Conversación

Based on the video, discuss in English the following questions with a partner.

1. In what ways do the food purchasing choices of this family differ from your own? In what ways are they alike?
2. How does the role of the pet in this video reflect that of your family or culture? How is it different?

Aplicación

With a partner, use a dictionary to prepare an ad in Spanish like that in the video. Present your ad to the class. How did your food choices vary from the ad? What was your "priceless" item?

The **Plaza de Mayo** in Buenos Aires, Argentina, is perhaps best known as a place of political protest. Aptly nicknamed **Plaza de Protestas** by the locals, it is the site of weekly demonstrations. Despite this reputation, for many it is also a traditional **plaza**, a spot to escape from the hustle of city life. In warmer months, office workers from neighboring buildings flock to the plaza during lunch hour. **Plaza de Mayo** is also a favorite spot for families, couples, and friends to gather, stroll, or simply sit and chat. Tourists come year-round to take in the iconic surroundings: **Plaza de Mayo** is flanked by the rose-colored presidential palace (**Casa Rosada**), city hall (**municipalidad**), a colonial era museum (**Cabildo**), and a spectacular cathedral (**Catedral Metropolitana**).

Vocabulario útil

abrazo	*hug*
¡Cuánto tiempo!	*It's been a long time!*
encuentro	*encounter*
plaza	*city or town square*
¡Qué bueno verte!	*It's great to see you!*
¡Qué suerte verlos!	*How lucky to see you!*

Preparación

Where do you and your friends usually meet? Are there public places where you get together? What activities do you take part in there?

Identificar

Identify the person or people who make(s) each of these statements.

1. ¿Cómo están ustedes?
2. ¡Qué bueno verte!
3. Bien, ¿y vos?
4. Hola.
5. ¡Qué suerte verlos!

a. Gonzalo
b. Mariana
c. Mark
d. Silvina

Encuentros en la plaza

Today we are at the Plaza de Mayo.

People come to walk and get some fresh air...

And children come to play...

Estados Unidos

El país en cifras°

- **Población° de los EE.UU.:** 317 millones
- **Población de origen hispano:** 50 millones
- **País de origen de hispanos en los EE.UU.:**

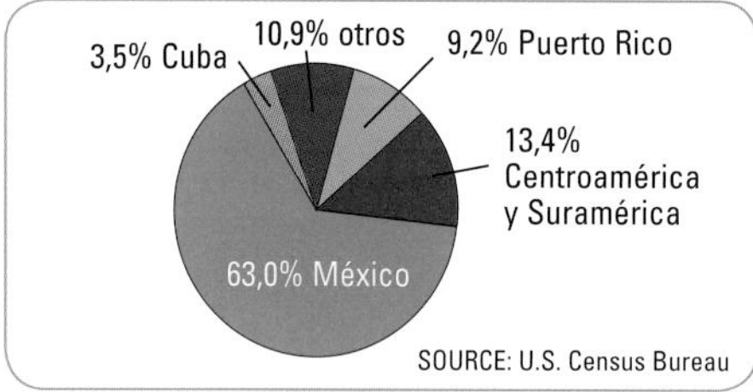

- **Estados con la mayor° población hispana:**

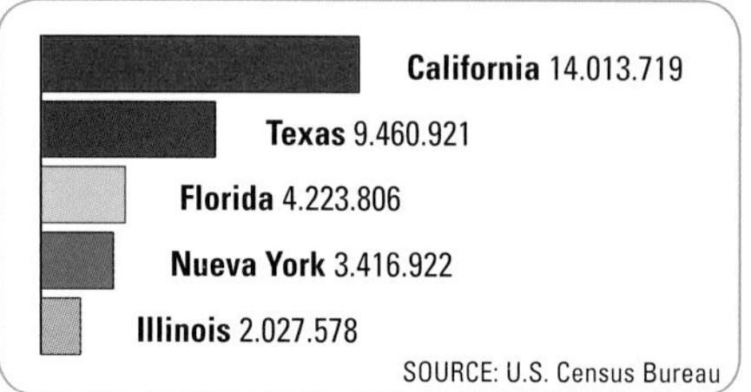

Canadá

El país en cifras

- **Población de Canadá:** 35 millones
- **Población de origen hispano:** 700.000
- **País de origen de hispanos en Canadá:**

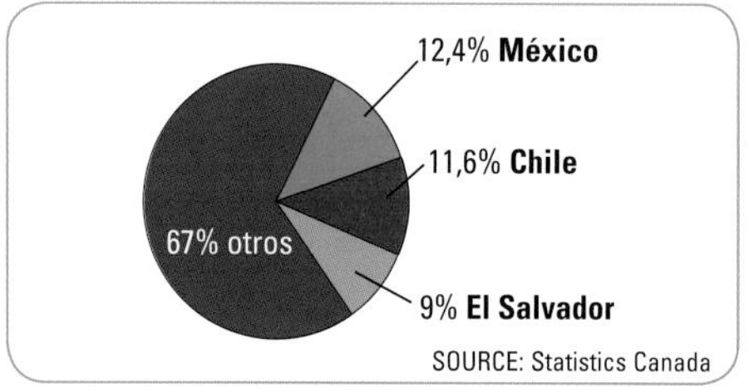

- **Ciudades° con la mayor población hispana:** Montreal, Toronto, Vancouver

en cifras *by the numbers* Población *Population* mayor *largest* Ciudades *Cities* creció *grew* más *more* cada *every* niños *children* Se estima *It is estimated* va a ser *it is going to be*

Mission District, en San Francisco

El Álamo, en San Antonio, Texas

¡Increíble pero cierto!

La población hispana en los EE.UU. creció° un 48% entre los años 2000 (dos mil) y 2011 (dos mil once) (16,7 millones de personas más°). Hoy, uno de cada° cinco niños° en los EE.UU. es de origen hispano. Se estima° que en el año 2034 va a ser° uno de cada tres.

Comida • La comida mexicana

La comida° mexicana es muy popular en los Estados Unidos. Los tacos, las enchiladas, las quesadillas y los frijoles frecuentemente forman parte de las comidas de muchos norteamericanos. También° son populares las variaciones de la comida mexicana en los Estados Unidos: el tex-mex y el cali-mex.

Lugares • La Pequeña Habana

La Pequeña Habana° es un barrio° de Miami, Florida, donde viven° muchos cubanoamericanos. Es un lugar° donde se encuentran° las costumbres° de la cultura cubana, los aromas y sabores° de su comida y la música salsa. La Pequeña Habana es una parte de Cuba en los Estados Unidos.

Costumbres • Desfile puertorriqueño

Cada junio, desde° 1958 (mil novecientos cincuenta y ocho), los puertorriqueños celebran su cultura con un desfile° en Nueva York. Es un gran espectáculo con carrozas° y música salsa, merengue y hip-hop. Muchos espectadores llevan° la bandera° de Puerto Rico en su ropa° o pintada en la cara°.

Comunidad • Hispanos en Canadá

En Canadá viven° muchos hispanos. Toronto y Montreal son las ciudades° con mayor° población hispana. Muchos de ellos tienen estudios universitarios° y hablan° una de las lenguas° oficiales: inglés o francés°. Los hispanos participan activamente en la vida cotidiana° y profesional de Canadá.

¿Qué aprendiste? Completa las oraciones con la información adecuada (*appropriate*).

1. Hay ________ de personas de origen hispano en los Estados Unidos.
2. Los cuatro estados con las poblaciones hispanas más grandes son (en orden) ________, Texas, Florida y ________.
3. Toronto, Montreal y ________ son las ciudades con más población hispana de Canadá.
4. Las quesadillas y las enchiladas son platos (*dishes*) ________.
5. La Pequeña ________ es un barrio de Miami.
6. En Miami hay muchas personas de origen ________.
7. Cada junio se celebra en Nueva York un gran desfile para personas de origen ________.
8. Muchos hispanos en Canadá hablan ________ o francés.

Conexión Internet Investiga estos temas en Internet.

1. Haz (*Make*) una lista de seis hispanos célebres de los EE.UU. o Canadá. Explica (*Explain*) por qué (*why*) son célebres.
2. Escoge (*Choose*) seis lugares en los Estados Unidos con nombres hispanos e investiga sobre el origen y el significado (*meaning*) de cada nombre.

comida *food* También *Also* La Pequeña Habana *Little Havana* barrio *neighborhood* viven *live* lugar *place* se encuentran *are found* costumbres *customs* sabores *flavors* Cada junio desde *Each June since* desfile *parade* con carrozas *with floats* llevan *wear* bandera *flag* ropa *clothing* cara *face* viven *live* ciudades *cities* mayor *most* tienen estudios universitarios *have a degree* hablan *speak* lenguas *languages* inglés o francés *English or French* vida cotidiana *daily life*

Saludos

Hola.	*Hello; Hi.*
Buenos días.	*Good morning.*
Buenas tardes.	*Good afternoon.*
Buenas noches.	*Good evening; Good night.*

Despedidas

Adiós.	*Goodbye.*
Nos vemos.	*See you.*
Hasta luego.	*See you later.*
Hasta la vista.	*See you later.*
Hasta pronto.	*See you soon.*
Hasta mañana.	*See you tomorrow.*
Saludos a...	*Greetings to…*
Chau.	*Bye.*

¿Cómo está?

¿Cómo está usted?	*How are you?* (form.)
¿Cómo estás?	*How are you?* (fam.)
¿Qué hay de nuevo?	*What's new?*
¿Qué pasa?	*What's happening?; What's going on?*
¿Qué tal?	*How are you?; How is it going?*
(Muy) bien, gracias.	*(Very) well, thanks.*
Nada.	*Nothing.*
No muy bien.	*Not very well.*
Regular.	*So-so; OK.*

Expresiones de cortesía

Con permiso.	*Pardon me; Excuse me.*
De nada.	*You're welcome.*
Lo siento.	*I'm sorry.*
(Muchas) gracias.	*Thank you (very much); Thanks (a lot).*
No hay de qué.	*You're welcome.*
Perdón.	*Pardon me; Excuse me.*
por favor	*please*

Títulos

señor (Sr.); don	*Mr.; sir*
señora (Sra.); doña	*Mrs.; ma'am*
señorita (Srta.)	*Miss*

Presentaciones

¿Cómo se llama usted?	*What's your name?* (form.)
¿Cómo te llamas?	*What's your name?* (fam.)
Me llamo...	*My name is…*
¿Y usted?	*And you?* (form.)
¿Y tú?	*And you?* (fam.)
Mucho gusto.	*Pleased to meet you.*
El gusto es mío.	*The pleasure is mine.*
Encantado/a.	*Delighted; Pleased to meet you.*
Igualmente.	*Likewise.*
Le presento a...	*I would like to introduce you to* (name). (form.)
Te presento a...	*I would like to introduce you to* (name). (fam.)
el nombre	*name*

¿De dónde es?

¿De dónde es usted?	*Where are you from?* (form.)
¿De dónde eres?	*Where are you from?* (fam.)
Soy de...	*I'm from…*

Palabras adicionales

¿cuánto(s)/a(s)?	*how much/many?*
¿de quién...?	*whose…?* (sing.)
¿de quiénes...?	*whose…?* (plural)
(no) hay	*there is (not); there are (not)*

Sustantivos

el autobús	*bus*
el chico	*boy*
la chica	*girl*
la computadora	*computer*
la comunidad	*community*
el/la conductor(a)	*driver*
la conversación	*conversation*
la cosa	*thing*
el cuaderno	*notebook*
el día	*day*
el diario	*diary*
el diccionario	*dictionary*
la escuela	*school*
el/la estudiante	*student*
la foto(grafía)	*photograph*
el hombre	*man*
el/la joven	*young person*
el lápiz	*pencil*
la lección	*lesson*
la maleta	*suitcase*
la mano	*hand*
el mapa	*map*
la mujer	*woman*
la nacionalidad	*nationality*
el número	*number*
el país	*country*
la palabra	*word*
el/la pasajero/a	*passenger*
el problema	*problem*
el/la profesor(a)	*teacher*
el programa	*program*
el/la turista	*tourist*
el video	*video*

Verbo

ser	*to be*

Numbers 0–30	*See page 40.*
Telling time	*See pages 48–49.*
Expresiones útiles	*See page 31.*

En la clase

2

Communicative Goals

You will learn how to:

- Talk about your classes and school life
- Discuss everyday activities
- Ask questions in Spanish
- Describe the location of people and things

A PRIMERA VISTA

- ¿Hay un chico y una chica en la foto?
- ¿Hay una computadora o dos?
- ¿Son turistas o estudiantes?
- ¿Qué hora es, la una de la mañana o de la tarde?

En la clase

Más vocabulario

la biblioteca	*library*
la cafetería	*cafeteria*
la casa	*house; home*
la escuela	*school*
el estadio	*stadium*
el laboratorio	*laboratory*
la librería	*bookstore*
la universidad	*university; college*
el/la compañero/a de clase	*classmate*
la clase	*class*
el curso	*course*
el examen	*test; exam*
el horario	*schedule*
la prueba	*test; quiz*
el semestre	*semester*
la tarea	*homework*
el trimestre	*trimester; quarter*
el arte	*art*
la biología	*biology*
las ciencias	*sciences*
la computación	*computer science*
la contabilidad	*accounting*
la economía	*economics*
el español	*Spanish*
la física	*physics*
la geografía	*geography*
la música	*music*

Variación léxica

pluma ⟷ bolígrafo
pizarra ⟷ tablero (*Col.*)

Práctica

1 Escuchar Listen to Ms. Morales talk about her Spanish classroom, then check the items she mentions.

puerta	❍	tiza	❍	plumas	❍
ventanas	❍	escritorios	❍	mochilas	❍
pizarra	❍	sillas	❍	papel	❍
borrador	❍	libros	❍	reloj	❍

2 Identificar You will hear a series of words. Write each one in the appropriate category.

Personas	Lugares	Materias
________	________	________
________	________	________
________	________	________

3 Emparejar Match each question with its most logical response. **¡Ojo!** (*Careful!*) One response will not be used.

1. ¿Qué clase es?
2. ¿Quiénes son?
3. ¿Quién es?
4. ¿De dónde es?
5. ¿A qué hora es la clase de inglés?
6. ¿Cuántos estudiantes hay?

a. Hay veinticinco.
b. Es un reloj.
c. Es de Perú.
d. Es la clase de química.
e. Es el señor Bastos.
f. Es a las nueve en punto.
g. Son los profesores.

4 Escoger Identify the word that does not belong in each group.

1. examen • casa • tarea • prueba
2. literatura • matemáticas • biblioteca • historia
3. pizarra • tiza • borrador • librería
4. lápiz • cafetería • papel • cuaderno
5. veinte • diez • pluma • treinta
6. conductor • laboratorio • autobús • pasajero

5 ¿Qué clase es? Name the class associated with the subject matter.

modelo

los elementos, los átomos *Es la clase de química.*

1. Abraham Lincoln, Winston Churchill
2. Picasso, Leonardo da Vinci
3. Newton, Einstein
4. África, el océano Pacífico
5. la cultura de España, verbos
6. Hemingway, Shakespeare
7. geometría, calculadora

Los días de la semana

septiembre

lunes	martes	miércoles	jueves	viernes	sábado	domingo
	1	2	3	4	5	6
7	8	9	10			

¡LENGUA VIVA!

The days of the week are never capitalized in Spanish.

• • •

Monday is considered the first day of the week in Spanish-speaking countries.

CONSULTA

Note that September in Spanish is **septiembre.** For all of the months of the year, go to **Senderos 1B**, **Contextos, Lección 5,** p. 64.

6 **¿Qué día es hoy?** Complete each statement with the correct day of the week.

1. Hoy es martes. Mañana es __________. Ayer fue (*Yesterday was*) __________.
2. Ayer fue sábado. Mañana es __________. Hoy es __________.
3. Mañana es viernes. Hoy es __________. Ayer fue __________.
4. Ayer fue domingo. Hoy es __________. Mañana es __________.
5. Hoy es jueves. Ayer fue __________. Mañana es __________.
6. Mañana es lunes. Hoy es __________. Ayer fue __________.

7 **Analogías** Use these words to complete the analogies. Some words will not be used.

arte	día	martes	pizarra
biblioteca	domingo	matemáticas	profesor
catorce	estudiante	mujer	reloj

1. maleta ⟷ pasajero ⊜ mochila ⟷ __________
2. chico ⟷ chica ⊜ hombre ⟷ __________
3. pluma ⟷ papel ⊜ tiza ⟷ __________
4. inglés ⟷ lengua ⊜ miércoles ⟷ __________
5. papel ⟷ cuaderno ⊜ libro ⟷ __________
6. quince ⟷ dieciséis ⊜ lunes ⟷ __________
7. Cervantes ⟷ literatura ⊜ Dalí ⟷ __________
8. autobús ⟷ conductor ⊜ clase ⟷ __________
9. los EE.UU. ⟷ mapa ⊜ hora ⟷ __________
10. veinte ⟷ veintitrés ⊜ jueves ⟷ __________

Comunicación

8 **Horario** Read Cristina's description of her schedule. Then indicate whether the following conclusions are **lógico** or **ilógico**, based on what you read.

¡ATENCIÓN!

Use **el** + [*day of the week*] when an activity occurs on a specific day and **los** + [*day of the week*] when an activity occurs regularly.

El lunes tengo un examen.

***On Monday** I have an exam.*

Los lunes y miércoles tomo biología.

***On Mondays and Wednesdays** I take biology.*

•••

Except for **sábados** and **domingos**, the singular and plural forms for days of the week are the same.

Las clases de inglés, matemáticas, español, e historia son a la misma (*same*) hora cada (*each*) día, de lunes a viernes. El professor Núñez enseña (*teaches*) la clase de inglés. Empieza (*It starts*) a las ocho. Tomo (*I take*) matématicas a las nueve menos diez, y español a las diez menos veinte. Me gusta (*I like*) la profesora Salazar que enseña la clase de historia. Los lunes y miércoles, voy (*I go*) al laboratorio para biología a la una. Los martes, jueves y viernes, tomo la clase de música. ¡Me gusta mucho la clase de música!

	Lógico	Ilógico
1. Cristina es estudiante.	❍	❍
2. Cristina toma seis clases durante la semana.	❍	❍
3. Cristina toma una clase los lunes a las tres de la tarde.	❍	❍
4. La profesora Salazar enseña la clase de historia.	❍	❍
5. El profesor Núñez enseña la clase de español.	❍	❍
6. Cristina toma clase de música los sábados.	❍	❍

9 **La semana** Write a paragraph about what a typical week looks like for you. Describe your schedule for the week, including classes, times, and teachers.

modelo

El lunes tomo la clase de matemáticas a las nueve con el profesor Smith. A las diez...

10 **Nuevos amigos** During the first week of class, you meet a new student in the cafeteria. With a partner, prepare a conversation using these cues.

Estudiante 1		Estudiante 2
Greet your new acquaintance.	→	Introduce yourself.
Find out about him or her.	→	Tell him or her about yourself.
Ask about your partner's class schedule.	→	Compare your schedule to your partner's.
Say nice to meet you and goodbye.	→	Say nice to meet you and goodbye.

¿Qué estudias?

Felipe, Marissa, Juan Carlos y Miguel visitan Chapultepec y hablan de las clases.

PERSONAJES

MARISSA

FELIPE

1

FELIPE Dos boletos, por favor.

2

EMPLEADO Dos boletos son 64 pesos.

FELIPE Aquí están 100 pesos.

EMPLEADO 100 menos 64 son 36 pesos de cambio.

3

FELIPE Ésta es la Ciudad de México.

4

FELIPE Oye, Marissa, ¿cuántas clases tomas?

MARISSA Tomo cuatro clases: español, historia, literatura y también geografía. Me gusta mucho la cultura mexicana.

5

MIGUEL Marissa, hablas muy bien el español... ¿Y dónde está tu diccionario?

MARISSA En casa de los Díaz. Felipe necesita practicar inglés.

MIGUEL ¡Ay, Maru! Chicos, nos vemos más tarde.

6

FELIPE Juan Carlos, ¿quién enseña la clase de química este semestre?

JUAN CARLOS El profesor Morales. Ah, ¿por qué tomo química y computación?

FELIPE Porque te gusta la tarea.

JUAN CARLOS **MIGUEL** **EMPLEADO** **MARU**

FELIPE Los lunes y los miércoles, economía a las 2:30. Tú tomas computación los martes en la tarde, y química, a ver... Los lunes, los miércoles y los viernes ¿a las 10? ¡Uf!

FELIPE Y Miguel, ¿cuándo regresa?

JUAN CARLOS Hoy estudia con Maru.

MARISSA ¿Quién es Maru?

MIGUEL ¿Hablas con tu mamá?

MARU Mamá habla. Yo escucho. Es la 1:30.

MIGUEL Ay, lo siento. Juan Carlos y Felipe...

MARU Ay, Felipe.

MARU Y ahora, ¿adónde? ¿A la biblioteca?

MIGUEL Sí, pero primero a la librería. Necesito comprar unos libros.

Expresiones útiles

Talking about classes

¿Cuántas clases tomas?
How many classes are you taking?
Tomo cuatro clases.
I'm taking four classes.
Este año, espero sacar buenas notas y, por supuesto, viajar por el país.
This year, I hope / I'm hoping to get good grades. And, of course, travel through the country.

Talking about likes/dislikes

Me gusta mucho la cultura mexicana.
I like Mexican culture a lot.
Me gustan las ciencias ambientales.
I like environmental science.
Me gusta dibujar.
I like to draw.
¿Te gusta este lugar?
Do you like this place?

Paying for tickets

Dos boletos, por favor.
Two tickets, please.
Dos boletos son sesenta y cuatro pesos.
Two tickets are sixty-four pesos.
Aquí están cien pesos.
Here's a hundred pesos.
Son treinta y seis pesos de cambio.
That's thirty-six pesos change.

Talking about location and direction

¿Dónde está tu diccionario?
Where is your dictionary?
Está en casa de los Díaz.
It's at the Díaz house.
Y ahora, ¿adónde? ¿A la biblioteca?
And now, where to? To the library?
Sí, pero primero a la librería.
Está al lado.
Yes, but first to the bookstore.
It's next door.

¿Qué pasó?

1 **Escoger** Choose the answer that best completes each sentence.

1. Marissa toma (*is taking*) __________ en la universidad.
   a. español, inglés, economía y música b. historia, inglés, sociología y biología
   c. español, historia, literatura y geografía
2. El profesor Morales enseña (*teaches*) __________.
   a. química b. matemáticas c. historia
3. Juan Carlos toma química __________.
   a. los miércoles, jueves y viernes b. los lunes, miércoles y viernes
   c. los lunes, martes y jueves
4. Miguel necesita ir a (*needs to go to*) __________.
   a. la biblioteca b. la cafetería c. la librería

2 **Identificar** Indicate which person would make each statement. The names may be used more than once.

1. ¿Maru es compañera de ustedes? __________
2. Mi mamá habla mucho. __________
3. El profesor Morales enseña la clase de química este semestre. __________
4. Mi diccionario está en casa de Felipe y Jimena. __________
5. Necesito estudiar con Maru. __________
6. Yo tomo clase de computación los martes por la tarde. __________

MARU

JUAN CARLOS

MARISSA

MIGUEL

NOTA CULTURAL

Maru is a shortened version of the name **María Eugenia.** Other popular "combination names" in Spanish are **Juanjo (Juan José)** and **Maite (María Teresa).**

3 **Completar** These sentences are similar to things said in the **Fotonovela**. Complete each sentence with the correct word(s).

Castillo de Chapultepec	estudiar	miércoles
clase	inglés	tarea

1. Marissa, éste es el __________________.
2. Felipe tiene (*has*) el diccionario porque (*because*) necesita practicar __________________.
3. A Juan Carlos le gusta mucho la __________________.
4. Hay clase de economía los lunes y __________________.
5. Miguel está con Maru para __________________.

NOTA CULTURAL

The **Castillo de Chapultepec** is one of Mexico City's most historic landmarks. Constructed in 1785, it was the residence of emperors and presidents. It has been open to the public since 1944 and now houses the National Museum of History.

4 **Preguntas personales** Answer your partner's questions about your classes.

1. ¿Qué clases tomas?
2. ¿Qué clases tomas los martes?
3. ¿Qué clases tomas los viernes?
4. ¿Quién enseña la clase de español?
5. ¿Te gusta la clase de español?

Pronunciación

Spanish vowels

a **e** **i** **o** **u**

Spanish vowels are never silent; they are always pronounced in a short, crisp way without the glide sounds used in English.

Álex **clase** **nada** **encantada**

The letter **a** is pronounced like the *a* in *father*, but shorter.

el **ene** **mesa** **elefante**

The letter **e** is pronounced like the *e* in *they*, but shorter.

Inés **chica** **tiza** **señorita**

The letter **i** sounds like the *ee* in *beet*, but shorter.

hola **con** **libro** **don Francisco**

The letter **o** is pronounced like the *o* in *tone*, but shorter.

uno **regular** **saludos** **gusto**

The letter **u** sounds like the *oo* in *room*, but shorter.

Práctica Practice the vowels by saying the names of these places in Spain.

1. Madrid
2. Alicante
3. Tenerife
4. Toledo
5. Barcelona
6. Granada
7. Burgos
8. La Coruña

Oraciones Read the sentences aloud, focusing on the vowels.

1. Hola. Me llamo Ramiro Morgado.
2. Enseño español en la escuela secundaria.
3. Tomo también literatura y contabilidad.
4. Ay, tengo clase de biología. ¡Nos vemos!

AYUDA

Although **hay** and **ay** are pronounced identically, they do not have the same meaning. As you learned in **Lección 1, hay** is a verb form that means *there is/are*. **Hay veinte libros.** (*There are twenty books.*) **¡Ay!** is an exclamation expressing pain, shock, or affliction: *Oh!; Oh, dear!*

Refranes Practice the vowels by reading these sayings aloud.

1 Easier said than done.
2 To each his own.

EN DETALLE

La escuela secundaria

Manuel, a 15-year-old student in Mexico, is taking an intense third level course focused on **la química**. This is a typical part of the studies for his grade. **Escuela secundaria** (*secondary school*), which in Mexico begins after six years of **escuela primaria** (*primary school*), has three grades for students between the ages of 12 and 15.

Students like Manuel must study courses in mathematics, science, Spanish, foreign languages (English or French), music, and more every year. After that, students choose a **plan de estudio** (*program of study*) in **preparatoria,** the three years (or two, depending on the program) of school after **escuela secundaria** and before university studies. The program of study that students choose requires them to study specific **materias** that are needed in preparation for their future career.

Some **bachilleratos** (*high school degrees*) are **terminales,** which means that when students graduate they are prepared with all of the skills and requirements to begin their field of work.

These students are not expected to continue studying. Some **modalidades** (*programs of study*) that are terminal include:

- **Educación Tecnológica Agropecuaria** (*Agriculture and Fishing*)
- **Comercio y Administración** (*Commerce, for administrative work*)

Other programs are designed for students who plan to continue their studies in a **carrera universitaria** (*college major*). Some programs that prepare students for university studies are:

- **Ciencias Biológicas**
- **Ciencias Contables, Económicas y Bancarias** (*Economic and Banking Sciences*)
- **Música y Arte**

Each program has courses that are designed for a specific career. This means that although all high school students may take a mathematics course, the type of mathematics studied varies according to the needs of each degree.

La escuela y la universidad

Some Mexican high schools are designed and managed by universities as well as by the Secretary of Education. One university that directs such schools is the **Universidad Nacional Autónoma de México (UNAM),** Mexico's largest university.

ACTIVIDADES

1 **¿Cierto o falso?** Indicate whether each statement is **cierto** or **falso.** Correct the false statements.

1. High schools are specialized in certain areas of study.
2. Students in Mexico cannot study art in school.
3. Students do not need to complete primary school before going to **escuela secundaria**.
4. The length of high school **planes de estudio** in Mexico varies between two and three years.
5. Students need to go to college to study to do administrative work.
6. All students must take the same mathematics courses at the high school level.
7. **La escuela secundaria** is for students from the ages of 16 to 18 years old.
8. All students in Mexico complete university studies.

ASÍ SE DICE

Clases y exámenes

aprobar	*to pass*
el colegio/la escuela	*school*
la escuela secundaria/ la preparatoria (Méx.)/ el liceo (Ven.)/ el instituto (Esp.)	*high school*
el examen parcial	*midterm exam*
el horario	*schedule*
la matrícula	*enrollment (in school)*
reprobar	*to fail*
sacar buenas/ malas notas	*to get good/ bad grades*

EL MUNDO HISPANO

La escuela en Latinoamérica

- **In Latin America**, public secondary schools are free of charge. Private schools, however, can be quite costly. At **la Escuela Campo Alegre** in Venezuela, annual tuition is about $25,000 a year.
- **Argentina** and **Chile** are the two Latin American countries with the most years of required schooling at 13 years each.
- **In Chile**, students begin the school year in March and finish in December. Of course—Chile lies south of the equator, so while it is winter in the United States, Chilean students are on their summer break!

PERFIL

El INFRAMEN

La ciudad de San Salvador

The **Instituto Nacional Francisco Menéndez (INFRAMEN)** is the largest public high school in El Salvador. So it should be: it is named after General Francisco Menéndez, an ex-president of the country who was the founder of **enseñanza secundaria** (*secondary studies*) for the entire country! The 1,900 students at the INFRAMEN can choose to complete one of four kinds of diplomas: general studies, health care, tourism, and business. The institution has changed locales (and even cities) many times since it was founded in 1885 and is currently located in the capital city of San Salvador. Students at the INFRAMEN begin their school year in mid January and finish in early November.

Conexión Internet

How do dress codes vary in schools across Latin America?

Go to **vhlcentral.com** to find more cultural information related to this **Cultura** section.

ACTIVIDADES

2 Comprensión Complete these sentences.

1. The INFRAMEN was founded in ________.
2. The programs of study available in the INFRAMEN are ______________________.
3. There are ________ students in the INFRAMEN.
4. General Francisco Menéndez was a ________ of El Salvador.
5. El ________ is a student's schedule.

3 ¡A estudiar! All students have classes they like and classes they don't. What are your favorite classes? Which are your least favorite? With a partner, discuss what you like and don't like about your classes and make a short list of what could be done to improve the classes you don't like.

2.1 Present tense of -ar verbs

ANTE TODO In order to talk about activities, you need to use verbs. Verbs express actions or states of being. In English and Spanish, the infinitive is the base form of the verb. In English, the infinitive is preceded by the word *to*: *to study*, *to be*. The infinitive in Spanish is a one-word form and can be recognized by its endings: **-ar**, **-er**, or **-ir**.

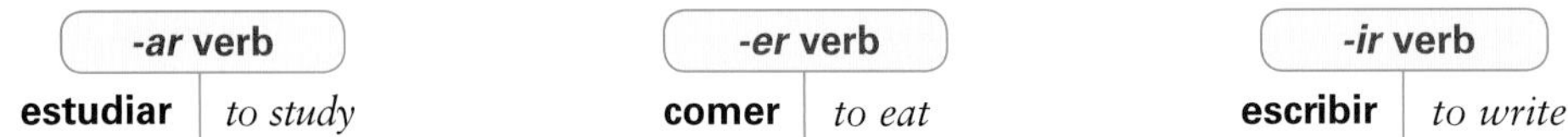

-ar verb		*-er* verb		*-ir* verb	
estudiar	*to study*	**comer**	*to eat*	**escribir**	*to write*

▶ In this lesson, you will learn the forms of regular **-ar** verbs.

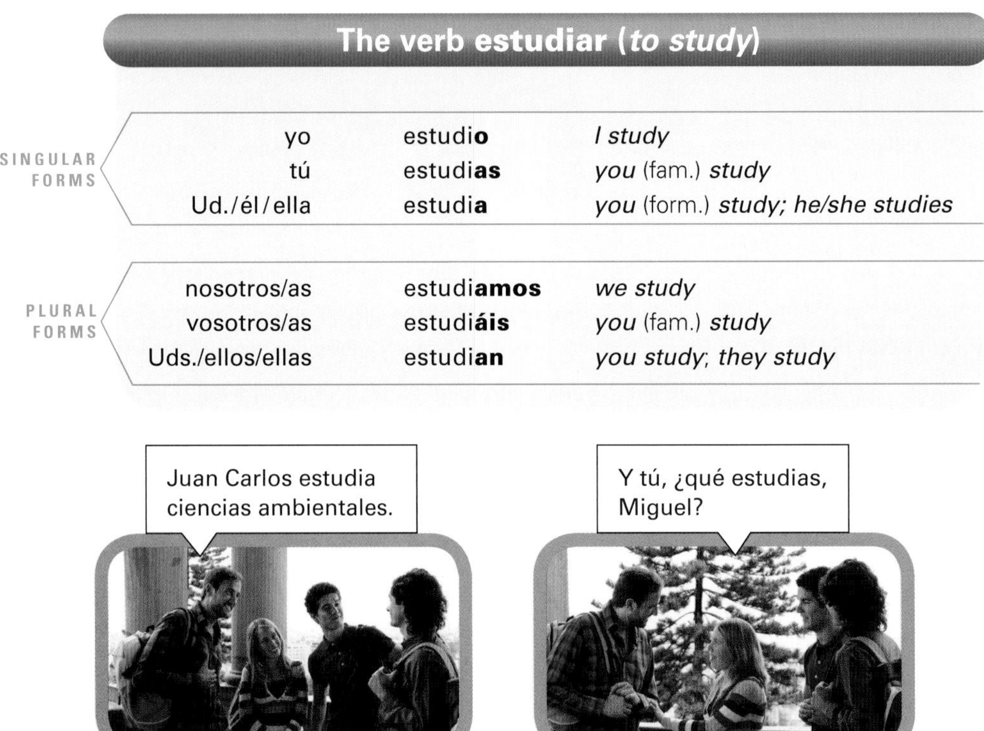

The verb estudiar (*to study*)

SINGULAR FORMS	yo	estudi**o**	*I study*
	tú	estudi**as**	*you* (fam.) *study*
	Ud./él/ella	estudi**a**	*you* (form.) *study; he/she studies*
PLURAL FORMS	nosotros/as	estudi**amos**	*we study*
	vosotros/as	estudi**áis**	*you* (fam.) *study*
	Uds./ellos/ellas	estudi**an**	*you study; they study*

▶ To create the forms of most regular verbs in Spanish, drop the infinitive endings (**-ar**, **-er**, **-ir**). You then add to the stem the endings that correspond to the different subject pronouns. This diagram will help you visualize verb conjugation.

Conjugation of *-ar* verbs

INFINITIVE	VERB STEM	CONJUGATED FORM
estudi**ar**	estudi-	yo estudi**o**
bail**ar**	bail-	tú bail**as**
trabaj**ar**	trabaj-	nosotros trabaj**amos**

Common *-ar* verbs

bailar	*to dance*	**estudiar**	*to study*
buscar	*to look for*	**explicar**	*to explain*
caminar	*to walk*	**hablar**	*to talk; to speak*
cantar	*to sing*	**llegar**	*to arrive*
cenar	*to have dinner*	**llevar**	*to carry*
comprar	*to buy*	**mirar**	*to look (at); to watch*
contestar	*to answer*	**necesitar (+ *inf.*)**	*to need*
conversar	*to converse, to chat*	**practicar**	*to practice*
desayunar	*to have breakfast*	**preguntar**	*to ask (a question)*
descansar	*to rest*	**preparar**	*to prepare*
desear (+ *inf.*)	*to desire; to wish*	**regresar**	*to return*
dibujar	*to draw*	**terminar**	*to end; to finish*
enseñar	*to teach*	**tomar**	*to take; to drink*
escuchar	*to listen (to)*	**trabajar**	*to work*
esperar (+ *inf.*)	*to wait (for); to hope*	**viajar**	*to travel*

▶ **¡Atención!** Unless referring to a person, the Spanish verbs **buscar**, **escuchar**, **esperar**, and **mirar** do not need to be followed by prepositions as they do in English.

Busco la tarea.
I'm looking for the homework.

Escucho la música.
I'm listening to the music.

Espero el autobús.
I'm waiting for the bus.

Miro la pizarra.
I'm looking at the blackboard.

COMPARE & CONTRAST

English uses three sets of forms to talk about the present: (1) the simple present (*Paco works*), (2) the present progressive (*Paco is working*), and (3) the emphatic present (*Paco does work*). In Spanish, the simple present can be used in all three cases.

Paco **trabaja** en la cafetería.

1. *Paco works in the cafeteria.*
2. *Paco is working in the cafeteria.*
3. *Paco does work in the cafeteria.*

In Spanish and English, the present tense is also sometimes used to express future action.

Marina **viaja** a Madrid mañana.

1. *Marina travels to Madrid tomorrow.*
2. *Marina will travel to Madrid tomorrow.*
3. *Marina is traveling to Madrid tomorrow.*

▶ When two verbs are used together with no change of subject, the second verb is generally in the infinitive. To make a sentence negative in Spanish, the word **no** is placed before the conjugated verb. In this case, **no** means *not*.

Deseo hablar con el señor Díaz.
I want to speak with Mr. Díaz.

Alicia **no** desea bailar ahora.
Alicia doesn't want to dance now.

▶ Spanish speakers often omit subject pronouns because the verb endings indicate who the subject is. In Spanish, subject pronouns are used for emphasis, clarification, or contrast.

—¿Qué enseñan?
What do they teach?

—**Ella** enseña arte y **él** enseña física.
She teaches art, and he teaches physics.

—¿Quién desea trabajar hoy?
Who wants to work today?

—**Yo** no deseo trabajar hoy.
I don't want to work today.

The verb gustar

▶ **Gustar** is different from other **-ar** verbs. To express your likes and dislikes, use the expression **(no) me gusta** + **el/la** + [*singular noun*] or **(no) me gustan** + **los/las** + [*plural noun*]. Note: You may use the phrase **a mí** for emphasis, but never the subject pronoun **yo**.

Me gusta la música clásica.
I like classical music.

Me gustan las clases de español y biología.
I like Spanish and biology classes.

A mí me gustan las artes.
I like the arts.

A mí no me gusta el programa.
I don't like the program.

▶ To talk about what you like and don't like to do, use **(no) me gusta** + [*infinitive(s)*]. Note that the singular **gusta** is always used, even with more than one infinitive.

No me gusta viajar en autobús.
I don't like to travel by bus.

Me gusta cantar y **bailar**.
I like to sing and dance.

▶ To ask a friend about likes and dislikes, use the pronoun **te** instead of **me**. Note: You may use **a ti** for emphasis, but never the subject pronoun **tú**.

—¿Te gusta la geografía?
Do you like geography?

—Sí, me gusta. Y a ti, ¿te gusta el inglés?
Yes, I like it. And you, do you like English?

▶ You can use this same structure to talk about other people by using the pronouns **nos**, **le**, and **les**.

Nos gusta dibujar. (nosotros)
We like to draw.

Nos gustan las clases de español e inglés. (nosotros)
We like Spanish class and English class.

No le gusta trabajar. (usted, él, ella)
You don't like to work.
He/She doesn't like to work.

Les gusta el arte. (ustedes, ellos, ellas)
You like art.
They like art.

¡ATENCIÓN!

Note that **gustar** does not behave like other **-ar** verbs. You must study its use carefully and pay attention to prepositions, pronouns, and agreement.

AYUDA

Use the construction **a** + [*name/pronoun*] to clarify to whom you are referring. This construction is not always necessary.

A Gabriela le gusta bailar.

A Sara y a él les gustan los animales.

A mí me gusta viajar.

¿**A ti** te gustan las clases?

¡INTÉNTALO! Provide the present tense forms of these verbs. The first items have been done for you.

hablar

1. Yo hablo español.
2. Ellos ________ español.
3. Inés ________ español.
4. Nosotras ________ español.
5. Tú ________ español.

gustar

1. Me gusta el café. (a mí)
2. ¿________ las clases? (a ti)
3. No ________ el café. (a ti)
4. No ________ las clases. (a mí)
5. No ________ el café. (a mí)

Práctica

1 **Completar** Complete the conversation with the appropriate forms of the verbs in parentheses.

JUAN ¡Hola, Linda! ¿Qué (1)__________ (llevar) en la mochila?

LINDA (2)__________ (llevar) las cosas que (3)__________ (necesitar) para la clase de español.

JUAN (4)__________ (necesitar) el libro de español?

LINDA Claro que sí.

JUAN ¿Los estudiantes en tu clase de español (5)__________ (estudiar) mucho?

LINDA Sí, nosotros (6)__________ (practicar) y (7)__________ (conversar) en español treinta minutos todos los días (*every day*).

2 **Oraciones** Form sentences using the words provided. Remember to conjugate the verbs and add any other necessary words.

1. ustedes / practicar / vocabulario
2. ¿preparar (tú) / tarea?
3. clase de español / terminar / once
4. ¿qué / buscar / ustedes?
5. (nosotros) buscar / pluma
6. (yo) comprar / calculadora

3 **Gustos** Read what these people do. Then use the information in parentheses to tell what they like.

modelo

Yo enseño en la escuela. (las clases) *Me gustan las clases.*

1. Tú deseas mirar cuadros (*paintings*) de Picasso. (el arte)
2. Soy estudiante de química. (estudiar)
3. Tú estudias italiano y español. (las lenguas extranjeras)
4. No descansas los sábados. (cantar y bailar)
5. Busco una computadora. (la computación)

4 **Actividades** Get together with a classmate and take turns asking each other if you do these activities. Which activities does your classmate like? Which do you both like?

modelo

tomar el autobús

Estudiante 1: *¿Tomas el autobús?*

Estudiante 2: *Sí, tomo el autobús, pero (but) no me gusta./ No, no tomo el autobús.*

bailar merengue	escuchar música rock	practicar el español
cantar en público	estudiar física	hablar italiano
dibujar bien	mirar la televisión	viajar a Europa

AYUDA

The Spanish **no** translates to both *no* and *not* in English. In negative answers to questions, you will need to use **no** twice:

¿Estudias geografía?

No, no estudio geografía.

Comunicación

5 **Actividades** Talk about the different activities you and your friends do in your daily life. Then specify which of those activities you like to do and which you don't. Use at least five of the **-ar** verbs you have learned.

modelo

Yo bailo hip hop en una academia. Mary dibuja...
Me gusta bailar. No me gusta dibujar.

6 **Describir** Write a description of what you see in each picture using the given verbs. Also mention whether or not you like the activities.

modelo

enseñar
La profesora enseña química. A mí me gusta la química.

1. caminar, hablar, llevar

2. buscar, descansar, estudiar

3. dibujar, cantar, escuchar

4. llevar, tomar, viajar

Síntesis

7 **Conversación** With a classmate, pretend that you are friends who have not seen each other for a few days. Have a conversation in which you catch up on things. Mention how you're feeling, what classes you're taking, which teachers teach those classes, and which classes you like and don't like.

2.2 Forming questions in Spanish

ANTE TODO There are three basic ways to ask questions in Spanish. Can you guess what they are by looking at the photos and photo captions on this page?

AYUDA

Say the example statements and questions on this page out loud. Your pitch indicates whether you are making a statement or asking a question. Then make up statements of your own and turn them into questions, using all three methods.

- One way to form a question is to raise the pitch of your voice at the end of a declarative sentence. When writing any question in Spanish, be sure to use an upside-down question mark (**¿**) at the beginning and a regular question mark (**?**) at the end of the sentence.

Statement	Question
Ustedes trabajan los sábados. *You work on Saturdays.*	¿Ustedes trabajan los sábados? *Do you work on Saturdays?*
Carlota busca un mapa. *Carlota is looking for a map.*	¿Carlota busca un mapa? *Is Carlota looking for a map?*

- You can also form a question by inverting the order of the subject and the verb of a declarative statement. The subject may even be placed at the end of the sentence.

Statement	Question
SUBJECT VERB **Ustedes trabajan** los sábados. *You work on Saturdays.*	VERB SUBJECT ¿**Trabajan ustedes** los sábados? *Do you work on Saturdays?*
SUBJECT VERB **Carlota regresa** a las seis. *Carlota returns at six.*	VERB SUBJECT ¿**Regresa** a las seis **Carlota**? *Does Carlota return at six?*

- Questions can also be formed by adding the tags **¿no?** or **¿verdad?** at the end of a statement.

Statement	Question
Ustedes trabajan los sábados. *You work on Saturdays.*	Ustedes trabajan los sábados, **¿no?** *You work on Saturdays, don't you?*
Carlota regresa a las seis. *Carlota returns at six.*	Carlota regresa a las seis, **¿verdad?** *Carlota returns at six, right?*

Question words

Interrogative words			
¿Adónde?	*Where (to)?*	**¿De dónde?**	*From where?*
¿Cómo?	*How?*	**¿Dónde?**	*Where?*
¿Cuál?, ¿Cuáles?	*Which?; Which one(s)?*	**¿Por qué?**	*Why?*
¿Cuándo?	*When?*	**¿Qué?**	*What?; Which?*
¿Cuánto/a?	*How much?*	**¿Quién?**	*Who?*
¿Cuántos/as?	*How many?*	**¿Quiénes?**	*Who* (plural)*?*

▶ To ask a question that requires more than a *yes* or *no* answer, use an interrogative word.

¿**Cuál** de ellos estudia en la biblioteca?
Which of them studies in the library?

¿**Cuántos** estudiantes hablan español?
How many students speak Spanish?

¿**Dónde** trabaja Ricardo?
Where does Ricardo work?

¿**Qué** clases tomas?
What classes are you taking?

¿**Adónde** caminamos?
Where are we walking (to)?

¿**Por qué** necesitas hablar con ella?
Why do you need to talk to her?

¿**Quién** enseña la clase de arte?
Who teaches the art class?

¿**Cuánta** tarea hay?
How much homework is there?

▶ When pronouncing this type of question, the pitch of your voice falls at the end of the sentence.

¿**Cómo** llegas a clase?
How do you get to class?

¿**Por qué** necesitas estudiar?
Why do you need to study?

▶ Notice the difference between **¿por qué?**, which is written as two words and has an accent, and **porque**, which is written as one word without an accent.

¿**Por qué** estudias español?
Why do you study Spanish?

¡**Porque** es divertido!
Because it's fun!

▶ In Spanish **no** can mean both *no* and *not*. Therefore, when answering a yes/no question in the negative, you need to use **no** twice.

¿Caminan a la escuela?
Do you walk to school?

No, no caminamos a la escuela.
No, we do not walk to the school.

¡INTÉNTALO! Make questions out of these statements. Use the intonation method in column 1 and the tag **¿no?** method in column 2.

Statement	Intonation	Tag questions
1. Hablas inglés.	¿Hablas inglés?	Hablas inglés, ¿no?
2. Trabajamos mañana.		
3. Ustedes desean bailar.		
4. Raúl estudia mucho.		
5. Enseño a las nueve.		
6. Luz mira la televisión.		

Práctica

1 **Preguntas** Change these sentences into questions by inverting the word order.

modelo

Ernesto habla con su compañero de clase.
¿Habla Ernesto con su compañero de clase? /
¿Habla con su compañero de clase Ernesto?

1. La profesora Cruz prepara la prueba.
2. Sandra y yo necesitamos estudiar.
3. Los chicos practican el vocabulario.
4. Jaime termina la tarea.
5. Tú trabajas en la biblioteca.

2 **Completar** Irene and Manolo are chatting in the library. Complete their conversation with the appropriate questions.

IRENE Hola, Manolo. (1)________________
MANOLO Bien, gracias. (2)________________
IRENE Muy bien. (3)________________
MANOLO Son las nueve.
IRENE (4)________________
MANOLO Estudio historia.
IRENE (5)________________
MANOLO Porque hay un examen mañana.
IRENE (6)________________
MANOLO Sí, me gusta mucho la clase.
IRENE (7)________________
MANOLO El profesor Padilla enseña la clase.
IRENE (8)________________
MANOLO No, no tomo biología.
IRENE (9)________________
MANOLO Regreso a mi casa a las tres.
IRENE (10)________________
MANOLO No, no deseo tomar una soda. ¡Deseo estudiar!

3 **Dos profesores** Create a dialogue, similar to the one in **Actividad 2**, between two teachers, Mr. Padilla and his colleague Mrs. Martínez. Use question words.

modelo

Prof. Padilla: *¿Qué enseñas este semestre?*
Prof. Martínez: *Enseño matemáticas.*

Comunicación

4 **Muchas preguntas** Listen to the conversation between Manuel and Ana. Then indicate whether the following conclusions are **lógico** or **ilógico**, based on what you heard.

	Lógico	Ilógico
1. Ana es profesora.	❍	❍
2. Diana es estudiante.	❍	❍
3. La profesora de español es de España.	❍	❍
4. Diana no toma la clase de computación porque hay mucha tarea.	❍	❍
5. Ana toma la clase de química.	❍	❍

5 **Un juego** With a classmate, play a game (**un juego**) of Jeopardy®. Remember to phrase your answers in the form of a question.

Es algo que...	**Es un lugar donde...**	**Es una persona que...**
It's something that...	*It's a place where...*	*It's a person that...*

modelo

Estudiante 1: Es un lugar donde estudiamos.
Estudiante 2: ¿Qué es la biblioteca?

Estudiante 2: Es algo que escuchamos.
Estudiante 1: ¿Qué es la música?

Estudiante 1: Es un director de España.
Estudiante 2: ¿Quién es Pedro Almodóvar?

NOTA CULTURAL

Pedro Almodóvar is an award-winning film director from Spain. His films are full of both humor and melodrama, and their controversial subject matter has often sparked great debate. His film ***Hable con ella*** won the Oscar for Best Original Screenplay in 2002. His 2006 hit ***Volver*** was nominated for numerous awards, and won the Best Screenplay and Best Actress award for the entire female cast at the Cannes Film Festival.

6  **El nuevo estudiante** Imagine you are a transfer student and today is your first day of Spanish class. Ask your partner questions to find out all you can about the class, your classmates, and the school. Then switch roles.

modelo

Estudiante 1: Hola, me llamo Samuel. ¿Cómo te llamas?
Estudiante 2: Me llamo Laura.
Estudiante 1: ¿Quiénes son ellos?
Estudiante 2: Son Melanie y Lucas.
Estudiante 1: En la escuela hay cursos de artes, ¿verdad?
Estudiante 2: Sí, hay clases de música y dibujo.
Estudiante 1: ¿Cuántos exámenes hay en esta clase?
Estudiante 2: Hay dos.

Síntesis

7 **Entrevista** Write an article about school life in your community. Write five questions you would ask students about their academic life.

2.3 Present tense of estar

CONSULTA

To review the forms of **ser**, see **Estructura 1.3**, pp. 43–45.

ANTE TODO In **Lección 1**, you learned how to conjugate and use the verb **ser** (*to be*). You will now learn a second verb which means *to be*, the verb **estar**. Although **estar** ends in **-ar**, it does not follow the pattern of regular **-ar** verbs. The **yo** form (**estoy**) is irregular. Also, all forms have an accented **á** except the **yo** and **nosotros/as** forms.

The verb estar (*to be*)

SINGULAR FORMS	yo	est**oy**	*I am*
	tú	est**ás**	*you* (fam.) *are*
	Ud./él/ella	est**á**	*you* (form.) *are; he/she is*
PLURAL FORMS	nosotros/as	est**amos**	*we are*
	vosotros/as	est**áis**	*you* (fam.) *are*
	Uds./ellos/ellas	est**án**	*you are; they are*

¡Estamos en Perú!

María está en la biblioteca.

COMPARE & CONTRAST

Compare the uses of the verb **estar** to those of the verb **ser**.

Uses of *estar*

Location

Estoy en casa.
I am at home.

Marissa **está** al lado de Felipe.
Marissa is next to Felipe.

Health

Juan Carlos **está** enfermo hoy.
Juan Carlos is sick today.

Well-being

—¿Cómo **estás**, Jimena?
How are you, Jimena?

—**Estoy** muy bien, gracias.
I'm very well, thank you.

Uses of *ser*

Identity

Hola, **soy** Maru.
Hello, I'm Maru.

Occupation

Soy estudiante.
I'm a student.

Origin

—¿**Eres** de México?
Are you from Mexico?

—Sí, **soy** de México.
Yes, I'm from Mexico.

Telling time

Son las cuatro.
It's four o'clock.

AYUDA

Use **la casa** to express *the house*, but **en casa** to express *at home*.

CONSULTA

To learn more about the difference between **ser** and **estar**, see **Senderos 1B, Estructura 5.3**, pp. 80–81.

▶ **Estar** is often used with certain prepositions and adverbs to describe the location of a person or an object.

Prepositions and adverbs often used with estar

al lado de	*next to*	**delante de**	*in front of*
a la derecha de	*to the right of*	**detrás de**	*behind*
a la izquierda de	*to the left of*	**en**	*in; on*
allá	*over there*	**encima de**	*on top of*
allí	*there*	**entre**	*between*
cerca de	*near*	**lejos de**	*far from*
con	*with*	**sin**	*without*
debajo de	*below*	**sobre**	*on; over*

La tiza **está al lado de** la pluma.
The chalk is next to the pen.

Los libros **están encima del** escritorio.
The books are on top of the desk.

El laboratorio **está cerca de** la clase.
The lab is near the classroom.

Maribel **está delante de** José.
Maribel is in front of José.

La maleta **está allí**.
The suitcase is there.

El estadio no **está lejos de** la librería.
The stadium isn't far from the bookstore.

El mapa **está entre** la pizarra y la puerta.
The map is between the blackboard and the door.

Los estudiantes **están en** la clase.
The students are in class.

La calculadora **está sobre** la mesa.
The calculator is on the table.

Los turistas **están allá**.
The tourists are over there.

Estamos lejos de casa.

La biblioteca está al lado de la librería.

¡INTÉNTALO! Provide the present tense forms of **estar**.

1. Ustedes ___están___ en la clase.
2. José ________ en la biblioteca.
3. Yo ________ bien, gracias.
4. Nosotras ________ en la cafetería.
5. Tú ________ en el laboratorio.
6. Elena ________ en la librería.
7. Ellas ________ en la clase.
8. Ana y yo ________ en la clase.
9. ¿Cómo ________ usted?
10. Javier y Maribel ________ en el estadio.
11. Nosotros ________ en la cafetería.
12. Yo ________ en el laboratorio.
13. Carmen y María ________ enfermas.
14. Tú ________ en la clase.

Práctica

1 **Completar** Daniela has just returned home from the library. Complete this conversation with the appropriate forms of **ser** or **estar**.

MAMÁ Hola, Daniela. ¿Cómo (1)__________?

DANIELA Hola, mamá. (2)__________ bien. ¿Dónde (3)__________ papá? ¡Ya (*Already*) (4)__________ las ocho de la noche!

MAMÁ No (5)__________ aquí. (6)__________ en la oficina.

DANIELA Y Andrés y Margarita, ¿dónde (7)__________ ellos?

MAMÁ (8)__________ en el restaurante La Palma con Martín.

DANIELA ¿Quién (9)__________ Martín?

MAMÁ (10)__________ un compañero de clase. (11)__________ de México.

DANIELA Ah. Y el restaurante La Palma, ¿dónde (12)__________?

MAMÁ (13)__________ cerca de la Plaza Mayor, en San Modesto.

DANIELA Gracias, mamá. Voy (*I'm going*) al restaurante. ¡Hasta pronto!

2 **Escoger** Choose the preposition that best completes each sentence.

1. La pluma está (encima de / detrás de) la mesa.
2. La ventana está (a la izquierda de / debajo de) la puerta.
3. La pizarra está (debajo de / delante de) los estudiantes.
4. Las sillas están (encima de / detrás de) los escritorios.
5. Los estudiantes llevan los libros (en / sobre) la mochila.
6. La biblioteca está (sobre / al lado de) la cafetería.
7. España está (cerca de / lejos de) Puerto Rico.
8. México está (cerca de / lejos de) los Estados Unidos.
9. Felipe trabaja (con / en) Ricardo en la cafetería.

3 **La librería** Indicate the location of five items in the drawing.

Los diccionarios están debajo de los libros de literatura.

Comunicación

4 **En la clase** Read Camila's e-mail to her friend, in which she describes her new school. Then, indicate whether each statement is **lógico** or **ilógico**, based on what you read.

Para: Andrés | Asunto:

Hola Andrés,
¿Cómo estás? Yo estoy muy bien, ¡adoro la nueva escuela! Hay dos cafeterías, una gran biblioteca y un laboratorio de biología. ¡Y mi salón de clases (*classroom*) está genial! Está cerca de la biblioteca. Tiene una puerta y dos ventanas, una mesa y una computadora para mí. También hay un reloj al lado de la puerta, y hay muchos escritorios y sillas para los estudiantes. ¿Y tú cómo estás? ¿Te gusta tu nueva escuela? ¿Cuántos estudiantes hay en tus clases de matemáticas?
¡Hasta pronto!
Camila

1. Camila es una estudiante de la clase de matemáticas.
2. El salón de clases está cerca del laboratorio de biología.
3. Hay una computadora en el salón de clases.
4. Camila y Andrés son profesores en la escuela.
5. Andrés es profesor de biología.

5 **¿Dónde estás...?** With a partner, take turns asking each other where you normally are at these times.

modelo

lunes / 10:00 a.m.
Estudiante 1: *¿Dónde estás los lunes a las diez de la mañana?*
Estudiante 2: *Estoy en la biblioteca.*

1. sábados / 6:00 a.m.
2. miércoles / 9:15 a.m.
3. lunes / 11:10 a.m.
4. jueves / 12:30 a.m.
5. viernes / 2:25 p.m.
6. martes / 3:50 p.m.
7. jueves / 5:45 p.m.
8. miércoles / 8:20 p.m.

Síntesis

6 **Entrevista** Answer your partner's questions.

1. ¿Cómo estás?
2. ¿Dónde estás ahora?
3. ¿Dónde está tu (*your*) diccionario de español?
4. ¿Dónde está tu casa?
5. ¿Cuándo hay un examen?
6. ¿Estudias mucho?
7. ¿Cuántas horas estudias para (*for*) una prueba?

2.4 Numbers 31 and higher

ANTE TODO You have already learned numbers 0–30. Now you will learn the rest of the numbers.

Numbers 31–100

▶ Numbers 31–99 follow the same basic pattern as 21–29.

Numbers 31–100

31	treinta y uno	**40**	cuarenta	**50**	cincuenta
32	treinta y dos	**41**	cuarenta y uno	**51**	cincuenta y uno
33	treinta y tres	**42**	cuarenta y dos	**52**	cincuenta y dos
34	treinta y cuatro	**43**	cuarenta y tres	**60**	sesenta
35	treinta y cinco	**44**	cuarenta y cuatro	**63**	sesenta y tres
36	treinta y seis	**45**	cuarenta y cinco	**64**	sesenta y cuatro
37	treinta y siete	**46**	cuarenta y seis	**70**	setenta
38	treinta y ocho	**47**	cuarenta y siete	**80**	ochenta
39	treinta y nueve	**48**	cuarenta y ocho	**90**	noventa
		49	cuarenta y nueve	**100**	cien, ciento

▶ **Y** is used in most numbers from **31** through **99**. Unlike numbers 21–29, these numbers must be written as three separate words.

Hay **noventa y dos** exámenes.
There are ninety-two exams.

Hay **cuarenta y dos** estudiantes.
There are forty-two students.

▶ With numbers that end in **uno** (31, 41, etc.), **uno** becomes **un** before a masculine noun and **una** before a feminine noun.

Hay **treinta y un** chicos.
There are thirty-one guys.

Hay **treinta y una** chicas.
There are thirty-one girls.

▶ **Cien** is used before nouns and in counting. The words **un**, **una**, and **uno** are never used before **cien** in Spanish. Use **cientos** to say *hundreds*.

Hay **cien** libros y **cien** sillas.
There are one hundred books and one hundred chairs.

¿Cuántos libros hay? **Cientos.**
How many books are there? Hundreds.

Numbers 101 and higher

▶ As shown in the chart, Spanish uses a period to indicate thousands and millions, rather than a comma, as is used in English.

Numbers 101 and higher

101	ciento uno	**1.000**	mil
200	doscientos/as	**1.100**	mil cien
300	trescientos/as	**2.000**	dos mil
400	cuatrocientos/as	**5.000**	cinco mil
500	quinientos/as	**100.000**	cien mil
600	seiscientos/as	**200.000**	doscientos/as mil
700	setecientos/as	**550.000**	quinientos/as cincuenta mil
800	ochocientos/as	**1.000.000**	un millón (de)
900	novecientos/as	**8.000.000**	ocho millones (de)

▶ Notice that you should use **ciento**, not **cien**, to count numbers over 100.

110 = **ciento diez** 118 = **ciento dieciocho** 150 = **ciento cincuenta**

▶ The numbers 200 through 999 agree in gender with the nouns they modify.

324 plum**as**
trescient**as** veinticuatro plum**as**

3.505 libr**os**
tres mil quinient**os** cinco libr**os**

▶ The word **mil**, which can mean *a thousand* and *one thousand*, is not usually used in the plural form to refer to an exact number, but it can be used to express the idea of *a lot*, *many*, or *thousands*. **Cientos** can also be used to express *hundreds* in this manner.

¡Hay **miles** de personas en el estadio!
There are thousands of people in the stadium!

Hay **cientos** de libros en la biblioteca.
There are hundreds of books in the library.

▶ To express a complex number (including years), string together all of its components.

55.422 cincuenta y cinco mil cuatrocientos veintidós

¡LENGUA VIVA!

In Spanish, years are not expressed as pairs of two-digit numbers as they are in English (1979, *nineteen seventy-nine*): **1776, mil setecientos setenta y seis; 1945, mil novecientos cuarenta y cinco; 2016, dos mil dieciséis.**

¡ATENCIÓN!

When **millón** or **millones** is used before a noun, the word **de** is placed between the two:

1.000.000 hombres = un millón de hombres

12.000.000 casas = doce millones de casas.

¡INTÉNTALO! Write out the Spanish equivalent of each number.

1. **102** ciento dos
2. **5.000.000** ________
3. **201** ________
4. **76** ________
5. **92** ________
6. **550.300** ________
7. **235** ________
8. **79** ________
9. **113** ________
10. **88** ________
11. **17.123** ________
12. **497** ________

Práctica y Comunicación

1 **Baloncesto** Provide these basketball scores in Spanish.

1. Ohio State 76, Michigan 65
2. Florida 92, Florida State 104
3. Stanford 83, UCLA 89
4. Purdue 81, Indiana 78
5. Princeton 67, Harvard 55
6. Duke 115, Virginia 121

2 **Completar** Following the pattern, write out the missing numbers in Spanish.

1. 50, 150, 250 ... 1.050
2. 5.000, 20.000, 35.000 ... 95.000
3. 100.000, 200.000, 300.000 ... 1.000.000
4. 100.000.000, 90.000.000, 80.000.000 ... 0

3 **Resolver** Solve the math problems. Write out the numbers in Spanish.

AYUDA

+ → **más**
– → **menos**
= → **son**

modelo

200 + 300 =

Doscientos más trescientos son quinientos.

1. 1.000 + 753 =
2. 1.000.000 – 30.000 =
3. 10.000 + 555 =
4. 15 + 150 =
5. 100.000 + 205.000 =
6. 29.000 – 10.000 =

4 **Los números de teléfono** Write a list of telephone numbers that are important to you. Write out the numbers.

modelo

mi celular: 635-1951 *seis-tres-cinco-diecinueve-cincuenta y uno*

Síntesis

5 **Preguntas** With a classmate, ask each other questions that require numbers in the answers. The questions could be about phone numbers, the number of people in your city or state, the year you finish school, etc.

modelo

Estudiante 1: *¿Cuándo terminas la escuela?*
Estudiante 2: *Termino la escuela en dos mil veintiuno.*

Recapitulación

Review the grammar concepts you have learned in this lesson by completing these activities.

1 **Completar** Complete the chart with the correct verb forms. **24 pts.**

yo	tú	nosotros	ellas
compro			
	deseas		
		miramos	
			preguntan

2 **Números** Write these numbers in Spanish. **16 pts.**

modelo

645: *seiscientos cuarenta y cinco*

1. **49:** ______
2. **97:** ______
3. **113:** ______
4. **632:** ______
5. **1.781:** ______
6. **3.558:** ______
7. **1.006.015:** ______
8. **67.224.370:** ______

3 **Preguntas** Write questions for these answers. **12 pts.**

1. —¿______ Patricia?
   —Patricia es de Colombia.
2. —¿______ él?
   —Él es mi amigo (*friend*).
3. —¿______ (tú)?
   —Hablo dos idiomas (*languages*).
4. —¿______ (ustedes)?
   —Deseamos tomar café.
5. —¿______?
   —Tomo biología porque me gustan las ciencias.
6. —¿______?
   —Camilo descansa por las mañanas.

RESUMEN GRAMATICAL

2.1 Present tense of *-ar* verbs *pp. 74–76*

estudiar	
estudio	estudiamos
estudias	estudiáis
estudia	estudian

The verb gustar

(no) me gusta + el/la + [*singular noun*]

(no) me gustan + los/las + [*plural noun*]

(no) me gusta + [*infinitive(s)*]

Note: You may use **a mí** for emphasis, but never **yo**.

To ask a friend about likes and dislikes, use **te** instead of **me**, but never **tú**.

¿Te gusta la historia?

2.2 Forming questions in Spanish *pp. 79–80*

- ¿Ustedes trabajan los sábados?
- ¿Trabajan ustedes los sábados?
- Ustedes trabajan los sábados, ¿verdad?/¿no?

Interrogative words

¿Adónde?	¿Cuánto/a?	¿Por qué?
¿Cómo?	¿Cuántos/as?	¿Qué?
¿Cuál(es)?	¿De dónde?	¿Quién(es)?
¿Cuándo?	¿Dónde?	

2.3 Present tense of *estar* *pp. 83–84*

- estar: estoy, estás, está, estamos, estáis, están

2.4 Numbers 31 and higher *pp. 87–88*

31	treinta y uno	101	ciento uno
32	treinta y dos (*and so on*)	200	doscientos/as
		500	quinientos/as
40	cuarenta	700	setecientos/as
50	cincuenta	900	novecientos/as
60	sesenta	1.000	mil
70	setenta	2.000	dos mil
80	ochenta	5.100	cinco mil cien
90	noventa	100.000	cien mil
100	cien, ciento	1.000.000	un millón (de)

4 **Al teléfono** Complete this telephone conversation with the correct forms of the verb **estar**. **16 pts.**

MARÍA TERESA Hola, señora López. (1) ¿ __________ Elisa en casa?

SRA. LÓPEZ Hola, ¿quién es?

MARÍA TERESA Soy María Teresa. Elisa y yo (2) __________ en la misma (*same*) clase de literatura.

SRA. LÓPEZ ¡Ah, María Teresa! ¿Cómo (3) __________ ?

MARÍA TERESA (4) __________ muy bien, gracias. Y usted, ¿cómo (5) __________ ?

SRA. LÓPEZ Bien, gracias. Pues, no, Elisa no (6) __________ en casa. Ella y su hermano (*her brother*) (7) __________ en la Biblioteca Cervantes.

MARÍA TERESA ¿Cervantes?

SRA. LÓPEZ Es la biblioteca que (8) __________ al lado del café Bambú.

MARÍA TERESA ¡Ah, sí! Gracias, señora López.

SRA. LÓPEZ Hasta luego, María Teresa.

5 **¿Qué te gusta?** Form complete sentences with the information provided to indicate what is liked. **28 pts.**

modelo

yo: las ciencias
Me gustan las ciencias.

1. yo: la clase de música __________
2. tú: las lenguas extranjeras __________
3. yo: escuchar la radio __________
4. tú: la historia __________
5. yo: las matemáticas __________
6. tú: viajar __________
7. yo: el arte __________

6 **Canción** Use the appropriate forms of the verb **gustar** to complete the beginning of a popular song by Manu Chao. **4 pts.**

"Me __________ los aviones°,
me gustas tú,
me __________ viajar,
me gustas tú,
me gusta la mañana,
me gustas tú."

aviones *airplanes*

Lectura

Antes de leer

Estrategia

Predicting content through formats

Recognizing the format of a document can help you to predict its content. For instance, invitations, greeting cards, and classified ads follow an easily identifiable format, which usually gives you a general idea of the information they contain. Look at the text and identify it based on its format.

Período	Hora	Clase
1	7:45 – 8:37	Matemáticas
2	8:43 – 9:30	Español
3	9:36 – 10:23	Inglés
4	10:29 – 11:16	Historia
Almuerzo	11:16 – 12:06	
5	12:12 – 12:59	Biología
6	1:05 – 1:52	Arte
7	1:58 – 2:45	Música

If you guessed that this is a page from a student's schedule, you are correct. You can now infer that the document contains information about a student's weekly schedule, including days, times, and activities.

Cognados

Make a list of the cognates in the text and guess their English meanings. What do cognates reveal about the content of the document?

Examinar el texto

Look at the format of the document entitled ***¡Español en Madrid!*** What type of text is it? What information do you expect to find in this type of document?

Después de leer

Correspondencias

Provide the letter of each item in Column B that matches the words in Column A. Two items will not be used.

1. profesores
2. vivienda
3. Madrid
4. número de teléfono
5. Español 2B
6. número de fax

a. (34) 91 523 4500
b. (34) 91 524 0210
c. 23 junio–30 julio
d. capital cultural de Europa
e. 16 junio–22 julio
f. especializados en enseñar español como lengua extranjera
g. (34) 91 523 4623
h. familias españolas

Escuela de Idiomas de Madrid

Madrid, la capital cultural de Europa, y la EIM te ofrecen cursos intensivos de verano° para aprender° español.

¿Dónde?
En el edificio de la EIM, cerca a la Plaza de Cibeles.

¿Quiénes son los profesores?
Son todos hablantes nativos del español especializados en enseñar el español como lengua extranjera.

¿Qué niveles se ofrecen?
Se ofrecen tres niveles° básicos:

1. Español Elemental, A, B y C
2. Español Intermedio, A y B
3. Español Avanzado, A y B

Viviendas
Para estudiantes extranjeros se ofrece vivienda° con familias españolas.

¿Cuándo?
Este verano desde° el 16 de junio hasta el 10 de agosto. Los cursos tienen una duración de 6 semanas.

Cursos	Empieza°	Termina
Español 1A	16 junio	22 julio
Español 1B	23 junio	30 julio
Español 1C	30 junio	10 agosto
Español 2A	16 junio	22 julio
Español 2B	23 junio	30 julio
Español 3A	16 junio	22 julio
Español 3B	23 junio	30 julio

Información
Para mayor información, sirvan comunicarse con la siguiente° oficina:

Escuela de Idiomas de Madrid
Programa de Español como Lengua Extranjera
Calle del Barquillo 1, 28005, 28039 Madrid, España
Tel. (34) 91 523 4500, **Fax** (34) 91 523 4623
www.uae.es

verano *summer* aprender *to learn* edificio *building* niveles *levels* vivienda *housing* desde *from* Empieza *Begins* siguiente *following*

¿Cierto o falso?
Indicate whether each statement is **cierto** or **falso**. Then correct the false statements.

	Cierto	Falso
1. La Escuela de Idiomas de Madrid ofrece (*offers*) cursos intensivos de italiano.	❍	❍
2. La lengua nativa de los profesores del programa es el inglés.	❍	❍
3. Se ofrecen dos niveles básicos de español.	❍	❍
4. Los estudiantes pueden vivir (*can live*) con familias españolas.	❍	❍
5. La escuela de idiomas que ofrece los cursos intensivos está en Salamanca.	❍	❍
6. Español 3B termina en agosto.	❍	❍
7. Si deseas información sobre (*about*) los cursos intensivos de español, es posible llamar al (34) 91 523 4500.	❍	❍
8. Español 1A empieza en julio.	❍	❍

Escritura

Estrategia

Brainstorming

How do you find ideas to write about? In the early stages of writing, brainstorming can help you generate ideas on a specific topic. You should spend ten to fifteen minutes brainstorming and jotting down any ideas about the topic. Whenever possible, try to write your ideas in Spanish. Express your ideas in single words or phrases, and jot them down in any order. While brainstorming, don't worry about whether your ideas are good or bad. Selecting and organizing ideas should be the second stage of your writing. Remember that the more ideas you write down while you're brainstorming, the more options you'll have to choose from later when you start to organize your ideas.

Me gusta

bailar
viajar
mirar la televisión
la clase de español
la clase de historia

No me gusta

cantar
dibujar
trabajar
la clase de química
la clase de biología

Tema

Una descripción

Write a description of yourself to post in a forum on a website in order to meet Spanish-speaking people. Include this information in your description:

- your name and where you are from, and a photo (optional) of yourself
- where you go to school
- the courses you are taking
- where you work (if you have a job)
- some of your likes and dislikes

¡Hola! Me llamo Alicia Roberts. Estudio matemáticas y economía. Me gusta dibujar, cantar y viajar.

Escuchar

Estrategia
Listening for cognates

You already know that cognates are words that have similar spellings and meanings in two or more languages: for example, *group* and **grupo** or *stereo* and **estéreo.** Listen for cognates to increase your comprehension of spoken Spanish.

To help you practice this strategy, you will now listen to two sentences. Make a list of all the cognates you hear.

Preparación

Based on the photograph, who do you think Armando and Julia are? What do you think they are talking about?

Ahora escucha

Now you are going to hear Armando and Julia's conversation. Make a list of the cognates they use.

Armando	Julia
______	______
______	______
______	______
______	______

Based on your knowledge of cognates, decide whether the following statements are **cierto** or **falso.**

	Cierto	Falso
1. Armando y Julia hablan de la familia.	❍	❍
2. Armando y Julia toman una clase de italiano.	❍	❍
3. Julia toma clase de historia.	❍	❍
4. Armando estudia lenguas extranjeras.	❍	❍
5. Julia toma una clase de religión.	❍	❍

Comprensión

Preguntas

Answer these questions about Armando and Julia's conversation.

1. ¿Qué clases toma Armando?

   ____

2. ¿Qué clases toma Julia?

   ____

Seleccionar

Choose the answer that best completes each sentence.

1. Armando toma ________ clases.
   a. cuatro b. tres c. seis
2. Julia toma dos clases de ________.
   a. matemáticas b. ciencias c. idiomas
3. Armando toma italiano y ________.
   a. historia b. música c. química

Preguntas personales

1. ¿Cuántas clases tomas?
2. ¿Qué clases tomas?
3. ¿Qué clases te gustan y qué clases no te gustan?

Anuncio de Jumbo

Viejito Pascuero°...

Preparación

Answer the following questions in English.

1. For what occasions do you give and get gifts?
2. When did you get a very special or needed gift? What was the gift?

Calendarios

During the months of cold weather and snow in North America, the southern hemisphere enjoys warm weather and longer days. Since Chile's summer lasts from December to February, school vacation coincides with these months. In Chile, the school year starts in early March and finishes toward the end of December. All schools, from preschools to universities, observe this scholastic calendar, with only a few days' variation between institutions.

Viejito Pascuero *Santa Claus (Chile)*

Vocabulario útil

ahorrar	*to save (money)*
Navidad	*Christmas*
pedirte	*to ask you*
quería	*I wanted*
te preocupa	*it worries you*

Comprensión

Answer the following questions, using both English and Spanish as directed.

1. In the video, what was the young boy doing?
2. Who else is in the video? How do you know who he is?
3. What did the boy ask? Give both the Spanish and the English equivalent.
4. What answer was he given? Give both the Spanish and the English equivalent.

Conversación

With a partner, take turns asking for something and being sure of the spelling. Each of you should ask for four different things. Follow the model.

modelo

Estudiante 1: *¿Qué quieres?*
Estudiante 2: *Quiero un diccionario.*
Estudiante 1: *¿Cómo se escribe "diccionario"?*
Estudiante 2: D-I-C-C-I-O-N-A-R-I-O

Aplicación

With a partner, describe your school calendar and vacations. Then research and describe the same for a Spanish-speaking culture. Include the following elements: at what age students start school, the first and last days of the school year, and the dates of school vacations. Present your descriptions to the class, comparing the two as you present.

Mexican author and diplomat Octavio Paz (March 31, 1914–April 19, 1998) studied both law and literature at the **Universidad Nacional Autónoma de México** (**UNAM**), but after graduating he immersed himself in the art of writing. An incredibly prolific writer of novels, poetry, and essays, Paz solidified his prestige as Mexico's preeminent author with his 1950 book ***El laberinto de la soledad***, a fundamental study of Mexican identity. Among the many awards he received in his lifetime are the **Premio Miguel de Cervantes** (1981) and Nobel Prize for Literature (1990). Paz foremost considered himself a poet and affirmed that poetry constitutes "**la religión secreta de la edad° moderna**".

Vocabulario útil	
¿Cuál es tu materia favorita?	*What is your favorite subject?*
¿Cuántos años tienes?	*How old are you?*
¿Qué estudias?	*What do you study?*
el/la alumno/a	*student*
la carrera (de medicina)	*(medical) degree program, major*
derecho	*law*
reconocido	*well-known*

Preparación

What is the name of your school? What classes are you taking this semester?

Emparejar

Match the first part of the sentence in the left column with the appropriate ending in the right column.

1. Los estudiantes Mexicanos de la UNAM viven en
2. México, D.F. es
3. La UNAM es
4. La UNAM ofrece

a. una universidad muy grande.
b. 74 carreras de estudio.
c. sus casas con sus padres.
d. la ciudad más grande (*biggest*) de Hispanoamérica.

Los estudios

—¿Qué estudias?
—Ciencias de la comunicación.

Estudio derecho en la UNAM.

¿Conoces a algún° profesor famoso que dé° clases... en la UNAM?

edad *age* ¿Conoces a algún...? *Do you know any...?* que dé *that teaches*

España

El país en cifras

- **Área:** 505.370 km² (kilómetros cuadrados) o 195.124 millas cuadradas°, incluyendo las islas Baleares y las islas Canarias
- **Población:** 47.043.000
- **Capital:** Madrid—5.762.000
- **Ciudades° principales:** Barcelona—5.029.000, Valencia—812.000, Sevilla, Zaragoza
- **Moneda°:** euro
- **Idiomas°:** español o castellano, catalán, gallego, valenciano, euskera

Regiones lingüísticas

Bandera de España

Plaza Mayor en Madrid

La Sagrada Familia en Barcelona

El baile flamenco

Españoles célebres

- **Miguel de Cervantes,** escritor° (1547–1616)
- **Pedro Almodóvar,** director de cine° (1949–)
- **Rosa Montero,** escritora y periodista° (1951–)
- **Fernando Alonso,** corredor de autos° (1981–)
- **Paz Vega,** actriz° (1976–)
- **Severo Ochoa,** Premio Nobel de Medicina, 1959; doctor y científico (1905–1993)

millas cuadradas *square miles* Ciudades *Cities* Moneda *Currency* Idiomas *Languages* escritor *writer* cine *film* periodista *reporter* corredor de autos *race car driver* actriz *actress* pueblo *town* Cada año *Every year* Durante todo un día *All day long* se tiran *throw at each other* varias toneladas *many tons*

¡Increíble pero cierto!

En Buñol, un pueblo° de Valencia, la producción de tomates es un recurso económico muy importante. Cada año° se celebra el festival de *La Tomatina*. Durante todo un día°, miles de personas se tiran° tomates. Llegan turistas de todo el país, y se usan varias toneladas° de tomates.

Gastronomía • José Andrés

José Andrés es un chef español famoso internacionalmente°. Le gusta combinar platos° tradicionales de España con las técnicas de cocina más innovadoras°. Andrés vive° en Washington, DC, es dueño° de varios restaurantes en los EE.UU. y presenta° un programa en PBS (foto, izquierda). También° ha estado° en *Late Show with David Letterman* y *Top Chef*.

Cultura • La diversidad

La riqueza° cultural y lingüística de España refleja la combinación de las diversas culturas que han habitado° en su territorio durante siglos°. El español es la lengua oficial del país, pero también son oficiales el catalán, el gallego, el euskera y el valenciano.

Sóc molt fan de la pàgina 335.

Ajuntament de Barcelona

Póster en catalán

Las meninas, Diego Velázquez, 1656

Artes • Velázquez y el Prado

El Prado, en Madrid, es uno de los museos más famosos del mundo°. En el Prado hay pinturas° importantes de Botticelli, de El Greco y de los españoles Goya y Velázquez. *Las meninas* es la obra° más conocida° de Diego Velázquez, pintor° oficial de la corte real° durante el siglo° XVII.

Comida • La paella

La paella es uno de los platos más típicos de España. Siempre se prepara° con arroz° y azafrán°, pero hay diferentes recetas°. La paella valenciana, por ejemplo, es de pollo° y conejo°, y la paella marinera es de mariscos°.

La costa de Ibiza

¿Qué aprendiste? Completa las oraciones con la información adecuada.

1. El chef español ____________ es muy famoso.
2. El arroz y el azafrán son ingredientes básicos de la ____________.
3. El Prado está en ____________.
4. José Andrés vive en ________________.
5. El chef José Andrés tiene un ____________ de televisión en PBS.
6. El gallego es una de las lenguas oficiales de ____________.

Conexión Internet Investiga estos temas en Internet.

1. Busca información sobre la Universidad de Salamanca u otra universidad española. ¿Qué cursos ofrece (*does it offer*)?
2. Busca información sobre un español o una española célebre (por ejemplo, un[a] político/a, un actor, una actriz, un[a] artista). ¿De qué parte de España es y por qué es célebre?

internacionalmente *internationally* **platos** *dishes* **más innovadoras** *most innovative* **vive** *lives* **dueño** *owner* **presenta** *hosts* **También** *Also* **ha estado** *has been* **riqueza** *richness* **han habitado** *have lived* **durante siglos** *for centuries* **mundo** *world* **pinturas** *paintings* **obra** *work* **más conocida** *best-known* **pintor** *painter* **corte real** *royal court* **siglo** *century* **Siempre se prepara** *It is always prepared* **arroz** *rice* **azafrán** *saffron* **recetas** *recipes* **pollo** *chicken* **conejo** *rabbit* **mariscos** *seafood*

La clase

el/la compañero/a de clase	*classmate*
el/la estudiante	*student*
el/la profesor(a)	*teacher*
el borrador	*eraser*
la calculadora	*calculator*
el escritorio	*desk*
el libro	*book*
el mapa	*map*
la mesa	*table*
la mochila	*backpack*
el papel	*paper*
la papelera	*wastebasket*
la pizarra	*blackboard*
la pluma	*pen*
la puerta	*door*
el reloj	*clock; watch*
la silla	*seat*
la tiza	*chalk*
la ventana	*window*
la biblioteca	*library*
la cafetería	*cafeteria*
la casa	*house; home*
el estadio	*stadium*
el laboratorio	*laboratory*
la librería	*bookstore*
la universidad	*university; college*
la clase	*class*
el curso, la materia	*course*
el examen	*test; exam*
el horario	*schedule*
la prueba	*test; quiz*
el semestre	*semester*
la tarea	*homework*
el trimestre	*trimester; quarter*

Las materias

la arqueología	*archeology*
el arte	*art*
la biología	*biology*
las ciencias	*sciences*
la computación	*computer science*
la contabilidad	*accounting*
la economía	*economics*
el español	*Spanish*
la física	*physics*
la geografía	*geography*
la historia	*history*
las humanidades	*humanities*
el inglés	*English*
las lenguas extranjeras	*foreign languages*
la literatura	*literature*
las matemáticas	*mathematics*
la música	*music*
el periodismo	*journalism*
la psicología	*psychology*
la química	*chemistry*
la sociología	*sociology*

Preposiciones y adverbios

al lado de	*next to*
a la derecha de	*to the right of*
a la izquierda de	*to the left of*
allá	*over there*
allí	*there*
cerca de	*near*
con	*with*
debajo de	*below*
delante de	*in front of*
detrás de	*behind*
en	*in; on*
encima de	*on top of*
entre	*between*
lejos de	*far from*
sin	*without*
sobre	*on; over*

Palabras adicionales

¿Adónde?	*Where (to)?*
ahora	*now*
¿Cuál?, ¿Cuáles?	*Which?; Which one(s)?*
¿Por qué?	*Why?*
porque	*because*

Verbos

bailar	*to dance*
buscar	*to look for*
caminar	*to walk*
cantar	*to sing*
cenar	*to have dinner*
comprar	*to buy*
contestar	*to answer*
conversar	*to converse, to chat*
desayunar	*to have breakfast*
descansar	*to rest*
desear	*to wish; to desire*
dibujar	*to draw*
enseñar	*to teach*
escuchar la radio/ música	*to listen (to) the radio/music*
esperar (+ *inf.*)	*to wait (for); to hope*
estar	*to be*
estudiar	*to study*
explicar	*to explain*
gustar	*to like*
hablar	*to talk; to speak*
llegar	*to arrive*
llevar	*to carry*
mirar	*to look (at); to watch*
necesitar (+ *inf.*)	*to need*
practicar	*to practice*
preguntar	*to ask (a question)*
preparar	*to prepare*
regresar	*to return*
terminar	*to end; to finish*
tomar	*to take; to drink*
trabajar	*to work*
viajar	*to travel*

Los días de la semana

¿Cuándo?	*When?*
¿Qué día es hoy?	*What day is it?*
Hoy es...	*Today is...*
la semana	*week*
lunes	*Monday*
martes	*Tuesday*
miércoles	*Wednesday*
jueves	*Thursday*
viernes	*Friday*
sábado	*Saturday*
domingo	*Sunday*

Numbers 31 and higher	*See pages 87–88.*
Expresiones útiles	*See page 69.*

La familia

3

Communicative Goals

You will learn how to:

- **Talk about your family and friends**
- **Describe people and things**
- **Express possession**

A PRIMERA VISTA

- ¿Cuántos chicos hay en la foto?
- ¿Hay una mujer detrás de la chica? ¿Y a la izquierda?
- ¿Hay una cosa en la mano del chico?
- ¿Conversan ellos? ¿Trabajan? ¿Descansan?
- ¿Están en su casa?

La familia

Más vocabulario

los abuelos	*grandparents*
el/la bisabuelo/a	*great-grandfather/ great-grandmother*
el/la gemelo/a	*twin*
el/la hermanastro/a	*stepbrother/stepsister*
el/la hijastro/a	*stepson/stepdaughter*
la madrastra	*stepmother*
el medio hermano/ la media hermana	*half-brother/ half-sister*
el padrastro	*stepfather*
los padres	*parents*
los parientes	*relatives*
el/la cuñado/a	*brother-in-law/ sister-in-law*
la nuera	*daughter-in-law*
el/la suegro/a	*father-in-law/ mother-in-law*
el yerno	*son-in-law*
el/la amigo/a	*friend*
el apellido	*last name*
la gente	*people*
el/la muchacho/a	*boy/girl*
el/la niño/a	*child*
el/la novio/a	*boyfriend/girlfriend*
la persona	*person*
el/la artista	*artist*
el/la ingeniero/a	*engineer*
el/la doctor(a), el/la médico/a	*doctor; physician*
el/la periodista	*journalist*
el/la programador(a)	*computer programmer*

Variación léxica

madre ⟷ mamá, mami (*colloquial*)
padre ⟷ papá, papi (*colloquial*)
muchacho/a ⟷ chico/a

La familia de José Miguel Pérez Santoro

Juan Santoro Sánchez

mi abuelo (*my grandfather*)

Ernesto Santoro González

mi tío (*uncle*)
hijo (*son*) **de Juan y Socorro**

Marina Gutiérrez de Santoro

mi tía (*aunt*)
esposa (*wife*) **de Ernesto**

Silvia Socorro Santoro Gutiérrez

mi prima (*cousin*)
hija (*daughter*) **de Ernesto y Marina**

Héctor Manuel Santoro Gutiérrez

mi primo (*cousin*)
nieto (*grandson*) **de Juan y Socorro**

Carmen Santoro Gutiérrez

mi prima
hija de Ernesto y Marina

¡LENGUA VIVA!

In Spanish-speaking countries, it is common for people to go by both their first name and middle name, such as **José Miguel** or **Juan Carlos.** You will learn more about names and naming conventions on p. 110.

Socorro González de Santoro

mi abuela (*my grandmother*)

Mirta Santoro de Pérez

mi madre (*mother*)
hija de Juan y Socorro

Rubén Ernesto Pérez Gómez

mi padre (*father*)
esposo de mi madre

José Miguel Pérez Santoro

hijo de Rubén y Mirta

Beatriz Alicia Pérez de Morales

mi hermana (*sister*)

Felipe Morales Zapata

esposo (*husband*) **de Beatriz Alicia**

Víctor Miguel Morales Pérez

mi sobrino (*nephew*)
hermano (*brother*) **de Anita**

Anita Morales Pérez

mi sobrina (*niece*)
nieta (*granddaughter*) **de mis padres**

los hijos (*children*) **de Beatriz Alicia y Felipe**

Práctica

1 Escuchar Listen to each statement made by José Miguel Pérez Santoro, then indicate whether it is **cierto** or **falso**, based on his family tree.

	Cierto	Falso		Cierto	Falso
1.	❍	❍	6.	❍	❍
2.	❍	❍	7.	❍	❍
3.	❍	❍	8.	❍	❍
4.	❍	❍	9.	❍	❍
5.	❍	❍	10.	❍	❍

2 Personas Indicate each word that you hear mentioned in the narration.

1. _____ cuñado
2. _____ tía
3. _____ periodista
4. _____ niño
5. _____ esposo
6. _____ abuelos
7. _____ ingeniera
8. _____ primo

3 Emparejar Provide the letter of the phrase that matches each description. Two items will not be used.

1. Mi hermano programa las computadoras.
2. Son los padres de mi esposo.
3. Son los hijos de mis (*my*) tíos.
4. Mi tía trabaja en un hospital.
5. Es el hijo de mi madrastra y el hijastro de mi padre.
6. Es el esposo de mi hija.
7. Es el hijo de mi hermana.
8. Mi primo dibuja y pinta mucho.
9. Mi hermanastra enseña en la universidad.
10. Mi padre trabaja con planos (*blueprints*).

a. Es médica.
b. Es mi hermanastro.
c. Es programador.
d. Es ingeniero.
e. Son mis suegros.
f. Es mi novio.
g. Es mi padrastro.
h. Son mis primos.
i. Es artista.
j. Es profesora.
k. Es mi sobrino.
l. Es mi yerno.

4 Definiciones Define these family terms in Spanish.

modelo
hijastro *Es el hijo de mi esposo/a, pero no es mi hijo.*

1. abuela
2. bisabuelo
3. tío
4. primas
5. suegra
6. cuñado
7. nietos
8. medio hermano

5 **Escoger** Complete the description of each photo using words you have learned in **Contextos**.

1. La ________ de Sara es grande.

2. Héctor y Lupita son ________.

3. Maira Díaz es ________.

4. Rubén habla con su ________.

5. Los dos ________ están en el parque.

6. Irene es ________.

7. Elena Vargas Soto es ________.

8. Don Manuel es el ________ de Martín.

Comunicación

6 **Preguntas personales** Answer your partner's questions.

1. ¿Cuántas personas hay en tu familia?
2. ¿Cómo se llaman tus padres? ¿De dónde son? ¿Dónde trabajan?
3. ¿Cuántos hermanos tienes? ¿Cómo se llaman? ¿Dónde estudian o trabajan?
4. ¿Cuántos primos tienes? ¿Cuáles son los apellidos de ellos? ¿Cuántos son niños y cuántos son adultos? ¿Hay más chicos o más chicas en tu familia?
5. ¿Quién es tu pariente favorito?

AYUDA

tu, tus *your* (sing., pl.)
mi, mis *my* (sing., pl.)
tienes *you have*
tengo *I have*

7 **Árbol genealógico** Write about a family tree. Use your own family or invent a family.

modelo

El abuelo se llama Robert Lange. Es de Nebraska...

8 **Una familia** With a partner, identify the members in the family tree by asking questions about how each family member is related to Graciela Vargas García.

modelo

Estudiante 1: ¿Quién es Beatriz Pardo de Vargas?
Estudiante 2: Es la abuela de Graciela.

CONSULTA

To see the cities where these family members live, look at the map in **Panorama** on p. 136.

Un domingo en familia

Marissa pasa el día en Xochimilco con la familia Díaz.

PERSONAJES

FELIPE

TÍA NAYELI

JIMENA Hola, tía Nayeli.

TÍA NAYELI ¡Hola, Jimena! ¿Cómo estás?

JIMENA Bien, gracias. Y, ¿dónde están mis primas?

TÍA NAYELI No sé. ¿Dónde están mis hijas? ¡Ah!

MARISSA ¡Qué bonitas son tus hijas! Y ¡qué simpáticas!

FELIPE Soy guapo y delgado.

JIMENA Ay, ¡por favor! Eres gordo, antipático y muy feo.

TÍO RAMÓN ¿Tienes una familia grande, Marissa?

MARISSA Tengo dos hermanos mayores, Zack y Jennifer, y un hermano menor, Adam.

MARISSA La verdad, mi familia es pequeña.

SRA. DÍAZ ¿Pequeña? Yo soy hija única. Bueno, y ¿qué más? ¿Tienes novio?

MARISSA No. Tengo mala suerte con los novios.

MARISSA Tía Nayeli, ¿cuántos años tienen tus hijas?

TÍA NAYELI Marta tiene ocho años y Valentina doce.

JIMENA

MARTA

VALENTINA

SRA. DÍAZ

TÍO RAMÓN

SR. DÍAZ

MARISSA

SRA. DÍAZ Chicas, ¿compartimos una trajinera?

MARISSA ¡Claro que sí! ¡Qué bonitas son!

SRA. DÍAZ ¿Vienes, Jimena?

JIMENA No, gracias. Tengo que leer.

MARISSA Me gusta mucho este sitio. Tengo ganas de visitar otros lugares en México.

SRA. DÍAZ ¡Debes viajar a Mérida!

TÍA NAYELI ¡Sí, con tus amigos! Debes visitar a Ana María, la hermana de Roberto y de Ramón.

(La Sra. Díaz habla por teléfono con la tía Ana María.)

SRA. DÍAZ ¡Qué bien! Excelente. Sí, la próxima semana. Muchísimas gracias.

MARISSA ¡Gracias, Sra. Díaz!

SRA. DÍAZ Tía Ana María.

MARISSA Tía Ana María.

SRA. DÍAZ ¡Un beso, chau!

MARISSA *Bye!*

Expresiones útiles

Talking about your family

¿Tienes una familia grande?
Do you have a big family?
Tengo dos hermanos mayores y un hermano menor.
I have two older siblings and a younger brother.
La verdad, mi familia es pequeña.
The truth is, my family is small.
¿Pequeña? Yo soy hija única.
Small? I'm an only child.

Describing people

¡Qué bonitas son tus hijas! Y ¡qué simpáticas!
Your daughters are so pretty! And so nice!
Soy guapo y delgado.
I'm handsome and slim.
¡Por favor! Eres gordo, antipático y muy feo.
Please! You're fat, unpleasant, and very ugly.

Talking about plans

¿Compartimos una trajinera?
Shall we share a trajinera*?*
¡Claro que sí! ¡Qué bonitas son!
Of course! They're so pretty!
¿Vienes, Jimena?
Are you coming, Jimena?
No, gracias. Tengo que leer.
No, thanks. I have to read.

Saying how old people are

¿Cuántos años tienen tus hijas?
How old are your daughters?
Marta tiene ocho años y Valentina doce.
Marta is eight and Valentina twelve.

Additional vocabulary

ensayo *essay*
pobrecito/a *poor thing*
próxima *next*
sitio *place*
todavía *still*
trajinera *type of barge*

¿Qué pasó?

1 **¿Cierto o falso?** Indicate whether each sentence is **cierto** or **falso**. Correct the false statements.

	Cierto	Falso
1. Marissa dice que (*says that*) tiene una familia grande.	❍	❍
2. La Sra. Díaz tiene dos hermanos.	❍	❍
3. Marissa no tiene novio.	❍	❍
4. Valentina tiene veinte años.	❍	❍
5. Marissa comparte una trajinera con la Sra. Díaz y la tía Nayeli.	❍	❍
6. A Marissa le gusta mucho Xochimilco.	❍	❍

NOTA CULTURAL

Xochimilco is famous for its system of canals and **chinampas**, or artificial islands, which have been used for agricultural purposes since Pre-Hispanic times. In 1987, UNESCO declared **Xochimilco** a World Heritage Site.

2 **Identificar** Indicate which person would make each statement. The names may be used more than once. **¡Ojo!** One name will not be used.

1. Felipe es antipático y feo.
2. Mis hermanos se llaman Jennifer, Adam y Zack.
3. ¡Soy un joven muy guapo!
4. Mis hijas tienen ocho y doce años.
5. ¡Qué bonitas son las trajineras!
6. Ana María es la hermana de Ramón y Roberto.
7. No puedo (*I can't*) compartir una trajinera porque tengo que leer.
8. Tus hijas son bonitas y simpáticas, tía Nayeli.

SRA. DÍAZ

JIMENA

MARISSA

FELIPE

TÍA NAYELI

NOTA CULTURAL

Trajineras are large passenger barges that you can rent in **Xochimilco**. Each boat is named and decorated and has a table and chairs so passengers can picnic while they ride.

3 **Escribir** Choose Marissa, Sra. Díaz, or tía Nayeli and write a brief description of her family. Be creative!

MARISSA

Marissa es de los EE.UU. ¿Cómo es su familia?

SRA. DÍAZ

La Sra. Díaz es de Cuba. ¿Cómo es su familia?

TÍA NAYELI

La tía Nayeli es de México. ¿Cómo es su familia?

4  **Conversar** Answer your partner's questions.

1. ¿Cuántos años tienes?
2. ¿Tienes una familia grande?
3. ¿Tienes hermanos o hermanas?
4. ¿Cuántos años tiene tu abuelo (tu hermana, tu primo, etc.)?
5. ¿De dónde son tus padres?

AYUDA

Here are some expressions to help you talk about age.

Yo tengo... años.
I am... years old.

Mi abuelo tiene... años.
My grandfather is... years old.

Pronunciación

Diphthongs and linking

hermano **niña** **cuñado**

In Spanish, **a**, **e**, and **o** are considered strong vowels. The weak vowels are **i** and **u**.

ruido **parientes** **periodista**

A diphthong is a combination of two weak vowels or of a strong vowel and a weak vowel. Diphthongs are pronounced as a single syllable.

la abuela

mi hijo **una clase excelente**

Two identical vowel sounds that appear together are pronounced like one long vowel.

con Natalia **sus sobrinos** **las sillas**

Two identical consonants together sound like a single consonant.

es ingeniera **mis abuelos** **sus hijos**

A consonant at the end of a word is linked with the vowel sound at the beginning of the next word.

mi hermano **su esposa** **nuestro amigo**

A vowel at the end of a word is linked with the vowel sound at the beginning of the next word.

Práctica Say these words aloud, focusing on the diphthongs.

1. historia
2. nieto
3. parientes
4. novia
5. residencia
6. prueba
7. puerta
8. ciencias
9. lenguas
10. estudiar
11. izquierda
12. ecuatoriano

Oraciones Read these sentences aloud to practice diphthongs and linking words.

1. Hola. Me llamo Anita Amaral. Soy del Ecuador.
2. Somos seis en mi familia.
3. Tengo dos hermanos y una hermana.
4. Mi papá es del Ecuador y mi mamá es de España.

Refranes Read these sayings aloud to practice diphthongs and linking sounds.

1 When one door closes, another opens.
2 Speak of the devil and he will appear.

EN DETALLE

¿Cómo te llamas?

In the Spanish-speaking world, it is common to have two last names: one paternal and one maternal. In some cases, the conjunctions **de** or **y** are used to connect the two. For example, in the name **Juan Martínez Velasco**, *Martínez* is the paternal surname (**el apellido paterno**), and *Velasco* is the maternal surname (**el apellido materno**). This convention of using two last names (**doble apellido**) is a European tradition that Spaniards brought to the Americas. It continues to be practiced in many countries, including Chile, Colombia, Mexico, Peru, and Venezuela. There are exceptions, however. In Argentina, the prevailing custom is for children to inherit only the father's last name.

When a woman marries in a country where two last names are used, legally she retains her two maiden surnames. However, socially she may take her husband's paternal surname in place of her inherited maternal surname. For example, **Karen Martínez Insignares**, the wife of Colombian singer **Juanes** (**Juan Esteban Aristizábal Vásquez**), might use the names **Karen Martínez Aristizábal** or **Karen Martínez de Aristizábal** in social situations (although officially her name remains **Karen Martínez Insignares**). Adopting a husband's last name for social purposes, though widespread, is only legally recognized in Ecuador and Peru.

Most parents do not break tradition upon naming their children; regardless of the surnames the mother uses, they use the father's first surname followed by the mother's first surname, as in the name **Juan Martínez Velasco**. However, one should note that both surnames come from the grandfathers, and therefore all **apellidos** are effectively paternal.

José Martínez García

Mercedes Velasco Pérez

Juan Martínez Velasco

Hijos en la casa

In Spanish-speaking countries, family and society place very little pressure on young adults to live on their own (**independizarse**), and children often live with their parents well into their thirties. For example, about 60% of Spaniards under 34 years of age live at home with their parents. This delay in moving out is both cultural and economic—lack of job security or low wages coupled with a high cost of living may make it impractical for young adults to live independently before they marry.

ACTIVIDADES

1 **¿Cierto o falso?** Indicate whether these statements are **cierto** or **falso**. Correct the false statements.

1. Most Spanish-speaking people have three last names.
2. Hispanic last names generally consist of the paternal last name followed by the maternal last name.
3. It is common to see **de** or **y** used in a Hispanic last name.
4. Someone from Argentina would most likely have two last names.
5. Generally, married women legally retain two maiden surnames.
6. In social situations, a married woman often uses her husband's last name in place of her inherited paternal surname.
7. Adopting a husband's surname is only legally recognized in Peru and Ecuador.
8. Hispanic last names are effectively a combination of the maternal surnames from the previous generation.

ASÍ SE DICE

Familia y amigos

el/la bisnieto/a	*great-grandson/daughter*
el/la chamaco/a (Méx.); el/la chamo/a (Ven.); el/la chaval(a) (Esp.); el/la pibe/a (Arg.)	el/la muchacho/a
mi colega (Esp.); mi cuate (Méx.); mi parcero/a (Col.); mi pana (Ven., P. Rico, Rep. Dom.)	*my pal; my buddy*
la madrina	*godmother*
el padrino	*godfather*
el/la tatarabuelo/a	*great-great-grandfather/ great-great-grandmother*

EL MUNDO HISPANO

Las familias

Although worldwide population trends show a decrease in average family size, households in many Spanish-speaking countries are still larger than their U.S. counterparts.

- **México** 4,0 personas
- **Colombia** 3,9 personas
- **Argentina** 3,6 personas
- **Uruguay** 3,0 personas
- **España** 2,9 personas
- **Estados Unidos** 2,6 personas

PERFIL

La familia real española

Undoubtedly, Spain's most famous family is **la familia real** (*Royal*). In 1962, the then prince **Juan Carlos de Borbón** married Princess **Sofía** of Greece. In the 1970s, **el Rey** (*King*) **Juan Carlos** and **la Reina** (*Queen*) **Sofía** helped transition Spain to democracy after a forty-year dictatorship. The royal couple has three children: las **infantas** (*Princesses*) **Elena** and **Cristina**, and a son, **el príncipe** (*Prince*) **Felipe**, whose official title was **el Príncipe de Asturias**. In 2004, Felipe married **Letizia Ortiz Rocasolano,** a journalist and TV presenter. They have two daughters, **las infantas Leonor** (born in 2005) and **Sofía** (born in 2007). In 2014, Juan Carlos decided to abdicate the throne in favor of his son.

Conexión Internet

What role do padrinos and madrinas have in today's Hispanic family?

Use the Web to find more cultural information related to this **Cultura** section.

ACTIVIDADES

2 Comprensión Complete these sentences.

1. Spain's royals were responsible for guiding in ___________.
2. In Spanish, your godmother is called ___________.
3. Princess Leonor is the ___________ of Queen Sofía.
4. Uruguay's average household has ___________ people.
5. If a Venezuelan calls you **mi pana**, you are that person's ___________.

3 Una familia famosa Create a genealogical tree of a famous family, using photos or drawings labeled with names and ages. Explain who the people are and their relationships to each other.

3.1 Descriptive adjectives

ANTE TODO Adjectives are words that describe people, places, and things. In Spanish, descriptive adjectives are used with the verb **ser** to point out characteristics such as nationality, size, color, shape, personality, and appearance.

Forms and agreement of adjectives

COMPARE & CONTRAST

In English, the forms of descriptive adjectives do not change to reflect the gender (masculine/feminine) and number (singular/plural) of the noun or pronoun they describe.

*Juan is **nice**.* *Elena is **nice**.* *They are **nice**.*

In Spanish, the forms of descriptive adjectives agree in gender and/or number with the nouns or pronouns they describe.

Juan es simpátic**o**. Elena es simpátic**a**. Ellos son simpátic**os**.

- Adjectives that end in **-o** have four different forms. The feminine singular is formed by changing the **-o** to **-a**. The plural is formed by adding **-s** to the singular forms.

Masculine		Feminine	
SINGULAR	PLURAL	SINGULAR	PLURAL
el muchach**o** alt**o**	los muchach**os** alt**os**	la muchach**a** alt**a**	las muchach**as** alt**as**

- Adjectives that end in **-e** or a consonant have the same masculine and feminine forms.

Masculine		Feminine	
SINGULAR	PLURAL	SINGULAR	PLURAL
el chico inteligent**e**	los chicos inteligent**es**	la chica inteligent**e**	las chicas inteligent**es**
el examen difíci**l**	los exámenes difíci**les**	la clase difíci**l**	las clases difíci**les**

- Adjectives that end in **-or** are variable in both gender and number.

Masculine		Feminine	
SINGULAR	PLURAL	SINGULAR	PLURAL
el hombre trabajad**or**	los hombres trabajad**ores**	la mujer trabajad**ora**	las mujeres trabajad**oras**

AYUDA

Many adjectives are cognates, that is, words that share similar spellings and meanings in Spanish and English. A cognate can be a noun like **profesor** or a descriptive adjective like **interesante**.

¡ATENCIÓN!

Note that **joven** takes an accent in its plural form. **Los jóvenes estudian mucho**.

¡ATENCIÓN!

Note that adjectives with an accent on the last syllable drop the accent in the feminine and plural forms.

inglés → inglesa
alemán → alemanes

▶ Use the masculine plural form to refer to groups that include males and females.

Manuel es alt**o**. Lola es alt**a**. Manuel y Lola son alt**os**.

Common adjectives

alto/a	*tall*	**gordo/a**	*fat*	**mucho/a**	*much; many; a lot of*
antipático/a	*unpleasant*	**grande**	*big*	**pelirrojo/a**	*red-haired*
bajo/a	*short (in height)*	**guapo/a**	*good-looking*	**pequeño/a**	*small*
bonito/a	*pretty*	**importante**	*important*	**rubio/a**	*blond(e)*
bueno/a	*good*	**inteligente**	*intelligent*	**simpático/a**	*nice; likeable*
delgado/a	*thin*	**interesante**	*interesting*	**tonto/a**	*foolish*
difícil	*difficult*	**joven**	*young*	**trabajador(a)**	*hard-working*
fácil	*easy*	**malo/a**	*bad*	**viejo/a**	*old*
feo/a	*ugly*	**mismo/a**	*same*		
		moreno/a	*brunet(te)*		

Adjectives of nationality

▶ Unlike in English, Spanish adjectives of nationality are **not** capitalized. Proper names of countries, however, are capitalized.

Some adjectives of nationality

alemán, alemana	*German*	**francés, francesa**	*French*
argentino/a	*Argentine*	**inglés, inglesa**	*English*
canadiense	*Canadian*	**italiano/a**	*Italian*
chino/a	*Chinese*	**japonés, japonesa**	*Japanese*
costarricense	*Costa Rican*	**mexicano/a**	*Mexican*
cubano/a	*Cuban*	**norteamericano/a**	*(North) American*
ecuatoriano/a	*Ecuadorian*	**puertorriqueño/a**	*Puerto Rican*
español(a)	*Spanish*	**ruso/a**	*Russian*
estadounidense	*from the U.S.*		

▶ Adjectives of nationality are formed like other descriptive adjectives. Those that end in **-o** change to **-a** when forming the feminine.

chin**o** → chin**a** mexican**o** → mexican**a**

The plural is formed by adding an **-s** to the masculine or feminine form.

argentin**o** → argentin**os** cuban**a** → cuban**as**

▶ Adjectives of nationality that end in **-e** have only two forms, singular and plural.

canadiens**e** → canadiens**es** estadounidens**e** → estadounidens**es**

▶ To form the feminine of adjectives of nationality that end in a consonant, add **–a**.

alemá**n** → alema**na** españo**l** → españo**la**
japoné**s** → japone**sa** inglé**s** → ingle**sa**

Position of adjectives

▶ Descriptive adjectives and adjectives of nationality generally follow the nouns they modify.

El niño **rubio** es de España.
The blond boy is from Spain.

La mujer **española** habla inglés.
The Spanish woman speaks English.

▶ Unlike descriptive adjectives, adjectives of quantity precede the modified noun.

Hay **muchos** libros en la biblioteca.
There are many books in the library.

Hablo con **dos** turistas puertorriqueños.
I am talking with two Puerto Rican tourists.

▶ **Bueno/a** and **malo/a** can appear before or after a noun. When placed before a masculine singular noun, the forms are shortened: **bueno** → **buen; malo** → **mal.**

Joaquín es un **buen** amigo.
Joaquín es un amigo **bueno**. → *Joaquín is a good friend.*

Hoy es un **mal** día.
Hoy es un día **malo**. → *Today is a bad day.*

▶ When **grande** appears before a singular noun, it is shortened to **gran**, and the meaning of the word changes: **gran** = *great* and **grande** = *big, large*.

Don Francisco es un **gran** hombre.
Don Francisco is a great man.

La familia de Inés es **grande**.
Inés' family is large.

¡LENGUA VIVA!

Like **bueno** and **grande, santo** (*saint*) is also shortened before masculine nouns (unless they begin with **To-** or **Do-**): **San Francisco, San José** (but: **Santo Tomás, Santo Domingo**). **Santa** is used with names of female saints: **Santa Bárbara, Santa Clara**.

¡INTÉNTALO! Provide the appropriate forms of the adjectives.

simpático

1. Mi hermano es simpático.
2. La profesora Martínez es ________.
3. Rosa y Teresa son ________.
4. Nosotros somos ________.

alemán

1. Hans es alemán.
2. Mis primas son ________.
3. Marcus y yo somos ________.
4. Mi tía es ________.

difícil

1. La química es difícil.
2. El curso es ________.
3. Las pruebas son ________.
4. Los libros son ________.

guapo

1. Su esposo es guapo.
2. Mis sobrinas son ________.
3. Los padres de ella son ________.
4. Marta es ________.

Práctica

1 **Emparejar** Find the words in column B that are the opposite of the words in column A. One word in B will not be used.

A	B
1. guapo	a. delgado
2. moreno	b. pequeño
3. alto	c. malo
4. gordo	d. feo
5. joven	e. viejo
6. grande	f. rubio
7. simpático	g. antipático
	h. bajo

2 **Completar** Indicate the nationalities of these people by selecting the correct adjectives and changing their forms when necessary.

NOTA CULTURAL

Alfonso Cuarón (1961–) became the first Mexican winner of the Best Director Academy Award for his film *Gravity* (2013).

1. Penélope Cruz es ________.
2. Alfonso Cuarón es un gran director de cine de México; es ________.
3. Ellen Page y Avril Lavigne son ________.
4. Giorgio Armani es un diseñador de modas (*fashion designer*) ________.
5. Daisy Fuentes es de La Habana, Cuba; ella es ________.
6. Emma Watson y Daniel Radcliffe son actores ________.
7. Heidi Klum y Michael Fassbender son ________.
8. Serena Williams y Michael Phelps son ________.

3 **Describir** Look at the drawing and describe each family member using as many adjectives as possible.

1. Susana Romero Barcos es ________.
2. Tomás Romero Barcos es ________.
3. Los dos hermanos son ________.
4. Josefina Barcos de Romero es ________.
5. Carlos Romero Sandoval es ________.
6. Alberto Romero Pereda es ________.
7. Tomás y su (*his*) padre son ________.
8. Susana y su (*her*) madre son ________.

Comunicación

4 **Busco novio** Read Cecilia's personal profile. Then indicate whether these conclusions are **lógico** or **ilógico**, based on what you read.

	Lógico	Ilógico
1. Cecilia es profesora.	❍	❍
2. Cecilia desea ser artista.	❍	❍
3. Cecilia dibuja.	❍	❍
4. Cecilia es tonta.	❍	❍
5. La amiga ideal de Cecilia es interesante.	❍	❍

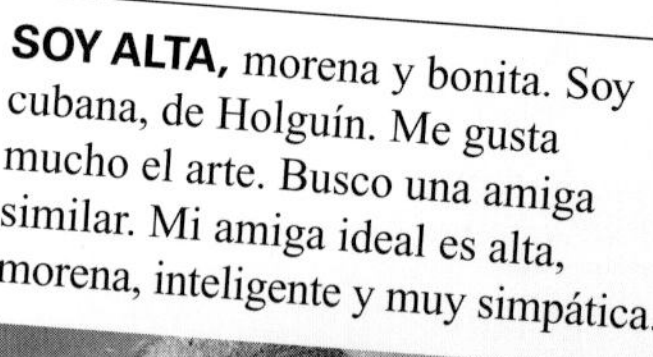
SOY ALTA, morena y bonita. Soy cubana, de Holguín. Me gusta mucho el arte. Busco una amiga similar. Mi amiga ideal es alta, morena, inteligente y muy simpática.

5 **Preguntas** Answer your partner's questions.

1. ¿Cómo eres tú?
2. ¿Cómo es tu casa?
3. ¿Cómo es tu escuela?
4. ¿Cómo es tu ciudad?
5. ¿Cómo es tu país?
6. ¿Cómo son tus amigos?

6 **Anuncio personal** Write a personal profile for your school newspaper. Describe yourself and your ideal best friend. Then compare you profile with a classmate's. How are you similar and how are you different? Are you looking for the same things in a best friend?

Síntesis

7 **¿Cómo es?** With a partner, take turns describing people, places, and things. You may want to use the items on the list. Tell your partner whether you agree (**Estoy de acuerdo**) or disagree (**No estoy de acuerdo**) with his/her descriptions.

modelo

San Francisco
Estudiante 1: *San Francisco es una ciudad (city) muy bonita.*
Estudiante 2: *No estoy de acuerdo. Es muy fea.*

Nueva York	los periodistas
Chicago	las clases de español/física/matemáticas/química
George Clooney	el/la presidente/a de los Estados Unidos
Taylor Swift	
los médicos	

3.2 Possessive adjectives

ANTE TODO Possessive adjectives, like descriptive adjectives, are words that are used to qualify people, places, or things. Possessive adjectives express the quality of ownership or possession.

Forms of possessive adjectives

SINGULAR FORMS	PLURAL FORMS	
mi	**mis**	*my*
tu	**tus**	*your* (fam.)
su	**sus**	*his, her, its, your* (form.)
nuestro/a	**nuestros/as**	*our*
vuestro/a	**vuestros/as**	*your* (fam.)
su	**sus**	*their, your*

COMPARE & CONTRAST

In English, possessive adjectives are invariable; that is, they do not agree in gender and number with the nouns they modify. Spanish possessive adjectives, however, do agree in number with the nouns they modify.

my cousin	*my cousins*	*my aunt*	*my aunts*
mi primo	**mis** primos	**mi** tía	**mis** tías

The forms **nuestro** and **vuestro** agree in both gender and number with the nouns they modify.

nuestr**o** prim**o** nuestr**os** prim**os** nuestr**a** tí**a** nuestr**as** tí**as**

- Possessive adjectives are always placed before the nouns they modify.

—¿Está **tu novio** aquí?
Is your boyfriend here?

—No, **mi novio** está en la biblioteca.
No, my boyfriend is in the library.

- Because **su** and **sus** have multiple meanings (*your, his, her, their, its*), you can avoid confusion by using this construction instead: [*article*] + [*noun*] + **de** + [*subject pronoun*].

sus parientes

los parientes **de él/ella**	*his/her relatives*
los parientes **de Ud./Uds.**	*your relatives*
los parientes **de ellos/ellas**	*their relatives*

AYUDA

Look at the context, focusing on nouns and pronouns, to help you determine the meaning of **su(s)**.

¡INTÉNTALO! Provide the appropriate form of each possessive adjective.

Singular

1. Es ___mi___ (*my*) libro.
2. ______ (*My*) familia es ecuatoriana.
3. ____ (*Your,* fam.) esposo es italiano.
4. ______ (*Our*) profesor es español.
5. Es ________ (*her*) reloj.
6. Es ________ (*your,* fam.) mochila.
7. Es ________ (*your,* form.) maleta.
8. _____ (*Their*) sobrina es alemana.

Plural

1. ___Sus___ (*Her*) primos son franceses.
2. ________ (*Our*) primos son canadienses.
3. Son ________ (*their*) lápices.
4. ________ (*Their*) nietos son japoneses.
5. Son ________ (*our*) plumas.
6. Son ________ (*my*) papeles.
7. ________ (*My*) amigas son inglesas.
8. Son ________ (*his*) cuadernos.

Práctica

1 **La familia de Manolo** Complete each sentence with the correct possessive adjective from the options in parentheses. Use the subject of each sentence as a guide.

1. Me llamo Manolo, y __________ (nuestro, mi, sus) hermano es Federico.
2. __________ (Nuestra, Sus, Mis) madre Silvia es profesora y enseña química.
3. Ella admira a __________ (tu, nuestro, sus) estudiantes porque trabajan mucho.
4. Yo estudio en la misma escuela, pero no tomo clases con __________ (mi, nuestras, tus) madre.
5. Federico trabaja en una oficina con __________ (mis, tu, nuestro) padre.
6. __________ (Mi, Su, Tu) oficina está en el centro de la Ciudad de México.
7. Javier y Óscar son __________ (mis, mi, sus) tíos de Oaxaca.
8. ¿Y tú? ¿Cómo es __________ (mi, su, tu) familia?

AYUDA

Remember that possessive adjectives don't agree in number or gender with the owner of an item; they always agree with the item(s) being possessed.

2 **Clarificar** Clarify each sentence with a prepositional phrase. Follow the model.

modelo

Su hermana es muy bonita. (ella)

La hermana de ella es muy bonita.

1. Su casa es muy grande. (ellos) ____________________
2. ¿Cómo se llama su hermano? (ellas) ____________________
3. Sus padres trabajan en el centro. (ella) ____________________
4. Sus abuelos son muy simpáticos. (él) ____________________
5. Maribel es su prima. (ella) ____________________
6. Su primo lee los libros. (ellos) ____________________

3 **¿Dónde está?** Look at the drawings and indicate where your belongings are.

CONSULTA

For a list of useful prepositions, refer to the table *Prepositions often used with **estar***, in **Estructura 2.3**, p. 84.

modelo

Mi mochila está encima del escritorio.

1. 

2. 

3. 

4. 

5. 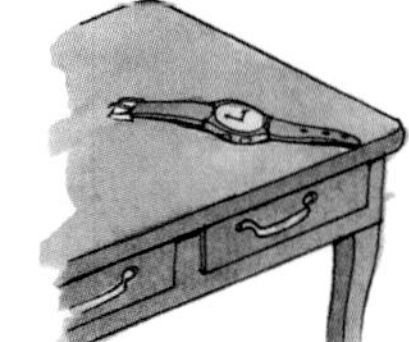

6. 

Comunicación

4 **Noticias de familia** Listen to Ana María talk about some family news. Then indicate whether the following conclusions are **lógico** or **ilógico**, based on what you heard.

	Lógico	Ilógico
1. Ana María es rubia.	❍	❍
2. Sus padres están en Bogotá.	❍	❍
3. Su primo es inteligente.	❍	❍
4. Su primo habla español.	❍	❍
5. La novia de su primo es argentina.	❍	❍

5 **Describir** With a partner, describe the people and places listed below.

modelo

la biblioteca de su escuela

La biblioteca de nuestra escuela es muy grande. Hay muchos libros en la biblioteca.

1. tu profesor favorito
2. tu profesora favorita
3. tu clase favorita
4. la cafetería de su escuela
5. tus padres
6. tus abuelos
7. tu mejor (*best*) amigo
8. tu mejor amiga

6 **Una familia famosa** Assume the identity of a member of a famous family, real or fictional (the Obamas, Clintons, Bushes, Kardashians, Simpsons, etc.), and write a description of "your" family. Reveal your identity at the end of your description.

modelo

Hay cuatro personas en mi familia. Mi padre es delgado y simpático. Él es de Philadelphia. Mi madre es muy inteligente y guapa. Mis padres son actores. Tengo una hermana menor. Nosotros también somos actores... Soy Jaden Smith.

Síntesis

7 **Describe a tu familia** With a partner, take turns asking each other questions about your families.

Estudiante 1: *¿Cómo es tu padre?*
Estudiante 2: *Mi padre es alto, guapo y muy inteligente.*

3.3 Present tense of -er and -ir verbs

ANTE TODO In **Lección 2,** you learned how to form the present tense of regular **-ar** verbs. You also learned about the importance of verb forms, which change to show who is performing the action. The chart below shows the forms from two other important groups, **-er** verbs and **-ir** verbs.

CONSULTA

To review the conjugation of **-ar** verbs, see **Estructura 2.1**, p. 74.

Present tense of -er and -ir verbs

		comer *(to eat)*	**escribir** *(to write)*
SINGULAR FORMS	yo	com**o**	escrib**o**
	tú	com**es**	escrib**es**
	Ud./él/ella	com**e**	escrib**e**
PLURAL FORMS	nosotros/as	com**emos**	escrib**imos**
	vosotros/as	com**éis**	escrib**ís**
	Uds./ellos/ellas	com**en**	escrib**en**

- **-Er** and **-ir** verbs have very similar endings. Study the preceding chart to detect the patterns that make it easier for you to use them to communicate in Spanish.

AYUDA

Here are some tips on learning Spanish verbs:

1) Learn to identify the verb's stem, to which all endings attach.

2) Memorize the endings that go with each verb and verb tense.

3) As often as possible, practice using different forms of each verb in speech and writing.

4) Devote extra time to learning irregular verbs, such as **ser** and **estar**.

Felipe y su tío comen.

Jimena lee.

- Like **-ar** verbs, the **yo** forms of **-er** and **-ir** verbs end in **-o.**

Yo com**o**. Yo escrib**o**.

- Except for the **yo** form, all of the verb endings for **-er** verbs begin with **-e**.

-es	**-emos**	**-en**
-e	**-éis**	

- **-Er** and **-ir** verbs have the exact same endings, except in the **nosotros/as** and **vosotros/as** forms.

nosotros: com**emos**, escrib**imos**

vosotros: com**éis**, escrib**ís**

Common -er and -ir verbs

-er verbs		-ir verbs	
aprender (a + *inf.*)	*to learn*	**abrir**	*to open*
beber	*to drink*	**asistir (a)**	*to attend*
comer	*to eat*	**compartir**	*to share*
comprender	*to understand*	**decidir (+ *inf.*)**	*to decide*
correr	*to run*	**describir**	*to describe*
creer (en)	*to believe (in)*	**escribir**	*to write*
deber (+ *inf.*)	*should*	**recibir**	*to receive*
leer	*to read*	**vivir**	*to live*

Ellos **corren** en el parque.

Él **escribe** una carta.

¡INTÉNTALO! Provide the appropriate present tense forms of these verbs.

correr

1. Graciela *corre*.
2. Tú ________.
3. Yo ________.
4. Sara y Ana ________.
5. Usted ________.
6. Ustedes ________.
7. La gente ________.
8. Marcos y yo ________.

abrir

1. Ellos *abren* la puerta.
2. Carolina ________ la maleta.
3. Yo ________ las ventanas.
4. Nosotras ________ los libros.
5. Usted ________ el cuaderno.
6. Tú ________ la ventana.
7. Ustedes ________ las maletas.
8. Los muchachos ________ los cuadernos.

aprender

1. Él *aprende* español.
2. Maribel y yo ________ inglés.
3. Tú ________ japonés.
4. Tú y tu hermanastra ________ francés.
5. Mi hijo ________ chino.
6. Yo ________ alemán.
7. Usted ________ inglés.
8. Nosotros ________ italiano.

Práctica

1 **Completar** Complete Susana's sentences about her family with the correct forms of the verbs in parentheses. One of the verbs will remain in the infinitive.

1. Mi familia y yo ________ (vivir) en Mérida, Yucatán.
2. Tengo muchos libros. Me gusta ________ (leer).
3. Mi hermano Alfredo es muy inteligente. Alfredo ________ (asistir) a clases los lunes, miércoles y viernes.
4. Los martes y jueves Alfredo y yo ________ (correr) en el Parque del Centenario.
5. Mis padres ________ (comer) mucha lasaña los domingos y se quedan dormidos (*they fall asleep*).
6. Yo ________ (creer) que (*that*) mis padres deben comer menos (*less*).

2 **Oraciones** Juan is talking about what he and his friends do after school. Form complete sentences by adding any other necessary elements.

modelo

yo / correr / amigos / lunes y miércoles

Yo corro con mis amigos los lunes y miércoles.

1. Manuela / asistir / clase / yoga
2. Eugenio / abrir / correo electrónico (*e-mail*)
3. Isabel y yo / leer / biblioteca
4. Sofía y Roberto / aprender / hablar / inglés
5. tú / comer / cafetería / escuela
6. mi novia y yo / compartir / libro de historia

3 **Consejos** Mario and his family are spending a year abroad to learn Japanese. Use the words below to indicate what he and/or his family members are doing or should do to adjust to life in Japan. Then, create one more sentence using a verb not on the list.

modelo

recibir libros / deber practicar japonés

Mario y su esposa reciben muchos libros en japonés.
Los hijos deben practicar japonés.

aprender japonés	decidir explorar el país
asistir a clases	escribir listas de palabras en japonés
beber té (*tea*)	leer novelas japonesas
deber comer cosas nuevas	vivir con una familia japonesa
¿?	¿?

Comunicación

4 **Entrevista** Answer your partner's questions.

1. ¿Dónde comes al mediodía? ¿Comes mucho?
2. ¿Dónde vives?
3. ¿Con quién vives?
4. ¿Qué cursos debes tomar el próximo (*next*) semestre?
5. ¿Lees el periódico (*newspaper*)? ¿Qué periódico lees y cuándo?
6. ¿Recibes muchos mensajes de texto (*text messages*)? ¿De quién(es)?
7. ¿Escribes poemas?
8. ¿Crees en fantasmas (*ghosts*)?

5 **Deberes** Talk about at least five things you should do to improve your life and the lives of others. Use **deber** (+ *inf.*) and other **-er** or **-ir** verbs.

Yo debo correr más...

6 **Descripción** With a partner, take turns choosing an action from the list. Then give a description. Your partner will have to guess the action you are describing.

abrir (un libro, una puerta, una mochila)
aprender (a bailar, a hablar francés, a dibujar)
asistir (a una clase de yoga, a un concierto de rock, a una clase interesante)
beber (agua, limonada)
comer (pasta, un sándwich, pizza)
compartir (un libro, un sándwich)
correr (en el parque, en un maratón)
escribir (una composición, un mensaje de texto [*text message*], con lápiz)
leer (una carta [*letter*] de amor, un mensaje electrónico [*e-mail message*], un periódico [*newspaper*])
recibir un regalo (*gift*)
¿?

modelo

Estudiante 1: Soy estudiante y tomo muchas clases. Vivo en Roma.
Estudiante 2: ¿Comes pasta?
Estudiante 1: No, no como pasta.
Estudiante 2: ¿Aprendes a hablar italiano?
Estudiante 1: ¡Sí!

Síntesis

7 **Un día típico** Write a description of a typical day in your life. Include at least six verbs.

A las nueve de la mañana mis amigas y yo bebemos un café.
Asisto a la clase de yoga a las nueve y media.....

3.4 Present tense of tener and venir

ANTE TODO The verbs **tener** (*to have*) and **venir** (*to come*) are among the most frequently used in Spanish. Because most of their forms are irregular, you will have to learn each one individually.

The verbs tener and venir

		tener	venir
SINGULAR FORMS	yo	ten**go**	ven**go**
	tú	tien**es**	vien**es**
	Ud./él/ella	tien**e**	vien**e**
PLURAL FORMS	nosotros/as	ten**emos**	ven**imos**
	vosotros/as	ten**éis**	ven**ís**
	Uds./ellos/ellas	tien**en**	vien**en**

- The endings are the same as those of regular **-er** and **-ir** verbs, except for the **yo** forms, which are irregular: **tengo, vengo.**
- In the **tú, Ud.,** and **Uds.** forms, the **e** of the stem changes to **ie,** as shown below.

INFINITIVE	VERB STEM	VERB FORM
tener →	ten- →	tú t**ie**nes
		Ud./él/ella t**ie**ne
		Uds./ellos/ellas t**ie**nen
venir →	ven- →	tú v**ie**nes
		Ud./él/ella v**ie**ne
		Uds./ellos/ellas v**ie**nen

- Only the **nosotros** and **vosotros** forms are regular. Compare them to the forms of **comer** and **escribir** that you learned on page 120.

	tener	comer	venir	escribir
nosotros/as	ten**emos**	com**emos**	ven**imos**	escrib**imos**
vosotros/as	ten**éis**	com**éis**	ven**ís**	escrib**ís**

AYUDA

Use what you already know about regular **-er** and **-ir** verbs to identify the irregularities in **tener** and **venir**.

1) Which verb forms use a regular stem? Which use an irregular stem?

2) Which verb forms use the regular endings? Which use irregular endings?

▶ In certain idiomatic or set expressions in Spanish, you use the construction **tener** + [*noun*] to express *to be* + [*adjective*]. This chart contains a list of the most common expressions with **tener**.

Expressions with tener

tener... años	*to be... years old*	**tener (mucha) prisa**	*to be in a (big) hurry*
tener (mucho) calor	*to be (very) hot*	**tener razón**	*to be right*
tener (mucho) cuidado	*to be (very) careful*	**no tener razón**	*to be wrong*
tener (mucho) frío	*to be (very) cold*	**tener (mucha) sed**	*to be (very) thirsty*
tener (mucha) hambre	*to be (very) hungry*	**tener (mucho) sueño**	*to be (very) sleepy*
tener (mucho) miedo (de)	*to be (very) afraid/ scared (of)*	**tener (mucha) suerte**	*to be (very) lucky*

—¿**Tienen** hambre ustedes?
Are you hungry?

—Sí, y **tenemos** sed también.
Yes, and we're thirsty, too.

▶ To express an obligation, use **tener que** (*to have to*) + [*infinitive*].

—¿Qué **tienes que** estudiar hoy?
What do you have to study today?

—**Tengo que** estudiar biología.
I have to study biology.

▶ To ask people if they feel like doing something, use **tener ganas de** (*to feel like*) + [*infinitive*].

—¿**Tienes ganas de** comer?
Do you feel like eating?

—No, **tengo ganas de** dormir.
No, I feel like sleeping.

¡INTÉNTALO! Provide the appropriate forms of **tener** and **venir**.

tener

1. Ellos _tienen_ dos hermanos.
2. Yo ________ una hermana.
3. El artista ________ tres primos.
4. Nosotros ________ diez tíos.
5. Eva y Diana ________ un sobrino.
6. Usted ________ cinco nietos.
7. Tú ________ dos hermanastras.
8. Ustedes ________ cuatro hijos.
9. Ella ________ una hija.

venir

1. Mis padres _vienen_ de México.
2. Tú ________ de España.
3. Nosotras ________ de Cuba.
4. Pepe ________ de Italia.
5. Yo ________ de Francia.
6. Ustedes ________ de Canadá.
7. Alfonso y yo ________ de Portugal.
8. Ellos ________ de Alemania.
9. Usted ________ de Venezuela.

Práctica

1 **Emparejar** Find the expression in column B that best matches an item in column A. Then, come up with a new item that corresponds with the leftover expression in column B.

A	B
1. el Polo Norte	a. tener calor
2. una sauna	b. tener sed
3. la comida salada (*salty food*)	c. tener frío
4. una persona muy inteligente	d. tener razón
5. un abuelo	e. tener ganas de
6. una dieta	f. tener hambre
	g. tener 75 años

2 **Completar** Complete the sentences with the correct forms of **tener** or **venir**.

1. Hoy nosotros __________ una reunión familiar (*family reunion*).
2. Yo __________ en autobús del aeropuerto de Quito.
3. Todos mis parientes __________, excepto mi tío Manolo y su esposa.
4. Ellos no __________ ganas de venir porque viven en Portoviejo.
5. Mi prima Susana y su novio no __________ hasta las ocho porque ella __________ que trabajar.
6. En las fiestas, mi hermana siempre (*always*) __________ muy tarde (*late*).
7. Nosotros __________ mucha suerte porque las reuniones son divertidas (*fun*).
8. Mi madre cree que mis sobrinos son muy simpáticos. Creo que ella __________ razón.

3 **Describir** Describe what these people are doing or feeling using an expression with **tener**.

1. __________________ 2. __________________ 3. __________________

4. __________________ 5. __________________ 6. __________________

Comunicación

4

Mi familia Listen to Francisco's description of his family. Then indicate whether the following conclusions are **lógico** or **ilógico**, based on what you heard.

	Lógico	Ilógico
1. Francisco tiene una familia grande.	❍	❍
2. A Francisco le gustan los números.	❍	❍
3. Francisco vive en la casa de sus padres durante el semestre.	❍	❍
4. Francisco desea ser artista.	❍	❍
5. Carlos y Dolores tienen gemelos.	❍	❍

5

Preguntas Answer your partner's questions.

1. ¿Tienes que estudiar hoy?
2. ¿Cuántos años tienes? ¿Y tus hermanos/as?
3. ¿Cuándo vienes a la escuela?
4. ¿Cuándo vienen tus amigos a tu casa o apartamento?
5. ¿De qué tienes miedo? ¿Por qué?
6. ¿Qué tienes ganas de hacer el sábado?

6

Obligaciones Talk about five things that you have to do but cannot do for various reasons, such as fear, lack of motivation, or being in a rush. Use expressions with **tener**.

modelo

Tengo que estudiar, pero no tengo ganas.

Síntesis

7

Minidrama Role-play this situation with a partner: you are introducing your best friend to your extended family. To avoid any surprises before you go, talk about who is coming and what each family member is like. Switch roles.

Recapitulación

Review the grammar concepts you have learned in this lesson by completing these activities.

1 Adjetivos Complete each phrase with the appropriate adjective from the list. Make all necessary changes. 18 pts.

antipático	interesante	mexicano
difícil	joven	moreno

1. Mi tía es ________. Vive en Guadalajara.
2. Mi primo no es rubio, es ________.
3. Mi amigo cree que la clase no es fácil; es ________.
4. Los libros son ________; me gustan mucho.
5. Mis hermanos son ________; no tienen muchos amigos.
6. Las gemelas tienen nueve años. Son ________.

2 Completar For each set of sentences, provide the appropriate form of the verb **tener** and the possessive adjective. Follow the model. 36 pts.

modelo

Él *tiene* un libro. Es *su* libro.

1. Esteban y Julio ________ una tía. Es ________ tía.
2. Yo ________ muchos amigos. Son ________ amigos.
3. Tú ________ tres primas. Son ________ primas.
4. María y tú ________ un hermano. Es ________ hermano.
5. Nosotras ________ unas mochilas. Son ________ mochilas.
6. Usted ________ dos sobrinos. Son ________ sobrinos.

3 Oraciones Arrange the words in the correct order to form complete logical sentences. **¡Ojo!** Don't forget to conjugate the verbs. 20 pts.

1. libros / unos / tener / interesantes / tú / muy
____
2. dos / leer / fáciles / compañera / tu / lecciones
____
3. mi / francés / ser / amigo / buen / Hugo
____
4. ser / simpáticas / dos / personas / nosotras
____
5. a / clases / menores / mismas / sus / asistir / hermanos / las
____

RESUMEN GRAMATICAL

3.1 Descriptive adjectives *pp. 112–114*

Forms and agreement of adjectives

Masculine		Feminine	
Singular	Plural	Singular	Plural
alto inteligente trabajador	altos inteligentes trabajadores	alta inteligente trabajadora	altas inteligentes trabajadoras

- Descriptive adjectives follow the noun: **el chico rubio**
- Adjectives of nationality also follow the noun: **la mujer española**
- Adjectives of quantity precede the noun: **muchos libros, dos turistas**
- When placed before a singular masculine noun, these adjectives are shortened.

  bueno → buen   malo → mal
- When placed before a singular noun, **grande** is shortened to **gran**.

3.2 Possessive adjectives *p. 117*

Singular		Plural	
mi	nuestro/a	mis	nuestros/as
tu	vuestro/a	tus	vuestros/as
su	su	sus	sus

3.3 Present tense of -er and -ir verbs *pp. 120–121*

comer		escribir	
como	comemos	escribo	escribimos
comes	coméis	escribes	escribís
come	comen	escribe	escriben

3.4 Present tense of tener and venir *pp. 124–125*

tener		venir	
tengo	tenemos	vengo	venimos
tienes	tenéis	vienes	venís
tiene	tienen	viene	vienen

4 **Carta** Complete this letter with the appropriate forms of the verbs in the word list. Not all verbs will be used. **22 pts.**

abrir	correr	recibir
asistir	creer	tener
compartir	escribir	venir
comprender	leer	vivir

Hola, Ángel:

¿Qué tal? (Yo) (1) ______ esta carta (*this letter*) en la biblioteca. Todos los días (2) ______ aquí y (3) ______ un buen libro. Yo (4) ______ que es importante leer por diversión. Mi hermano no (5) ______ por qué me gusta leer. Él sólo (6) ______ los libros de texto. Pero nosotros (7) ______ unos intereses. Por ejemplo, los dos somos atléticos; por las mañanas nosotros (8) ______. También nos gustan las ciencias; por las tardes (9) ______ a nuestra clase de biología. Nosotros (10) ______ en un apartamento que está cerca de la escuela. Y tú, ¿cómo estás? ¿(Tú) (11) ______ mucho trabajo (*work*)?

5 **Proverbio** Complete this proverb with the correct forms of the verbs in parentheses. **4 pts.**

"Dos andares° ______ (tener) el dinero°, ______ (venir) despacio° y se va° ligero°."

andares *speeds* dinero *money* despacio *slowly* se va *it leaves* ligero *quickly*

Lectura

Antes de leer

Estrategia

Guessing meaning from context

As you read in Spanish, you'll often come across words you haven't learned. You can guess what they mean by looking at the surrounding words and sentences. Look at the following text and guess what **tía abuela** means, based on the context.

¡Hola, Claudia!
¿Qué hay de nuevo?
¿Sabes qué? Ayer fui a ver a mi tía abuela, la hermana de mi abuela. Tiene 85 años, pero es muy independiente. Vive en un apartamento en Quito con su prima Lorena, quien también tiene 85 años.

If you guessed *great-aunt*, you are correct, and you can conclude from this word and the format clues that this is a letter about someone's visit with his or her great-aunt.

Examinar el texto

Quickly read through the paragraphs and find two or three words you don't know. Using the context as your guide, guess what these words mean. Then glance at the paragraphs where these words appear and try to predict what the paragraphs are about.

Examinar el formato

Look at the format of the reading. What clues do the captions, photos, and layout give you about its content?

Gente . . . Las familias

1. Me llamo Armando y tengo setenta años, pero no me considero viejo. Tengo seis nietas y un nieto. Vivo con mi hija y tengo la oportunidad de pasar mucho tiempo con ella y con mi nieto. Por las tardes salgo a pasear° por el parque con él y por la noche le leo cuentos°.

Armando. Tiene seis nietas y un nieto.

2. Mi prima Victoria y yo nos llevamos muy bien. Estudiamos juntas° en la universidad y compartimos un apartamento. Ella es muy inteligente y me ayuda° con los estudios. Además°, es muy simpática y generosa. Si necesito cualquier° cosa, ¡ella me la compra!

Diana. Vive con su prima.

3. Me llamo Ramona y soy paraguaya, aunque° ahora vivo en los Estados Unidos. Tengo tres hijos, uno de nueve años, uno de doce y el mayor de quince. Es difícil a veces, pero mi esposo y yo tratamos° de ayudarlos y comprenderlos siempre°.

Ramona. Sus hijos son muy importantes para ella.

4. Tengo mucha suerte. Aunque mis padres están divorciados, tengo una familia muy unida. Tengo dos hermanos y dos hermanas. Me gusta hablar y salir a fiestas con ellos. Ahora tengo novio en la universidad y él no conoce a mis hermanos. ¡Espero que se lleven bien!

Ana María. Su familia es muy unida.

5. Antes quería° tener hermanos, pero ya no° es tan importante. Ser hijo único tiene muchas ventajas°: no tengo que compartir mis cosas con hermanos, no hay discusiones° y, como soy nieto único también, ¡mis abuelos piensan° que soy perfecto!

Fernando. Es hijo único.

6. Como soy joven todavía°, no tengo ni esposa ni hijos. Pero tengo un sobrino, el hijo de mi hermano, que es muy especial para mí. Se llama Benjamín y tiene diez años. Es un muchacho muy simpático. Siempre tiene hambre y por lo tanto vamos° frecuentemente a comer hamburguesas. Nos gusta también ir al cine° a ver películas de acción. Hablamos de todo. ¡Creo que ser tío es mejor que ser padre!

Santiago. Cree que ser tío es divertido.

salgo a pasear *I go take a walk* **cuentos** *stories* **juntas** *together* **me ayuda** *she helps me* **Además** *Besides* **cualquier** *any* **aunque** *although* **tratamos** *we try* **siempre** *always* **quería** *I wanted* **ya no** *no longer* **ventajas** *advantages* **discusiones** *arguments* **piensan** *think* **todavía** *still* **vamos** *we go* **ir al cine** *to go to the movies*

Después de leer

Emparejar

Glance at the paragraphs and see how the words and phrases in column A are used in context. Then find their definitions in column B.

A	B
1. me la compra	a. the oldest
2. nos llevamos bien	b. movies
3. no conoce	c. the youngest
4. películas	d. buys it for me
5. mejor que	e. borrows it from me
6. el mayor	f. we see each other
	g. doesn't know
	h. we get along
	i. portraits
	j. better than

Seleccionar

Choose the sentence that best summarizes each paragraph.

1. Párrafo 1
   a. Me gusta mucho ser abuelo.
   b. No hablo mucho con mi nieto.
   c. No tengo nietos.
2. Párrafo 2
   a. Mi prima es antipática.
   b. Mi prima no es muy trabajadora.
   c. Mi prima y yo somos muy buenas amigas.
3. Párrafo 3
   a. Tener hijos es un gran sacrificio, pero es muy bonito también.
   b. No comprendo a mis hijos.
   c. Mi esposo y yo no tenemos hijos.
4. Párrafo 4
   a. No hablo mucho con mis hermanos.
   b. Comparto mis cosas con mis hermanos.
   c. Mis hermanos y yo somos como (*like*) amigos.
5. Párrafo 5
   a. Me gusta ser hijo único.
   b. Tengo hermanos y hermanas.
   c. Vivo con mis abuelos.
6. Párrafo 6
   a. Mi sobrino tiene diez años.
   b. Me gusta mucho ser tío.
   c. Mi esposa y yo no tenemos hijos.

Escritura

Estrategia

Using idea maps

How do you organize ideas for a first draft? Often, the organization of ideas represents the most challenging part of the process. Idea maps are useful for organizing pertinent information. Here is an example of an idea map you can use:

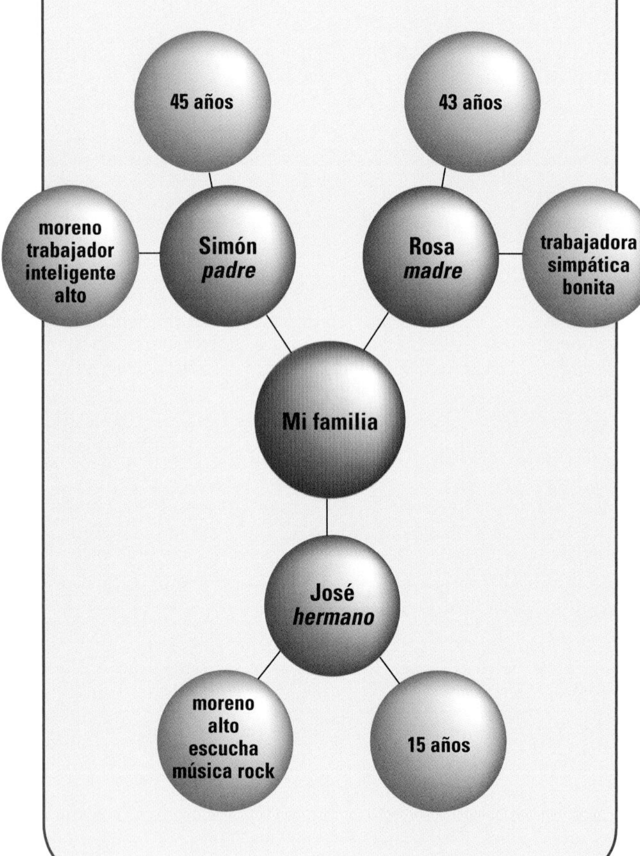

Tema

Escribir un mensaje electrónico

A friend you met in a chat room for Spanish speakers wants to know about your family. Using some of the verbs and adjectives you have learned in this lesson, write a brief e-mail describing your family or an imaginary family, including:

- Names and relationships
- Physical characteristics
- Hobbies and interests

Here are some useful expressions for writing an e-mail or letter in Spanish:

Salutations

Estimado/a Julio/Julia:	*Dear Julio/Julia,*
Querido/a Miguel/Ana María:	*Dear Miguel/Ana María,*

Closings

Un abrazo,	*A hug,*
Abrazos,	*Hugs,*
Con cariño,	*Affectionately,*
¡Hasta pronto!	*See you soon!*
¡Hasta la próxima semana!	*See you next week!*

Escuchar

Estrategia

Asking for repetition/ Replaying the recording

Sometimes it is difficult to understand what people say, especially in a noisy environment. During a conversation, you can ask someone to repeat by saying **¿Cómo?** (*What?*) or **¿Perdón?** (*Pardon me?*). In class, you can ask your teacher to repeat by saying **Repita, por favor** (*Repeat, please*). If you don't understand a recorded activity, you can simply replay it.

To help you practice this strategy, you will listen to a short paragraph. Ask your teacher to repeat it or replay the recording, and then summarize what you heard.

Preparación

Based on the photograph, where do you think Cristina and Laura are? What do you think Laura is saying to Cristina?

Ahora escucha

Now you are going to hear Laura and Cristina's conversation. Use **R** to indicate which adjectives describe Cristina's boyfriend, Rafael. Use **E** for adjectives that describe Laura's boyfriend, Esteban. Some adjectives will not be used.

____ **rubio**	____ **interesante**
____ **feo**	____ **antipático**
____ **alto**	____ **inteligente**
____ **trabajador**	____ **moreno**
____ **un poco gordo**	____ **viejo**

Comprensión

Identificar

Which person would make each statement: Cristina or Laura?

	Cristina	Laura
1. Mi novio habla sólo de fútbol y de béisbol.	❍	❍
2. Tengo un novio muy interesante y simpático.	❍	❍
3. Mi novio es alto y moreno.	❍	❍
4. Mi novio trabaja mucho.	❍	❍
5. Mi amiga no tiene buena suerte con los muchachos.	❍	❍
6. El novio de mi amiga es un poco gordo, pero guapo.	❍	❍

¿Cierto o falso?

Indicate whether each sentence is **cierto** or **falso**, then correct the false statements.

	Cierto	Falso
1. Esteban es un chico interesante y simpático.	❍	❍
2. Laura tiene mala suerte con los chicos.	❍	❍
3. Rafael es muy interesante.	❍	❍
4. Laura y su novio hablan de muchas cosas.	❍	❍

Diminutivo

¡Oh! ¡Un saquito te compró mamá!

Preparación

How do you feel about shopping sprees? Do you like spending time in shopping malls? What would you rather do: buy things for yourself or gifts for others?

Diminutivos are suffixes used to indicate a small size, young age, or to express affection. They are also used to talk to babies and toddlers, and to communicate that something is cute. The most commonly used diminutive suffix in Spanish is **–ito/ita**, which can be used with nouns and names (**niñito/a, Miguelito, Susanita**), adjectives (**pequeñito/a**), and adverbs (**lueguito, ahorita**). When words end in consonants like n, r, or z, such as in **lápiz** and **lección**, **-ito/ita** becomes **–cito/cita**; for example: **lapicito** and **leccioncita**. However, there are many exceptions, such as **novio/a**, which diminutive is **noviecito/a**. Diminutives can also be created using the suffix **–illo/illa** (**cuadernillo, problemilla**).

Vocabulario útil

¿Te falta mucho?	*Have you got long to go?*
apurarse	*to hurry*
saquito	*small/cute coat*
par de zapatitos	*pair of small shoes*
conjuntito	*small outfit*
cerrar	*to close*

Comprensión

Fill in the blanks, choosing the correct option from the word bank.

hija/a	prisa	su	cierra
regresar	esposo	zapatos	

1. Marcos es el ________ de Claudia.
2. Claudia compra ________ y otras cosas para ella en el centro comercial (*shopping mall*).
3. Marcos y Claudia tienen una ________.
4. El centro comercial ________ en diez minutos.
5. Claudia busca un regalo (*gift*) para ________ hija.
6. Claudia tiene ________ porque debe ________ pronto a casa.

Conversación

Talk with a classmate about these questions:

1. In the video, why did the man think the woman was buying presents for their baby daughter?
2. Why do you think the woman was using diminutives such as **saquito**, **zapatitos**, and **conjuntito**?

Aplicación

Work in small groups to create an ad for **Banco Galicia**, using adjectives from this lesson and applying different diminutives to nouns you include in the ad. Present it to the class, and discuss afterward which ads seem most effective and why.

If a Spanish-speaking friend told you he was going to a **reunión familiar,** what type of event would you picture? Most likely, your friend would not be referring to an annual event reuniting family members from far-flung cities. In Hispanic culture, family gatherings are often more frequent and relaxed, and thus do not require intensive planning or juggling of schedules. Some families gather every Sunday afternoon to enjoy a leisurely meal; others may prefer to hold get-togethers on a Saturday evening, with food, music, and dancing. In any case, gatherings tend to be laid-back events in which family members spend hours chatting, sharing stories, and telling jokes.

Vocabulario útil

el Día de la Madre	*Mother's Day*
estamos celebrando	*we are celebrating*
familia grande y feliz	*a big, happy family*
familia numerosa	*a large family*
hacer (algo) juntos	*to do (something) together*
el patio interior	*courtyard*
pelear	*to fight*
reuniones familiares	*family gatherings, reunions*

Preparación

What is a "typical family" like where you live? Is there such a thing? What members of a family usually live together?

Completar

Complete this paragraph with the correct options.

Los Valdivieso y los Bolaños son dos ejemplos de familias en Ecuador. Los Valdivieso son una familia (1) ________ (difícil/numerosa). Viven en una casa (2) ________ (grande/buena). En el patio, hacen (*they do*) muchas reuniones (3) ________ (familiares/con amigos). Los Bolaños son una familia pequeña. Ellos comen (4) ________ (separados/juntos) y preparan canelazo, una bebida (*drink*) típica ecuatoriana.

tan *so*

La familia

1 **—Érica, ¿y cómo se llaman tus padres?**
—Mi mamá, Lorena y mi papá, Miguel.

2 **¡Qué familia tan° grande tiene!**

3 **Te presento a la familia Bolaños.**

Ecuador

El país en cifras

- **Área:** 283.560 km² (109.483 millas²), *incluyendo las islas Galápagos, aproximadamente el área de Colorado*
- **Población:** 15.439.000
- **Capital:** Quito — 1.622.000
- **Ciudades° principales:** Guayaquil — 2.634.000, Cuenca, Machala, Portoviejo
- **Moneda:** dólar estadounidense
- **Idiomas:** español (oficial), quichua

La lengua oficial de Ecuador es el español, pero también se hablan° otras° lenguas en el país. Aproximadamente unos 4.000.000 de ecuatorianos hablan lenguas indígenas; la mayoría° de ellos habla quichua. El quichua es el dialecto ecuatoriano del quechua, la lengua de los incas.

Muchos indígenas de Ecuador hablan quichua.

Bandera de Ecuador

Indígenas del Amazonas

La ciudad de Quito y la Cordillera de los Andes

Catedral de Guayaquil

Ecuatorianos célebres

- **Francisco Eugenio de Santa Cruz y Espejo,** médico, periodista y patriota (1747–1795)
- **Juan León Mera,** novelista (1832–1894)
- **Eduardo Kingman,** pintor° (1913–1997)
- **Rosalía Arteaga,** abogada°, política y ex vicepresidenta (1956–)
- **Iván Vallejo Ricafuerte,** montañista (1959–)

Ciudades *cities* se hablan *are spoken* otras *other* mayoría *majority* pintor *painter* abogada *lawyer* sur *south* mundo *world* pies *feet* dos veces más alto que *twice as tall as*

¡Increíble pero cierto!

El volcán Cotopaxi, situado a unos 60 kilómetros al sur° de Quito, es considerado el volcán activo más alto del mundo°. Tiene una altura de 5.897 metros (19.340 pies°). Es dos veces más alto que° el monte Santa Elena (2.550 metros o 9.215 pies) en el estado de Washington.

Lugares • Las islas Galápagos

Muchas personas vienen de lejos a visitar las islas Galápagos porque son un verdadero tesoro° ecológico. Aquí Charles Darwin estudió° las especies que inspiraron° sus ideas sobre la evolución. Como las Galápagos están lejos del continente, sus plantas y animales son únicos. Las islas son famosas por sus tortugas° gigantes.

Artes • Oswaldo Guayasamín

Oswaldo Guayasamín fue° uno de los artistas latinoamericanos más famosos del mundo. Fue escultor° y muralista. Su expresivo estilo viene del cubismo y sus temas preferidos son la injusticia y la pobreza° sufridas° por los indígenas de su país.

Deportes • El *trekking*

El sistema montañoso de los Andes cruza° y divide Ecuador en varias regiones. La Sierra, que tiene volcanes, grandes valles y una variedad increíble de plantas y animales, es perfecta para el *trekking*. Muchos turistas visitan Ecuador cada° año para hacer° *trekking* y escalar montañas°.

Lugares • Latitud 0

Hay un monumento en Ecuador, a unos 22 kilómetros (14 millas) de Quito, donde los visitantes están en el hemisferio norte y el hemisferio sur a la vez°. Este monumento se llama la Mitad del Mundo° y es un destino turístico muy popular.

Explosión del volcán Tungurahua

¿Qué aprendiste? Completa las oraciones con la información correcta.

1. La ciudad más grande (*biggest*) de Ecuador es ________.
2. La capital de Ecuador es ________.
3. Unos 4.000.000 de ecuatorianos hablan ________.
4. Darwin estudió el proceso de la evolución en ________.
5. Dos temas del arte de ________ son la pobreza y la ________.
6. Un monumento muy popular es ________.
7. La Sierra es un lugar perfecto para el ________.
8. El volcán ________ es el volcán activo más alto del mundo.

Conexión Internet Investiga estos temas en Internet.

1. Busca información sobre una ciudad de Ecuador. ¿Te gustaría (*Would you like*) visitar la ciudad? ¿Por qué?
2. Haz una lista de tres animales o plantas que viven sólo en las islas Galápagos. ¿Dónde hay animales o plantas similares?

verdadero tesoro *true treasure* **estudió** *studied* **inspiraron** *inspired* **tortugas** *tortoises* **fue** *was* **escultor** *sculptor* **pobreza** *poverty* **sufridas** *suffered* **cruza** *crosses* **cada** *every* **hacer** to do **escalar montañas** *to climb mountains* **a la vez** at *the same time* **Mitad del Mundo** *Equatorial Line Monument (lit. Midpoint of the World)*

La familia

el/la abuelo/a	*grandfather/ grandmother*
los abuelos	*grandparents*
el apellido	*last name*
el/la bisabuelo/a	*great-grandfather/ great-grandmother*
el/la cuñado/a	*brother-in-law/ sister-in-law*
el/la esposo/a	*husband/wife; spouse*
la familia	*family*
el/la gemelo/a	*twin*
el/la hermanastro/a	*stepbrother/ stepsister*
el/la hermano/a	*brother/sister*
el/la hijastro/a	*stepson/ stepdaughter*
el/la hijo/a	*son/daughter*
los hijos	*children*
la madrastra	*stepmother*
la madre	*mother*
el/la medio/a hermano/a	*half-brother/ half-sister*
el/la nieto/a	*grandson/ granddaughter*
la nuera	*daughter-in-law*
el padrastro	*stepfather*
el padre	*father*
los padres	*parents*
los parientes	*relatives*
el/la primo/a	*cousin*
el/la sobrino/a	*nephew/niece*
el/la suegro/a	*father-in-law/ mother-in-law*
el/la tío/a	*uncle/aunt*
el yerno	*son-in-law*

Otras personas

el/la amigo/a	*friend*
la gente	*people*
el/la muchacho/a	*boy/girl*
el/la niño/a	*child*
el/la novio/a	*boyfriend/girlfriend*
la persona	*person*

Profesiones

el/la artista	*artist*
el/la doctor(a), el/la médico/a	*doctor; physician*
el/la ingeniero/a	*engineer*
el/la periodista	*journalist*
el/la programador(a)	*computer programmer*

Adjetivos

alto/a	*tall*
antipático/a	*unpleasant*
bajo/a	*short (in height)*
bonito/a	*pretty*
buen, bueno/a	*good*
delgado/a	*thin*
difícil	*difficult*
fácil	*easy*
feo/a	*ugly*
gordo/a	*fat*
grande	*big*
guapo/a	*good-looking*
importante	*important*
inteligente	*intelligent*
interesante	*interesting*
joven (sing.), jóvenes (pl.)	*young*
mal, malo/a	*bad*
mismo/a	*same*
moreno/a	*brunet(te)*
mucho/a	*much; many; a lot of*
pelirrojo/a	*red-haired*
pequeño/a	*small*
rubio/a	*blond(e)*
simpático/a	*nice; likeable*
tonto/a	*foolish*
trabajador(a)	*hard-working*
viejo/a	*old*

Nacionalidades

alemán, alemana	*German*
argentino/a	*Argentine*
canadiense	*Canadian*
chino/a	*Chinese*
costarricense	*Costa Rican*
cubano/a	*Cuban*
ecuatoriano/a	*Ecuadorian*
español(a)	*Spanish*
estadounidense	*from the U.S.*
francés, francesa	*French*
inglés, inglesa	*English*
italiano/a	*Italian*
japonés, japonesa	*Japanese*
mexicano/a	*Mexican*
norteamericano/a	*(North) American*
puertorriqueño/a	*Puerto Rican*
ruso/a	*Russian*

Verbos

abrir	*to open*
aprender (a + *inf.*)	*to learn*
asistir (a)	*to attend*
beber	*to drink*
comer	*to eat*
compartir	*to share*
comprender	*to understand*
correr	*to run*
creer (en)	*to believe (in)*
deber (+ *inf.*)	*should*
decidir (+ *inf.*)	*to decide*
describir	*to describe*
escribir	*to write*
leer	*to read*
recibir	*to receive*
tener	*to have*
venir	*to come*
vivir	*to live*

Possessive adjectives	*See page 117.*
Expressions with *tener*	*See page 125.*
Expresiones útiles	*See page 107.*

Consulta

Guide to Vocabulary

Note on alphabetization

For purposes of alphabetization, **ch** and **ll** are not treated as separate letters, but **ñ** follows **n**. Therefore, in this glossary you will find that **año**, for example, appears after **anuncio.**

Abbreviations used in this glossary

adj.	adjective	*form.*	formal	*pl.*	plural
adv.	adverb	*indef.*	indefinite	*poss.*	possessive
art.	article	*interj.*	interjection	*prep.*	preposition
conj.	conjunction	*i.o.*	indirect object	*pron.*	pronoun
def.	definite	*m.*	masculine	*ref.*	reflexive
d.o.	direct object	*n.*	noun	*sing.*	singular
f.	feminine	*obj.*	object	*sub.*	subject
fam.	familiar	*p.p.*	past participle	*v.*	verb

Spanish–English

A

a *prep.* at; to 1.1
¿A qué hora...? At what time...? 1.1
a bordo aboard
a dieta on a diet 3.3
a la derecha de to the right of 1.2
a la izquierda de to the left of 1.2
a la plancha grilled 2.2
a la(s) + *time* at + *time* 1.1
a menos que *conj.* unless 3.1
a menudo *adv.* often 2.4
a nombre de in the name of 1.5
a plazos in installments 3.2
A sus órdenes. At your service.
a tiempo *adv.* on time 2.4
a veces *adv.* sometimes 2.4
a ver let's see
abeja *f.* bee
abierto/a *adj.* open 1.5, 3.2
abogado/a *m., f.* lawyer 3.4
abrazar(se) *v.* to hug; to embrace (each other) 2.5
abrazo *m.* hug
abrigo *m.* coat 1.6
abril *m.* April 1.5
abrir *v.* to open 1.3
abuelo/a *m., f.* grandfather/grandmother 1.3
abuelos *pl.* grandparents 1.3
aburrido/a *adj.* bored; boring 1.5
aburrir *v.* to bore 2.1
aburrirse *v.* to get bored 3.5
acabar de (+ *inf.*) *v.* to have just *done something* 1.6
acampar *v.* to camp 1.5
accidente *m.* accident 2.4
acción *f.* action 3.5
de acción action (genre) 3.5
aceite *m.* oil 2.2
aceptar: ¡Acepto casarme contigo! I'll marry you! 3.5
acompañar *v.* to accompany 3.2
aconsejar *v.* to advise 2.6
acontecimiento *m.* event 3.6
acordarse (de) (o:ue) *v.* to remember 2.1
acostarse (o:ue) *v.* to go to bed 2.1
activo/a *adj.* active 3.3
actor *m.* actor 3.4
actriz *f.* actress 3.4
actualidades *f., pl.* news; current events 3.6
adelgazar *v.* to lose weight; to slim down 3.3
además (de) *adv.* furthermore; besides 2.4
adicional *adj.* additional
adiós *m.* goodbye 1.1
adjetivo *m.* adjective
administración de empresas *f.* business administration 1.2
adolescencia *f.* adolescence 2.3
¿adónde? *adv.* where (to)? (destination) 1.2
aduana *f.* customs
aeróbico/a *adj.* aerobic 3.3
aeropuerto *m.* airport 1.5
afectado/a *adj.* affected 3.1
afeitarse *v.* to shave 2.1
aficionado/a *m., f.* fan 1.4
afirmativo/a *adj.* affirmative
afuera *adv.* outside 1.5
afueras *f., pl.* suburbs; outskirts 2.6
agencia de viajes *f.* travel agency 1.5
agente de viajes *m., f.* travel agent 1.5
agosto *m.* August 1.5
agradable *adj.* pleasant
agua *f.* water 2.2
agua mineral mineral water 2.2
aguantar *v.* to endure, to hold up 3.2
ahora *adv.* now 1.2
ahora mismo right now 1.5
ahorrar *v.* to save (money) 3.2
ahorros *m., pl.* savings 3.2
aire *m.* air 3.1
ajo *m.* garlic 2.2
al (*contraction of* a + el) 1.4
al aire libre open-air 1.6
al contado in cash 3.2
(al) este (to the) east 3.2
al lado de next to; beside 1.2
(al) norte (to the) north 3.2
(al) oeste (to the) west 3.2
(al) sur (to the) south 3.2
alcoba *f.* bedroom
alegrarse (de) *v.* to be happy 3.1
alegre *adj.* happy; joyful 1.5
alegría *f.* happiness 2.3
alemán, alemana *adj.* German 1.3
alérgico/a *adj.* allergic 2.4
alfombra *f.* carpet; rug 2.6
algo *pron.* something; anything 2.1
algodón *m.* cotton 1.6
alguien *pron.* someone; somebody; anyone 2.1
algún, alguno/a(s) *adj.* any; some 2.1
alimento *m.* food
alimentación *f.* diet
aliviar *v.* to reduce 3.3
aliviar el estrés/la tensión to reduce stress/tension 3.3
allá *adv.* over there 1.2
allí *adv.* there 1.2
alma *f.* soul 2.3
almacén *m.* department store 1.6
almohada *f.* pillow 2.6
almorzar (o:ue) *v.* to have lunch 1.4
almuerzo *m.* lunch 1.4, 2.2

aló *interj.* hello (*on the telephone*) 2.5
alquilar *v.* to rent 2.6
alquiler *m.* rent (payment) 2.6
altar *m.* altar 2.3
altillo *m.* attic 2.6
alto/a *adj.* tall 1.3
aluminio *m.* aluminum 3.1
ama de casa *m., f.* housekeeper; caretaker 2.6
amable *adj.* nice; friendly 1.5
amarillo/a *adj.* yellow 1.6
amigo/a *m., f.* friend 1.3
amistad *f.* friendship 2.3
amor *m.* love 2.3
  amor a primera vista love at first sight 2.3
anaranjado/a *adj.* orange 1.6
ándale *interj.* come on 3.2
andar *v.* **en patineta** to skateboard 1.4
ángel *m.* angel 2.3
anillo *m.* ring 3.5
animal *m.* animal 3.1
aniversario (de bodas) *m.* (wedding) anniversary 2.3
anoche *adv.* last night 1.6
anteayer *adv.* the day before yesterday 1.6
antes *adv.* before 2.1
  antes (de) que *conj.* before 3.1
  antes de *prep.* before 2.1
antibiótico *m.* antibiotic 2.4
antipático/a *adj.* unpleasant 1.3
anunciar *v.* to announce; to advertise 3.6
anuncio *m.* advertisement 3.4
año *m.* year 1.5
  año pasado last year 1.6
apagar *v.* to turn off 2.5
aparato *m.* appliance
apartamento *m.* apartment 2.6
apellido *m.* last name 1.3
apenas *adv.* hardly; scarcely 2.4
aplaudir *v.* to applaud 3.5
aplicación *f.* app 2.5
apreciar *v.* to appreciate 3.5
aprender (a + ***inf.*****)** *v.* to learn 1.3
apurarse *v.* to hurry; to rush 3.3
aquel, aquella *adj.* that (over there) 1.6
aquél, aquélla *pron.* that (over there) 1.6
aquello *neuter, pron.* that; that thing; that fact 1.6
aquellos/as *pl. adj.* those (over there) 1.6
aquéllos/as *pl. pron.* those (ones) (over there) 1.6
aquí *adv.* here 1.1
  Aquí está(n)... Here is/are... 1.5
árbol *m.* tree 3.1
archivo *m.* file 2.5
arete *m.* earring 1.6
argentino/a *adj.* Argentine 1.3
armario *m.* closet 2.6
arqueología *f.* archeology 1.2
arqueólogo/a *m., f.* archeologist 3.4
arquitecto/a *m., f.* architect 3.4
arrancar *v.* to start (*a car*) 2.5
arreglar *v.* to fix; to arrange 2.5; to neaten; to straighten up 2.6
arreglarse *v.* to get ready 2.1; to fix oneself (*clothes, hair, etc. to go out*) 2.1
arroba *f.* @ symbol 2.5
arroz *m.* rice 2.2
arte *m.* art 1.2
artes *f., pl.* arts 3.5
artesanía *f.* craftsmanship; crafts 3.5
artículo *m.* article 3.6
artista *m., f.* artist 1.3
artístico/a *adj.* artistic 3.5
arveja *f.* pea 2.2
asado/a *adj.* roast 2.2
ascenso *m.* promotion 3.4
ascensor *m.* elevator 1.5
así *adv.* like this; so (*in such a way*) 2.4
asistir (a) *v.* to attend 1.3
aspiradora *f.* vacuum cleaner 2.6
aspirante *m., f.* candidate; applicant 3.4
aspirina *f.* aspirin 2.4
atún *m.* tuna 2.2
aumentar *v.* to grow; to get bigger 3.1
aumentar *v.* **de peso** to gain weight 3.3
aumento *m.* increase
  aumento de sueldo pay raise 3.4
aunque although
autobús *m.* bus 1.1
automático/a *adj.* automatic
auto(móvil) *m.* auto(mobile) 1.5
autopista *f.* highway 2.5
ave *f.* bird 3.1
avenida *f.* avenue
aventura *f.* adventure 3.5
  de aventuras adventure (genre) 3.5
avergonzado/a *adj.* embarrassed 1.5
avión *m.* airplane 1.5
¡Ay! *interj.* Oh!
  ¡Ay, qué dolor! Oh, what pain!
ayer *adv.* yesterday 1.6
ayudar(se) *v.* to help (each other) 2.5
azúcar *m.* sugar 2.2
azul *adj. m., f.* blue 1.6

B

bailar *v.* to dance 1.2
bailarín/bailarina *m., f.* dancer 3.5
baile *m.* dance 3.5
bajar(se) de *v.* to get off of/out of (a vehicle) 2.5
bajo/a *adj.* short (*in height*) 1.3
balcón *m.* balcony 2.6
balde *m.* bucket 1.5
ballena *f.* whale 3.1
baloncesto *m.* basketball 1.4
banana *f.* banana 2.2
banco *m.* bank 3.2
banda *f.* band 3.5
bandera *f.* flag
bañarse *v.* to bathe; to take a bath 2.1
baño *m.* bathroom 2.1
barato/a *adj.* cheap 1.6
barco *m.* boat 1.5
barrer *v.* to sweep 2.6
  barrer el suelo *v.* to sweep the floor 2.6
barrio *m.* neighborhood 2.6
bastante *adv.* enough; rather 2.4
basura *f.* trash 2.6
baúl *m.* trunk 2.5
beber *v.* to drink 1.3
bebida *f.* drink 2.2
béisbol *m.* baseball 1.4
bellas artes *f., pl.* fine arts 3.5
belleza *f.* beauty 3.2
beneficio *m.* benefit 3.4
besar(se) *v.* to kiss (each other) 2.5
beso *m.* kiss 2.3
biblioteca *f.* library 1.2
bicicleta *f.* bicycle 1.4
bien *adv.* well 1.1
bienestar *m.* well-being 3.3
bienvenido(s)/a(s) *adj.* welcome 1.1
billete *m.* paper money; ticket
billón *m.* trillion
biología *f.* biology 1.2
bisabuelo/a *m., f.* great-grandfather/great-grandmother 1.3
bistec *m.* steak 2.2
blanco/a *adj.* white 1.6
blog *m.* blog 2.5
(blue)jeans *m., pl.* jeans 1.6
blusa *f.* blouse 1.6
boca *f.* mouth 2.4
boda *f.* wedding 2.3
boleto *m.* ticket 1.2, 3.5
bolsa *f.* purse, bag 1.6
bombero/a *m., f.* firefighter 3.4
bonito/a *adj.* pretty 1.3
borrador *m.* eraser 1.2
borrar *v.* to erase 2.5
bosque *m.* forest 3.1
  bosque tropical tropical forest; rain forest 3.1
bota *f.* boot 1.6
botella *f.* bottle 2.3
botones *m., f. sing.* bellhop 1.5
brazo *m.* arm 2.4
brindar *v.* to toast (*drink*) 2.3
bucear *v.* to scuba dive 1.4
buen, bueno/a *adj.* good 1.3, 1.6
  buena forma good shape (*physical*) 3.3

Buenas noches. Good evening; Good night. 1.1
Buenas tardes. Good afternoon. 1.1
Bueno. Hello. (*on telephone*) 2.5
Buenos días. Good morning. 1.1
bulevar *m.* boulevard
buscador *m.* browser 2.5
buscar *v.* to look for 1.2
buzón *m.* mailbox 3.2

C

caballero *m.* gentleman, sir 2.2
caballo *m.* horse 1.5
cabe: no cabe duda de there's no doubt 3.1
cabeza *f.* head 2.4
cada *adj. m., f.* each 1.6
caerse *v.* to fall (down) 2.4
café *m.* café 1.4; *adj. m., f.* brown 1.6; *m.* coffee 2.2
cafeína *f.* caffeine 3.3
cafetera *f.* coffee maker 2.6
cafetería *f.* cafeteria 1.2
caído/a *p.p.* fallen 3.2
caja *f.* cash register 1.6
cajero/a *m., f.* cashier
cajero automático *m.* ATM 3.2
calavera de azúcar *f.* skull made out of sugar 2.3
calcetín (calcetines) *m.* sock(s) 1.6
calculadora *f.* calculator 1.2
calentamiento global *m.* global warming 3.1
calentarse (e:ie) *v.* to warm up 3.3
calidad *f.* quality 1.6
calle *f.* street 2.5
calor *m.* heat
caloría *f.* calorie 3.3
calzar *v.* to take size... shoes 1.6
cama *f.* bed 1.5
cámara de video *f.* video camera 2.5
cámara digital *f.* digital camera 2.5
camarero/a *m., f.* waiter/waitress 2.2
camarón *m.* shrimp 2.2
cambiar (de) *v.* to change 2.3
cambio: de cambio in change 1.2
cambio *m.* **climático** climate change 3.1
cambio *m.* **de moneda** currency exchange
caminar *v.* to walk 1.2
camino *m.* road
camión *m.* truck; bus
camisa *f.* shirt 1.6
camiseta *f.* t-shirt 1.6
campo *m.* countryside 1.5
canadiense *adj.* Canadian 1.3
canal *m.* (TV) channel 2.5; 3.5
canción *f.* song 3.5
candidato/a *m., f.* candidate 3.6
canela *f.* cinnamon 2.4
cansado/a *adj.* tired 1.5
cantante *m., f.* singer 3.5
cantar *v.* to sing 1.2
capital *f.* capital city
capó *m.* hood 2.5
cara *f.* face 2.1
caramelo *m.* caramel 2.3
cargador *m.* charger 2.5
carne *f.* meat 2.2
carne de res *f.* beef 2.2
carnicería *f.* butcher shop 3.2
caro/a *adj.* expensive 1.6
carpintero/a *m., f.* carpenter 3.4
carrera *f.* career 3.4
carretera *f.* highway; (main) road 2.5
carro *m.* car; automobile 2.5
carta *f.* letter 1.4; (playing) card 1.5
cartel *m.* poster 2.6
cartera *f.* wallet 1.4, 1.6
cartero *m.* mail carrier 3.2
casa *f.* house; home 1.2
casado/a *adj.* married 2.3
casarse (con) *v.* to get married (to) 2.3
casi *adv.* almost 2.4
catorce fourteen 1.1
cazar *v.* to hunt 3.1
cebolla *f.* onion 2.2
cederrón *m.* CD-ROM
celebrar *v.* to celebrate 2.3
cementerio *m.* cemetery 2.3
cena *f.* dinner 2.2
cenar *v.* to have dinner 1.2
centro *m.* downtown 1.4
centro comercial shopping mall 1.6
cepillarse los dientes/el pelo *v.* to brush one's teeth/one's hair 2.1
cerámica *f.* pottery 3.5
cerca de *prep.* near 1.2
cerdo *m.* pork 2.2
cereales *m., pl.* cereal; grains 2.2
cero *m.* zero 1.1
cerrado/a *adj.* closed 1.5
cerrar (e:ie) *v.* to close 1.4
césped *m.* grass
ceviche *m.* marinated fish dish 2.2
ceviche de camarón *m.* lemon-marinated shrimp 2.2
chaleco *m.* vest
champiñón *m.* mushroom 2.2
champú *m.* shampoo 2.1
chaqueta *f.* jacket 1.6
chatear *v.* to chat 2.5
chau *fam. interj.* bye 1.1
cheque *m.* (bank) check 3.2
cheque (de viajero) *m.* (traveler's) check 3.2
chévere *adj., fam.* terrific
chico/a *m., f.* boy/girl 1.1
chino/a *adj.* Chinese 1.3
chocar (con) *v.* to run into
chocolate *m.* chocolate 2.3
choque *m.* collision 3.6
chuleta *f.* chop (*food*) 2.2
chuleta de cerdo *f.* pork chop 2.2
cibercafé *m.* cybercafé 2.5
ciclismo *m.* cycling 1.4
cielo *m.* sky 3.1
cien(to) one hundred 1.2
ciencias *f., pl.* sciences 1.2
ciencias ambientales environmental science 1.2
de ciencia ficción *f.* science fiction (genre) 3.5
científico/a *m., f.* scientist 3.4
cierto/a *adj.* certain 3.1
es cierto it's certain 3.1
no es cierto it's not certain 3.1
cima *f.* top, peak 3.3
cinco five 1.1
cincuenta fifty 1.2
cine *m.* movie theater 1.4
cinta *f.* (audio)tape
cinta caminadora *f.* treadmill 3.3
cinturón *m.* belt 1.6
circulación *f.* traffic 2.5
cita *f.* date; appointment 2.3
ciudad *f.* city
ciudadano/a *m., f.* citizen 3.6
Claro (que sí). *fam.* Of course.
clase *f.* class 1.2
clase de ejercicios aeróbicos *f.* aerobics class 3.3
clásico/a *adj.* classical 3.5
cliente/a *m., f.* customer 1.6
clínica *f.* clinic 2.4
cobrar *v.* to cash (a check) 3.2
coche *m.* car; automobile 2.5
cocina *f.* kitchen; stove 2.3, 2.6
cocinar *v.* to cook 2.6
cocinero/a *m., f.* cook, chef 3.4
cofre *m.* hood 3.2
cola *f.* line 3.2
colesterol *m.* cholesterol 3.3
color *m.* color 1.6
comedia *f.* comedy; play 3.5
comedor *m.* dining room 2.6
comenzar (e:ie) *v.* to begin 1.4
comer *v.* to eat 1.3
comercial *adj.* commercial; business-related 3.4
comida *f.* food; meal 1.4, 2.2
como like; as 2.2
¿cómo? what?; how? 1.1, 1.2
¿Cómo es...? What's... like?
¿Cómo está usted? *form.* How are you? 1.1
¿Cómo estás? *fam.* How are you? 1.1
¿Cómo se llama usted? (*form.*) What's your name? 1.1
¿Cómo te llamas? *fam.* What's your name? 1.1

cómoda *f.* chest of drawers 2.6
cómodo/a *adj.* comfortable 1.5
compañero/a de clase *m., f.* classmate 1.2
compañero/a de cuarto *m., f.* roommate 1.2
compañía *f.* company; firm 3.4
compartir *v.* to share 1.3
compositor(a) *m., f.* composer 3.5
comprar *v.* to buy 1.2
compras *f., pl.* purchases
ir de compras to go shopping 1.5
comprender *v.* to understand 1.3
comprobar *v.* to check
comprometerse (con) *v.* to get engaged (to) 2.3
computación *f.* computer science 1.2
computadora *f.* computer 1.1
computadora portátil *f.* portable computer; laptop 2.5
comunicación *f.* communication 3.6
comunicarse (con) *v.* to communicate (with) 3.6
comunidad *f.* community 1.1
con *prep.* with 1.2
Con él/ella habla. Speaking. (*on telephone*) 2.5
con frecuencia *adv.* frequently 2.4
Con permiso. Pardon me; Excuse me. 1.1
con tal (de) que *conj.* provided (that) 3.1
concierto *m.* concert 3.5
concordar *v.* to agree
concurso *m.* game show; contest 3.5
conducir *v.* to drive 1.6, 2.5
conductor(a) *m., f.* driver 1.1
conexión *f.* **inalámbrica** wireless connection 2.5
confirmar *v.* to confirm 1.5
confirmar *v.* **una reservación** *f.* to confirm a reservation 1.5
confundido/a *adj.* confused 1.5
congelador *m.* freezer 2.6
congestionado/a *adj.* congested; stuffed-up 2.4
conmigo *pron.* with me 1.4, 2.3
conocer *v.* to know; to be acquainted with 1.6
conocido/a *adj.; p.p.* known
conseguir (e:i) *v.* to get; to obtain 1.4
consejero/a *m., f.* counselor; advisor 3.4
consejo *m.* advice
conservación *f.* conservation 3.1
conservar *v.* to conserve 3.1
construir *v.* to build
consultorio *m.* doctor's office 2.4
consumir *v.* to consume 3.3
contabilidad *f.* accounting 1.2
contador(a) *m., f.* accountant 3.4
contaminación *f.* pollution 3.1
contaminación del aire/del agua air/water pollution 3.1
contaminado/a *adj.* polluted 3.1
contaminar *v.* to pollute 3.1
contar (o:ue) *v.* to count; to tell 1.4
contento/a *adj.* content 1.5
contestadora *f.* answering machine
contestar *v.* to answer 1.2
contigo *fam. pron.* with you 1.5, 2.3
contratar *v.* to hire 3.4
control *m.* **remoto** remote control 2.5
controlar *v.* to control 3.1
conversación *f.* conversation 1.1
conversar *v.* to converse, to chat 1.2
corazón *m.* heart 2.4
corbata *f.* tie 1.6
corredor(a) *m., f.* **de bolsa** stockbroker 3.4
correo *m.* mail; post office 3.2
correo de voz *m.* voice mail 2.5
correo electrónico *m.* e-mail 1.4
correr *v.* to run 1.3
cortesía *f.* courtesy
cortinas *f., pl.* curtains 2.6
corto/a *adj.* short (*in length*) 1.6
cosa *f.* thing 1.1
costar (o:ue) *v.* to cost 1.6
costarricense *adj.* Costa Rican 1.3
cráter *m.* crater 3.1
creer *v.* to believe 1.3, 3.1
creer (en) *v.* to believe (in) 1.3
no creer *v.* not to believe 3.1
creído/a *adj., p.p.* believed 3.2
crema de afeitar *f.* shaving cream 1.5, 2.1
crimen *m.* crime; murder 3.6
cruzar *v.* to cross 3.2
cuaderno *m.* notebook 1.1
cuadra *f.* (city) block 3.2
¿cuál(es)? which?; which one(s)? 1.2
¿Cuál es la fecha de hoy? What is today's date? 1.5
cuadro *m.* picture 2.6
cuando *conj.* when 2.1; 3.1
¿cuándo? when? 1.2
¿cuánto(s)/a(s)? how much/how many? 1.1, 1.2
¿Cuánto cuesta...? How much does... cost? 1.6
¿Cuántos años tienes? How old are you?
cuarenta forty 1.2
cuarto de baño *m.* bathroom 2.1
cuarto *m.* room 1.2; 2.1
cuarto/a *adj.* fourth 1.5
menos cuarto quarter to (time) 1.1
y cuarto quarter after (time) 1.1
cuatro four 1.1
cuatrocientos/as four hundred 1.2
cubano/a *adj.* Cuban 1.3
cubiertos *m., pl.* silverware
cubierto/a *p.p.* covered
cubrir *v.* to cover
cuchara *f.* (table or large) spoon 2.6
cuchillo *m.* knife 2.6
cuello *m.* neck 2.4
cuenta *f.* bill 2.2; account 3.2
cuenta corriente *f.* checking account 3.2
cuenta de ahorros *f.* savings account 3.2
cuento *m.* short story 3.5
cuerpo *m.* body 2.4
cuidado *m.* care
cuidar *v.* to take care of 3.1
cultura *f.* culture 1.2, 3.5
cumpleaños *m., sing.* birthday 2.3
cumplir años *v.* to have a birthday
cuñado/a *m., f.* brother-in-law/sister-in-law 1.3
currículum *m.* résumé 3.4
curso *m.* course 1.2

D

danza *f.* dance 3.5
dañar *v.* to damage; to break down 2.4
dar *v.* to give 1.6
dar un consejo *v.* to give advice
darse con *v.* to bump into; to run into (something) 2.4
darse prisa *v.* to hurry; to rush 3.3
de *prep.* of; from 1.1
¿De dónde eres? *fam.* Where are you from? 1.1
¿De dónde es usted? *form.* Where are you from? 1.1
¿De parte de quién? Who is speaking/calling? (*on telephone*) 2.5
¿de quién...? whose...? (*sing.*) 1.1
¿de quiénes...? whose...? (*pl.*) 1.1
de algodón (made) of cotton 1.6
de aluminio (made) of aluminum 3.1
de buen humor in a good mood 1.5
de compras shopping 1.5
de cuadros plaid 1.6
de excursión hiking 1.4
de hecho in fact
de ida y vuelta roundtrip 1.5
de la mañana in the morning; A.M. 1.1
de la noche in the evening; at night; P.M. 1.1
de la tarde in the afternoon; in the early evening; P.M. 1.1
de lana (made) of wool 1.6
de lunares polka-dotted 1.6
de mal humor in a bad mood 1.5
de moda in fashion 1.6

De nada. You're welcome. 1.1
de niño/a as a child 2.4
de parte de on behalf of 2.5
de plástico (made) of plastic 3.1
de rayas striped 1.6
de repente suddenly 1.6
de seda (made) of silk 1.6
de vaqueros western (genre) 3.5
de vez en cuando from time to time 2.4
de vidrio (made) of glass 3.1
debajo de *prep.* below; under 1.2
deber (+ *inf.*) *v.* should; must; ought to 1.3
deber *m.* responsibility; obligation 3.6
debido a due to (the fact that)
débil *adj.* weak 3.3
decidir (+ *inf.*) *v.* to decide 1.3
décimo/a *adj.* tenth 1.5
decir (e:i) *v.* **(que)** to say (that); to tell (that) 1.4
decir la respuesta to say the answer 1.4
decir la verdad to tell the truth 1.4
decir mentiras to tell lies 1.4
declarar *v.* to declare; to say 3.6
dedo *m.* finger 2.4
dedo del pie *m.* toe 2.4
deforestación *f.* deforestation 3.1
dejar *v.* to let; to quit; to leave behind 3.4
dejar de (+ *inf.*) *v.* to stop (*doing something*) 3.1
dejar una propina *v.* to leave a tip
del (*contraction of* de + el) of the; from the 1.1
delante de *prep.* in front of 1.2
delgado/a *adj.* thin; slender 1.3
delicioso/a *adj.* delicious 2.2
demás *adj.* the rest
demasiado *adv.* too much 1.6
dentista *m., f.* dentist 2.4
dentro de (diez años) within (ten years) 3.4; inside
dependiente/a *m., f.* clerk 1.6
deporte *m.* sport 1.4
deportista *m.* sports person
deportivo/a *adj.* sports-related 1.4
depositar *v.* to deposit 3.2
derecha *f.* right 1.2
a la derecha de to the right of 1.2
derecho *adv.* straight (ahead) 3.2
derechos *m., pl.* rights 3.6
desarrollar *v.* to develop 3.1
desastre (natural) *m.* (natural) disaster 3.6
desayunar *v.* to have breakfast 1.2
desayuno *m.* breakfast 2.2
descafeinado/a *adj.* decaffeinated 3.3
descansar *v.* to rest 1.2
descargar *v.* to download 2.5
descompuesto/a *adj.* not working; out of order 2.5
describir *v.* to describe 1.3
descrito/a *p.p.* described 3.2
descubierto/a *p.p.* discovered 3.2
descubrir *v.* to discover 3.1
desde *prep.* from 1.6
desear *v.* to wish; to desire 1.2
desempleo *m.* unemployment 3.6
desierto *m.* desert 3.1
desigualdad *f.* inequality 3.6
desordenado/a *adj.* disorderly 1.5
despacio *adv.* slowly 2.4
despedida *f.* farewell; goodbye
despedir (e:i) *v.* to fire 3.4
despedirse (de) (e:i) *v.* to say goodbye (to) 3.6
despejado/a *adj.* clear (*weather*)
despertador *m.* alarm clock 2.1
despertarse (e:ie) *v.* to wake up 2.1
después *adv.* afterwards; then 2.1
después de after 2.1
después de que *conj.* after 3.1
destruir *v.* to destroy 3.1
detrás de *prep.* behind 1.2
día *m.* day 1.1
día de fiesta holiday 2.3
diario *m.* diary 1.1; newspaper 3.6
diario/a *adj.* daily 2.1
dibujar *v.* to draw 1.2
dibujo *m.* drawing
dibujos animados *m., pl.* cartoons 3.5
diccionario *m.* dictionary 1.1
dicho/a *p.p.* said 3.2
diciembre *m.* December 1.5
dictadura *f.* dictatorship 3.6
diecinueve nineteen 1.1
dieciocho eighteen 1.1
dieciséis sixteen 1.1
diecisiete seventeen 1.1
diente *m.* tooth 2.1
dieta *f.* diet 3.3
comer una dieta equilibrada to eat a balanced diet 3.3
diez ten 1.1
difícil *adj.* difficult; hard 1.3
Diga. Hello. (*on telephone*) 2.5
diligencia *f.* errand 3.2
dinero *m.* money 1.6
dirección *f.* address 3.2
dirección electrónica *f.* e-mail address 2.5
director(a) *m., f.* director; (*musical*) conductor 3.5
dirigir *v.* to direct 3.5
disco compacto compact disc (CD) 2.5
discriminación *f.* discrimination 3.6
discurso *m.* speech 3.6
diseñador(a) *m., f.* designer 3.4
diseño *m.* design
disfraz *m.* costume 2.3
disfrutar (de) *v.* to enjoy; to reap the benefits (of) 3.3
disminuir *v.* to reduce 3.4
diversión *f.* fun activity; entertainment; recreation 1.4
divertido/a *adj.* fun
divertirse (e:ie) *v.* to have fun 2.3
divorciado/a *adj.* divorced 2.3
divorciarse (de) *v.* to get divorced (from) 2.3
divorcio *m.* divorce 2.3
doblar *v.* to turn 3.2
doble *adj.* double 1.5
doce twelve 1.1
doctor(a) *m., f.* doctor 1.3; 2.4
documental *m.* documentary 3.5
documentos de viaje *m., pl.* travel documents
doler (o:ue) *v.* to hurt 2.4
dolor *m.* ache; pain 2.4
dolor de cabeza *m.* headache 2.4
doméstico/a *adj.* domestic 2.6
domingo *m.* Sunday 1.2
don *m.* Mr.; sir 1.1
doña *f.* Mrs.; ma'am 1.1
donde *adv.* where
¿Dónde está...? Where is...? 1.2
¿dónde? where? 1.1, 1.2
dormir (o:ue) *v.* to sleep 1.4
dormirse (o:ue) *v.* to go to sleep; to fall asleep 2.1
dormitorio *m.* bedroom 2.6
dos two 1.1
dos veces *f.* twice; two times 1.6
doscientos/as two hundred 1.2
drama *m.* drama; play 3.5
dramático/a *adj.* dramatic 3.5
dramaturgo/a *m., f.* playwright 3.5
ducha *f.* shower 2.1
ducharse *v.* to shower; to take a shower 2.1
duda *f.* doubt 3.1
dudar *v.* to doubt 3.1
no dudar *v.* not to doubt 3.1
dueño/a *m., f.* owner 2.2
dulces *m., pl.* sweets; candy 2.3
durante *prep.* during 2.1
durar *v.* to last 3.6

E

e *conj.* *(used instead of* y *before words beginning with* **i** *and* **hi***)* and
echar *v.* to throw
echar (una carta) al buzón *v.* to put (a letter) in the mailbox; to mail 3.2
ecología *f.* ecology 3.1
ecológico/a *adj.* ecological 3.1
ecologista *m., f.* ecologist 3.1
economía *f.* economics 1.2
ecoturismo *m.* ecotourism 3.1

ecuatoriano/a *adj.* Ecuadorian 1.3
edad *f.* age 2.3
edificio *m.* building 2.6
edificio de apartamentos apartment building 2.6
(en) efectivo *m.* cash 1.6
ejercer *v.* to practice/exercise (a degree/profession) 3.4
ejercicio *m.* exercise 3.3
ejercicios aeróbicos aerobic exercises 3.3
ejercicios de estiramiento stretching exercises 3.3
ejército *m.* army 3.6
el *m., sing., def. art.* the 1.1
él *sub. pron.* he 1.1; *obj. pron.* him
elecciones *f., pl.* election 3.6
electricista *m., f.* electrician 3.4
electrodoméstico *m.* electric appliance 2.6
elegante *adj. m., f.* elegant 1.6
elegir (e:i) *v.* to elect 3.6
ella *sub. pron.* she 1.1; *obj. pron.* her
ellos/as *sub. pron.* they 1.1; *obj. pron.* them
embarazada *adj.* pregnant 2.4
emergencia *f.* emergency 2.4
emitir *v.* to broadcast 3.6
emocionante *adj. m., f.* exciting
empezar (e:ie) *v.* to begin 1.4
empleado/a *m., f.* employee 1.5
empleo *m.* job; employment 3.4
empresa *f.* company; firm 3.4
en *prep.* in; on 1.2
en casa at home
en caso (de) que *conj.* in case (that) 3.1
en cuanto *conj.* as soon as 3.1
en efectivo in cash 3.2
en exceso in excess; too much 3.3
en línea in-line 1.4
en punto on the dot; exactly; sharp (*time*) 1.1
en qué in what; how
¿En qué puedo servirles? How can I help you? 1.5
en vivo live 2.1
enamorado/a (de) *adj.* in love (with) 1.5
enamorarse (de) *v.* to fall in love (with) 2.3
encantado/a *adj.* delighted; pleased to meet you 1.1
encantar *v.* to like very much; to love (*inanimate objects*) 2.1
encima de *prep.* on top of 1.2
encontrar (o:ue) *v.* to find 1.4
encontrar(se) (o:ue) *v.* to meet (each other); to run into (each other) 2.5
encontrarse con to meet up with 2.1
encuesta *f.* poll; survey 3.6
energía *f.* energy 3.1
energía nuclear nuclear energy 3.1
energía solar solar energy 3.1
enero *m.* January 1.5
enfermarse *v.* to get sick 2.4
enfermedad *f.* illness 2.4
enfermero/a *m., f.* nurse 2.4
enfermo/a *adj.* sick 2.4
enfrente de *adv.* opposite; facing 3.2
engordar *v.* to gain weight 3.3
enojado/a *adj.* angry 1.5
enojarse (con) *v.* to get angry (with) 2.1
ensalada *f.* salad 2.2
ensayo *m.* essay 1.3
enseguida *adv.* right away
enseñar *v.* to teach 1.2
ensuciar *v.* to get (something) dirty 2.6
entender (e:ie) *v.* to understand 1.4
enterarse *v.* to find out 3.4
entonces *adv.* so, then 1.5, 2.1
entrada *f.* entrance 2.6; ticket
entre *prep.* between; among 1.2
entregar *v.* to hand in 2.5
entremeses *m., pl.* hors d'oeuvres; appetizers 2.2
entrenador(a) *m., f.* trainer 3.3
entrenarse *v.* to practice; to train 3.3
entrevista *f.* interview 3.4
entrevistador(a) *m., f.* interviewer 3.4
entrevistar *v.* to interview 3.4
envase *m.* container 3.1
enviar *v.* to send; to mail 3.2
equilibrado/a *adj.* balanced 3.3
equipaje *m.* luggage 1.5
equipo *m.* team 1.4
equivocado/a *adj.* wrong 1.5
eres *fam.* you are 1.1
es he/she/it is 1.1
Es bueno que... It's good that... 2.6
es cierto it's certain 3.1
es extraño it's strange 3.1
es igual it's the same 1.5
Es importante que... It's important that... 2.6
es imposible it's impossible 3.1
es improbable it's improbable 3.1
Es malo que... It's bad that... 2.6
Es mejor que... It's better that... 2.6
Es necesario que... It's necessary that... 2.6
es obvio it's obvious 3.1
es posible it's possible 3.1
es probable it's probable 3.1
es ridículo it's ridiculous 3.1
es seguro it's certain 3.1
es terrible it's terrible 3.1
es triste it's sad 3.1
Es urgente que... It's urgent that... 2.6
Es la una. It's one o'clock. 1.1
es una lástima it's a shame 3.1
es verdad it's true 3.1
esa(s) *f., adj.* that; those 1.6
ésa(s) *f., pron.* that (one); those (ones) 1.6
escalar *v.* to climb 1.4
escalar montañas to climb mountains 1.4
escalera *f.* stairs; stairway 2.6
escalón *m.* step 3.3
escanear *v.* to scan 2.5
escoger *v.* to choose 2.2
escribir *v.* to write 1.3
escribir un mensaje electrónico to write an e-mail 1.4
escribir una carta to write a letter 1.4
escrito/a *p.p.* written 3.2
escritor(a) *m., f.* writer 3.5
escritorio *m.* desk 1.2
escuchar *v.* to listen (to) 1.2
escuchar la radio to listen to the radio 1.2
escuchar música to listen to music 1.2
escuela *f.* school 1.1
esculpir *v.* to sculpt 3.5
escultor(a) *m., f.* sculptor 3.5
escultura *f.* sculpture 3.5
ese *m., sing., adj.* that 1.6
ése *m., sing., pron.* that one 1.6
eso *neuter, pron.* that; that thing 1.6
esos *m., pl., adj.* those 1.6
ésos *m., pl., pron.* those (ones) 1.6
España *f.* Spain
español *m.* Spanish (*language*) 1.2
español(a) *adj. m., f.* Spanish 1.3
espárragos *m., pl.* asparagus 2.2
especialidad: las especialidades del día today's specials 2.2
especialización *f.* major 1.2
espectacular *adj.* spectacular
espectáculo *m.* show 3.5
espejo *m.* mirror 2.1
esperar *v.* to hope; to wish 3.1
esperar (+ *inf.*) *v.* to wait (for); to hope 1.2
esposo/a *m., f.* husband/wife; spouse 1.3
esquí (acuático) *m.* (water) skiing 1.4
esquiar *v.* to ski 1.4
esquina *f.* corner 3.2
está he/she/it is, you are
Está bien. That's fine.
Está (muy) despejado. It's (very) clear. (*weather*)
Está lloviendo. It's raining. 1.5
Está nevando. It's snowing. 1.5
Está (muy) nublado. It's (very) cloudy. (*weather*) 1.5
esta(s) *f., adj.* this; these 1.6

esta noche tonight
ésta(s) *f., pron.* this (one); these (ones) 1.6
establecer *v.* to establish 3.4
estación *f.* station; season 1.5
estación de autobuses bus station 1.5
estación del metro subway station 1.5
estación de tren train station 1.5
estacionamiento *m.* parking lot 3.2
estacionar *v.* to park 2.5
estadio *m.* stadium 1.2
estado civil *m.* marital status 2.3
Estados Unidos *m., pl.* (EE.UU.; E.U.) United States
estadounidense *adj. m., f.* from the United States 1.3
estampilla *f.* stamp 3.2
estante *m.* bookcase; bookshelves 2.6
estar *v.* to be 1.2
estar a dieta to be on a diet 3.3
estar aburrido/a to be bored 1.5
estar afectado/a (por) to be affected (by) 3.1
estar cansado/a to be tired 1.5
estar contaminado/a to be polluted 3.1
estar de acuerdo to agree 3.5
Estoy de acuerdo. I agree. 3.5
No estoy de acuerdo. I don't agree. 3.5
estar de moda to be in fashion 1.6
estar de vacaciones *f., pl.* to be on vacation 1.5
estar en buena forma to be in good shape 3.3
estar enfermo/a to be sick 2.4
estar harto/a de... to be sick of... 3.6
estar listo/a to be ready 1.5
estar perdido/a to be lost 3.2
estar roto/a to be broken
estar seguro/a to be sure 1.5
estar torcido/a to be twisted; to be sprained 2.4
No está nada mal. It's not bad at all. 1.5
estatua *f.* statue 3.5
este *m.* east 3.2
este *m., sing., adj.* this 1.6
éste *m., sing., pron.* this (one) 1.6
estéreo *m.* stereo 2.5
estilo *m.* style
estiramiento *m.* stretching 3.3
esto *neuter pron.* this; this thing 1.6
estómago *m.* stomach 2.4
estornudar *v.* to sneeze 2.4
estos *m., pl., adj.* these 1.6
éstos *m., pl., pron.* these (ones) 1.6
estrella *f.* star 3.1
estrella de cine *m., f.* movie star 3.5
estrés *m.* stress 3.3
estudiante *m., f.* student 1.1, 1.2
estudiantil *adj. m., f.* student 1.2
estudiar *v.* to study 1.2
estufa *f.* stove 2.6
estupendo/a *adj.* stupendous 1.5
etapa *f.* stage 2.3
evitar *v.* to avoid 3.1
examen *m.* test; exam 1.2
examen médico physical exam 2.4
excelente *adj. m., f.* excellent 1.5
exceso *m.* excess 3.3
excursión *f.* hike; tour; excursion 1.4
excursionista *m., f.* hiker
éxito *m.* success
experiencia *f.* experience
explicar *v.* to explain 1.2
explorar *v.* to explore
expresión *f.* expression
extinción *f.* extinction 3.1
extranjero/a *adj.* foreign 3.5
extrañar *v.* to miss 3.4
extraño/a *adj.* strange 3.1

F

fábrica *f.* factory 3.1
fabuloso/a *adj.* fabulous 1.5
fácil *adj.* easy 1.3
falda *f.* skirt 1.6
faltar *v.* to lack; to need 2.1
familia *f.* family 1.3
famoso/a *adj.* famous
farmacia *f.* pharmacy 2.4
fascinar *v.* to fascinate 2.1
favorito/a *adj.* favorite 1.4
fax *m.* fax (machine)
febrero *m.* February 1.5
fecha *f.* date 1.5
¡Felicidades! Congratulations! 2.3
¡Felicitaciones! Congratulations! 2.3
feliz *adj.* happy 1.5
¡Feliz cumpleaños! Happy birthday! 2.3
fenomenal *adj.* great, phenomenal 1.5
feo/a *adj.* ugly 1.3
festival *m.* festival 3.5
fiebre *f.* fever 2.4
fiesta *f.* party 2.3
fijo/a *adj.* fixed, set 1.6
fin *m.* end 1.4
fin de semana weekend 1.4
finalmente *adv.* finally
firmar *v.* to sign (*a document*) 3.2
física *f.* physics 1.2
flan (de caramelo) *m.* baked (caramel) custard 2.3
flexible *adj.* flexible 3.3
flor *f.* flower 3.1
folclórico/a *adj.* folk; folkloric 3.5
folleto *m.* brochure
forma *f.* shape 3.3
formulario *m.* form 3.2
foto(grafía) *f.* photograph 1.1
francés, francesa *adj. m., f.* French 1.3
frecuentemente *adv.* frequently
frenos *m., pl.* brakes
frente (frío) *m.* (cold) front 1.5
fresco/a *adj.* cool
frijoles *m., pl.* beans 2.2
frío/a *adj.* cold
frito/a *adj.* fried 2.2
fruta *f.* fruit 2.2
frutería *f.* fruit store 3.2
fuera *adv.* outside
fuerte *adj. m., f.* strong 3.3
fumar *v.* to smoke 3.3
(no) fumar *v.* (not) to smoke 3.3
funcionar *v.* to work 2.5; to function
fútbol *m.* soccer 1.4
fútbol americano *m.* football 1.4
futuro/a *adj.* future
en el futuro in the future

G

gafas (de sol) *f., pl.* (sun)glasses 1.6
gafas (oscuras) *f., pl.* (sun)glasses
galleta *f.* cookie 2.3
ganar *v.* to win 1.4; to earn (money) 3.4
ganga *f.* bargain 1.6
garaje *m.* garage; (mechanic's) repair shop 2.5; garage (*in a house*) 2.6
garganta *f.* throat 2.4
gasolina *f.* gasoline 2.5
gasolinera *f.* gas station 2.5
gastar *v.* to spend (*money*) 1.6
gato *m.* cat 3.1
gemelo/a *m., f.* twin 1.3
genial *adj.* great 3.4
gente *f.* people 1.3
geografía *f.* geography 1.2
gerente *m., f.* manager 2.2, 3.4
gimnasio *m.* gymnasium 1.4
gobierno *m.* government 3.1
golf *m.* golf 1.4
gordo/a *adj.* fat 1.3
grabar *v.* to record 2.5
gracias *f., pl.* thank you; thanks 1.1
Gracias por invitarme. Thanks for inviting me. 2.3
graduarse (de/en) *v.* to graduate (from/in) 2.3
grande *adj.* big; large 1.3
grasa *f.* fat 3.3
gratis *adj. m., f.* free of charge 3.2
grave *adj.* grave; serious 2.4
gripe *f.* flu 2.4
gris *adj. m., f.* gray 1.6

gritar *v.* to scream, to shout
grito *m.* scream **1.5**
guantes *m., pl.* gloves **1.6**
guapo/a *adj.* handsome; good-looking **1.3**
guardar *v.* to save (on a computer) **2.5**
guerra *f.* war **3.6**
guía *m., f.* guide
gustar *v.* to be pleasing to; to like **1.2**
  Me gustaría... I would like...
gusto *m.* pleasure **1.1**
  El gusto es mío. The pleasure is mine. **1.1**
  Mucho gusto. Pleased to meet you. **1.1**
  ¡Qué gusto verlo/la! *(form.) How nice to see you!* **3.6**
  ¡Qué gusto verte! *(fam.) How nice to see you!* **3.6**

H

haber *(auxiliar) v.* to have (done something) **3.3**
habitación *f.* room **1.5**
  habitación doble double room **1.5**
  habitación individual single room **1.5**
hablar *v.* to talk; to speak **1.2**
hacer *v.* to do; to make **1.4**
  Hace buen tiempo. The weather is good. **1.5**
  Hace (mucho) calor. It's (very) hot. (*weather*) **1.5**
  Hace fresco. It's cool. (*weather*) **1.5**
  Hace (mucho) frío. It's (very) cold. (*weather*) **1.5**
  Hace mal tiempo. The weather is bad. **1.5**
  Hace (mucho) sol. It's (very) sunny. (*weather*) **1.5**
  Hace (mucho) viento. It's (very) windy. (*weather*) **1.5**
  hacer cola to stand in line **3.2**
  hacer diligencias to run errands **3.2**
  hacer ejercicio to exercise **3.3**
  hacer ejercicios aeróbicos to do aerobics **3.3**
  hacer ejercicios de estiramiento to do stretching exercises **3.3**
  hacer el papel (de) to play the role (of) **3.5**
  hacer gimnasia to work out **3.3**
  hacer juego (con) to match (with) **1.6**
  hacer la cama to make the bed **2.6**
  hacer las maletas to pack (one's) suitcases **1.5**
  hacer quehaceres domésticos to do household chores **2.6**
  hacer (wind)surf to (wind) surf **1.5**
  hacer turismo to go sightseeing
  hacer un viaje to take a trip **1.5**
  ¿Me harías el honor de casarte conmigo? Would you do me the honor of marrying me? **3.5**
hacia *prep.* toward **3.2**
hambre *f.* hunger
hamburguesa *f.* hamburger **2.2**
hasta *prep.* until **1.6**; toward
  Hasta la vista. See you later. **1.1**
  Hasta luego. See you later. **1.1**
  Hasta mañana. See you tomorrow. **1.1**
  Hasta pronto. See you soon. **1.1**
  hasta que *conj.* until **3.1**
hay there is; there are **1.1**
  Hay (mucha) contaminación. It's (very) smoggy.
  Hay (mucha) niebla. It's (very) foggy.
  Hay que It is necessary that
  No hay de qué. You're welcome. **1.1**
  No hay duda de There's no doubt **3.1**
hecho/a *p.p.* done **3.2**
heladería *f.* ice cream shop **3.2**
helado/a *adj.* iced **2.2**
helado *m.* ice cream **2.3**
hermanastro/a *m., f.* stepbrother/stepsister **1.3**
hermano/a *m., f.* brother/sister **1.3**
hermano/a mayor/menor *m., f.* older/younger brother/sister **1.3**
hermanos *m., pl.* siblings (brothers and sisters) **1.3**
hermoso/a *adj.* beautiful **1.6**
hierba *f.* grass **3.1**
hijastro/a *m., f.* stepson/stepdaughter **1.3**
hijo/a *m., f.* son/daughter **1.3**
  hijo/a único/a *m., f.* only child **1.3**
  hijos *m., pl.* children **1.3**
híjole *interj.* wow **1.6**
historia *f.* history **1.2**; story **3.5**
hockey *m.* hockey **1.4**
hola *interj.* hello; hi **1.1**
hombre *m.* man **1.1**
  hombre de negocios *m.* businessman **3.4**
hora *f.* hour **1.1**; the time
horario *m.* schedule **1.2**
horno *m.* oven **2.6**
  horno de microondas *m.* microwave oven **2.6**
horror *m.* horror **3.5**
  de horror horror (genre) **3.5**
hospital *m.* hospital **2.4**
hotel *m.* hotel **1.5**
hoy *adv.* today **1.2**
  hoy día *adv.* nowadays
  Hoy es... Today is... **1.2**
hueco *m.* hole **1.4**
huelga *f.* strike (*labor*) **3.6**
hueso *m.* bone **2.4**
huésped *m., f.* guest **1.5**
huevo *m.* egg **2.2**
humanidades *f., pl.* humanities **1.2**
huracán *m.* hurricane **3.6**

I

ida *f.* one way (*travel*)
idea *f.* idea **3.6**
iglesia *f.* church **1.4**
igualdad *f.* equality **3.6**
igualmente *adv.* likewise **1.1**
impermeable *m.* raincoat **1.6**
importante *adj. m., f.* important **1.3**
importar *v.* to be important to; to matter **2.1**
imposible *adj. m., f.* impossible **3.1**
impresora *f.* printer **2.5**
imprimir *v.* to print **2.5**
improbable *adj. m., f.* improbable **3.1**
impuesto *m.* tax **3.6**
incendio *m.* fire **3.6**
increíble *adj. m., f.* incredible **1.5**
indicar cómo llegar *v.* to give directions **3.2**
individual *adj.* single (*room*) **1.5**
infección *f.* infection **2.4**
informar *v.* to inform **3.6**
informe *m.* report; paper (*written work*) **3.6**
ingeniero/a *m., f.* engineer **1.3**
inglés *m.* English (*language*) **1.2**
inglés, inglesa *adj.* English **1.3**
inodoro *m.* toilet **2.1**
insistir (en) *v.* to insist (on) **2.6**
inspector(a) de aduanas *m., f.* customs inspector **1.5**
inteligente *adj. m., f.* intelligent **1.3**
intento *m.* attempt **2.5**
intercambiar *v.* to exchange
interesante *adj. m., f.* interesting **1.3**
interesar *v.* to be interesting to; to interest **2.1**
internacional *adj. m., f.* international **3.6**
Internet Internet **2.5**
inundación *f.* flood **3.6**
invertir (e:ie) *v.* to invest **3.4**
invierno *m.* winter **1.5**
invitado/a *m., f.* guest **2.3**
invitar *v.* to invite **2.3**
inyección *f.* injection **2.4**
ir *v.* to go **1.4**
  ir a (+ *inf.*) to be going to do something **1.4**
  ir de compras to go shopping **1.5**
  ir de excursión (a las montañas) to go on a hike (in the mountains) **1.4**
  ir de pesca to go fishing

ir de vacaciones to go on vacation 1.5
ir en autobús to go by bus 1.5
ir en auto(móvil) to go by auto(mobile); to go by car 1.5
ir en avión to go by plane 1.5
ir en barco to go by boat 1.5
ir en metro to go by subway
ir en moto(cicleta) to go by motorcycle 1.5
ir en taxi to go by taxi 1.5
ir en tren to go by train
irse *v.* to go away; to leave 2.1
italiano/a *adj.* Italian 1.3
izquierda *f.* left 1.2
a la izquierda de to the left of 1.2

J

jabón *m.* soap 2.1
jamás *adv.* never; not ever 2.1
jamón *m.* ham 2.2
japonés, japonesa *adj.* Japanese 1.3
jardín *m.* garden; yard 2.6
jefe, jefa *m., f.* boss 3.4
jengibre *m.* ginger 2.4
joven *adj. m., f., sing.* (**jóvenes** *pl.*) young 1.3
joven *m., f., sing.* (**jóvenes** *pl.*) young person 1.1
joyería *f.* jewelry store 3.2
jubilarse *v.* to retire (*from work*) 2.3
juego *m.* game
jueves *m., sing.* Thursday 1.2
jugador(a) *m., f.* player 1.4
jugar (u:ue) *v.* to play 1.4
jugar a las cartas *f., pl.* to play cards 1.5
jugo *m.* juice 2.2
jugo de fruta *m.* fruit juice 2.2
julio *m.* July 1.5
jungla *f.* jungle 3.1
junio *m.* June 1.5
juntos/as *adj.* together 2.3
juventud *f.* youth 2.3

K

kilómetro *m.* kilometer 2.5

L

la *f., sing., def. art.* the 1.1; *f., sing., d.o. pron.* her, it, *form.* you 1.5
laboratorio *m.* laboratory 1.2
lago *m.* lake 3.1
lámpara *f.* lamp 2.6
lana *f.* wool 1.6
langosta *f.* lobster 2.2
lápiz *m.* pencil 1.1
largo/a *adj.* long 1.6
las *f., pl., def. art.* the 1.1; *f., pl., d.o. pron.* them; you 1.5
lástima *f.* shame 3.1
lastimarse *v.* to injure oneself 2.4
lastimarse el pie to injure one's foot 2.4
lata *f.* (*tin*) can 3.1
lavabo *m.* sink 2.1
lavadora *f.* washing machine 2.6
lavandería *f.* laundromat 3.2
lavaplatos *m., sing.* dishwasher 2.6
lavar *v.* to wash 2.6
lavar (el suelo, los platos) to wash (the floor, the dishes) 2.6
lavarse *v.* to wash oneself 2.1
lavarse la cara to wash one's face 2.1
lavarse las manos to wash one's hands 2.1
le *sing., i.o. pron.* to/for him, her, *form.* you 1.6
Le presento a… *form.* I would like to introduce you to (name). 1.1
lección *f.* lesson 1.1
leche *f.* milk 2.2
lechuga *f.* lettuce 2.2
leer *v.* to read 1.3
leer el correo electrónico to read e-mail 1.4
leer un periódico to read a newspaper 1.4
leer una revista to read a magazine 1.4
leído/a *p.p.* read 3.2
lejos de *prep.* far from 1.2
lengua *f.* language 1.2
lenguas extranjeras *f., pl.* foreign languages 1.2
lentes de contacto *m., pl.* contact lenses
lentes (de sol) (sun)glasses
lento/a *adj.* slow 2.5
les *pl., i.o. pron.* to/for them, you 1.6
letrero *m.* sign 3.2
levantar *v.* to lift 3.3
levantar pesas to lift weights 3.3
levantarse *v.* to get up 2.1
ley *f.* law 3.1
libertad *f.* liberty; freedom 3.6
libre *adj. m., f.* free 1.4
librería *f.* bookstore 1.2
libro *m.* book 1.2
licencia de conducir *f.* driver's license 2.5
limón *m.* lemon 2.2
limpiar *v.* to clean 2.6
limpiar la casa *v.* to clean the house 2.6
limpio/a *adj.* clean 1.5
línea *f.* line 1.4
listo/a *adj.* ready; smart 1.5
literatura *f.* literature 1.2
llamar *v.* to call 2.5
llamar por teléfono to call on the phone
llamarse *v.* to be called; to be named 2.1
llanta *f.* tire 2.5
llave *f.* key 1.5; wrench 2.5
llegada *f.* arrival 1.5
llegar *v.* to arrive 1.2
llenar *v.* to fill 2.5, 3.2
llenar el tanque to fill the tank 2.5
llenar (un formulario) to fill out (a form) 3.2
lleno/a *adj.* full 2.5
llevar *v.* to carry 1.2; to wear; to take 1.6
llevar una vida sana to lead a healthy lifestyle 3.3
llevarse bien/mal (con) to get along well/badly (with) 2.3
llorar *v.* to cry 3.3
llover (o:ue) *v.* to rain 1.5
Llueve. It's raining. 1.5
lluvia *f.* rain
lo *m., sing. d.o. pron.* him, it, *form.* you 1.5
¡Lo he pasado de película! I've had a fantastic time! 3.6
lo mejor the best (thing)
lo que that which; what 2.6
Lo siento. I'm sorry. 1.1
loco/a *adj.* crazy 1.6
locutor(a) *m., f.* (TV or radio) announcer 3.6
lodo *m.* mud
los *m., pl., def. art.* the 1.1; *m. pl., d.o. pron.* them, you 1.5
luchar (contra/por) *v.* to fight; to struggle (against/for) 3.6
luego *adv.* then 2.1; later 1.1
lugar *m.* place 1.2, 1.4
luna *f.* moon 3.1
lunares *m.* polka dots
lunes *m., sing.* Monday 1.2
luz *f.* light; electricity 2.6

M

madrastra *f.* stepmother 1.3
madre *f.* mother 1.3
madurez *f.* maturity; middle age 2.3
maestro/a *m., f.* teacher 3.4
magnífico/a *adj.* magnificent 1.5
maíz *m.* corn 2.2
mal, malo/a *adj.* bad 1.3
maleta *f.* suitcase 1.1
mamá *f.* mom
mandar *v.* to order 2.6; to send; to mail 3.2
manejar *v.* to drive 2.5
manera *f.* way
mano *f.* hand 1.1
manta *f.* blanket 2.6
mantener *v.* to maintain 3.3
mantenerse en forma to stay in shape 3.3
mantequilla *f.* butter 2.2
manzana *f.* apple 2.2

mañana *f.* morning, a.m. 1.1; tomorrow 1.1
mapa *m.* map 1.1, 1.2
maquillaje *m.* makeup 2.1
maquillarse *v.* to put on makeup 2.1
mar *m.* sea 1.5
maravilloso/a *adj.* marvelous 1.5
mareado/a *adj.* dizzy; nauseated 2.4
margarina *f.* margarine 2.2
mariscos *m., pl.* shellfish 2.2
marrón *adj. m., f.* brown 1.6
martes *m., sing.* Tuesday 1.2
marzo *m.* March 1.5
más *adv.* more 1.2
  más de (+ *number*) more than 2.2
  más tarde later (on) 2.1
  más... que more... than 2.2
masaje *m.* massage 3.3
matemáticas *f., pl.* mathematics 1.2
materia *f.* course 1.2
matrimonio *m.* marriage 2.3
máximo/a *adj.* maximum 2.5
mayo *m.* May 1.5
mayonesa *f.* mayonnaise 2.2
mayor *adj.* older 1.3
  el/la mayor *adj.* oldest 2.2
me *sing., d.o. pron.* me 1.5; *sing. i.o. pron.* to/for me 1.6
  Me gusta... I like... 1.2
  Me gustaría(n)... I would like... 3.3
  Me llamo... My name is... 1.1
  Me muero por... I'm dying to (for)...
mecánico/a *m., f.* mechanic 2.5
mediano/a *adj.* medium
medianoche *f.* midnight 1.1
medias *f., pl.* pantyhose, stockings 1.6
medicamento *m.* medication 2.4
medicina *f.* medicine 2.4
médico/a *m., f.* doctor 1.3; *adj.* medical 2.4
medio/a *adj.* half 1.3
  medio ambiente *m.* environment 3.1
  medio/a hermano/a *m., f.* half-brother/half-sister 1.3
  mediodía *m.* noon 1.1
  medios de comunicación *m., pl.* means of communication; media 3.6
  y media thirty minutes past the hour (time) 1.1
mejor *adj.* better 2.2
  el/la mejor *m., f.* the best 2.2
mejorar *v.* to improve 3.1
melocotón *m.* peach 2.2
menor *adj.* younger 1.3
  el/la menor *m., f.* youngest 2.2
menos *adv.* less 2.4
  menos cuarto..., menos quince... quarter to... (*time*) 1.1
  menos de (+ *number*) fewer than 2.2
  menos... que less... than 2.2
mensaje *m.* **de texto** text message 2.5
mensaje electrónico *m.* e-mail message 1.4
mentira *f.* lie 1.4
menú *m.* menu 2.2
mercado *m.* market 1.6
  mercado al aire libre open-air market 1.6
merendar (e:ie) *v.* to snack 2.2; to have an afternoon snack
merienda *f.* afternoon snack 3.3
mes *m.* month 1.5
mesa *f.* table 1.2
mesita *f.* end table 2.6
  mesita de noche night stand 2.6
meterse en problemas *v.* to get into trouble 3.1
metro *m.* subway 1.5
mexicano/a *adj.* Mexican 1.3
mí *pron., obj. of prep.* me 2.3
mi(s) *poss. adj.* my 1.3
microonda *f.* microwave 2.6
  horno de microondas *m.* microwave oven 2.6
miedo *m.* fear
miel *f.* honey 2.4
mientras *conj.* while 2.4
miércoles *m., sing.* Wednesday 1.2
mil *m.* one thousand 1.2
  mil millones billion
milla *f.* mile
millón *m.* million 1.2
millones (de) *m.* millions (of)
mineral *m.* mineral 3.3
minuto *m.* minute
mío(s)/a(s) *poss.* my; (of) mine 2.5
mirar *v.* to look (at); to watch 1.2
  mirar (la) televisión to watch television 1.2
mismo/a *adj.* same 1.3
mochila *f.* backpack 1.2
moda *f.* fashion 1.6
moderno/a *adj.* modern 3.5
molestar *v.* to bother; to annoy 2.1
monitor *m.* (computer) monitor 2.5
  monitor(a) *m., f.* trainer
mono *m.* monkey 3.1
montaña *f.* mountain 1.4
montar *v.* **a caballo** to ride a horse 1.5
montón: un montón de a lot of 1.4
monumento *m.* monument 1.4
morado/a *adj.* purple 1.6
moreno/a *adj.* brunet(te) 1.3
morir (o:ue) *v.* to die 2.2
mostrar (o:ue) *v.* to show 1.4
moto(cicleta) *f.* motorcycle 1.5
motor *m.* motor
muchacho/a *m., f.* boy/girl 1.3
mucho/a *adj.*, a lot of; much; many 1.3
  (Muchas) gracias. Thank you (very much); Thanks (a lot). 1.1
  muchas veces *adv.* a lot; many times 2.4
  Mucho gusto. Pleased to meet you. 1.1
mudarse *v.* to move (from one house to another) 2.6
muebles *m., pl.* furniture 2.6
muerte *f.* death 2.3
muerto/a *p.p.* died 3.2
mujer *f.* woman 1.1
  mujer de negocios *f.* business woman 3.4
  mujer policía *f.* female police officer
multa *f.* fine
mundial *adj. m., f.* worldwide
mundo *m.* world 2.2
muro *m.* wall 3.3
músculo *m.* muscle 3.3
museo *m.* museum 1.4
música *f.* music 1.2, 3.5
musical *adj. m., f.* musical 3.5
músico/a *m., f.* musician 3.5
muy *adv.* very 1.1
  (Muy) bien, gracias. (Very) well, thanks. 1.1

N

nacer *v.* to be born 2.3
nacimiento *m.* birth 2.3
nacional *adj. m., f.* national 3.6
nacionalidad *f.* nationality 1.1
nada nothing 1.1; not anything 2.1
  nada mal not bad at all 1.5
nadar *v.* to swim 1.4
nadie *pron.* no one, nobody, not anyone 2.1
naranja *f.* orange 2.2
nariz *f.* nose 2.4
natación *f.* swimming 1.4
natural *adj. m., f.* natural 3.1
naturaleza *f.* nature 3.1
navegador *m.* **GPS** GPS 2.5
navegar (en Internet) *v.* to surf (the Internet) 2.5
Navidad *f.* Christmas 2.3
necesario/a *adj.* necessary 2.6
necesitar (+ *inf.*) *v.* to need 1.2
negar (e:ie) *v.* to deny 3.1
  no negar (e:ie) *v.* not to deny 3.1
negocios *m., pl.* business; commerce 3.4
negro/a *adj.* black 1.6
nervioso/a *adj.* nervous 1.5
nevar (e:ie) *v.* to snow 1.5
  Nieva. It's snowing. 1.5
ni...ni neither... nor 2.1
niebla *f.* fog

nieto/a *m., f.* grandson/ granddaughter **1.3**
nieve *f.* snow
ningún, ninguno/a(s) *adj.* no; none; not any **2.1**
niñez *f.* childhood **2.3**
niño/a *m., f.* child **1.3**
no no; not **1.1**
¿no? right? **1.1**
no cabe duda de there is no doubt **3.1**
no es seguro it's not certain **3.1**
no es verdad it's not true **3.1**
No está nada mal. It's not bad at all. **1.5**
no estar de acuerdo to disagree
No estoy seguro. I'm not sure.
no hay there is not; there are not **1.1**
No hay de qué. You're welcome. **1.1**
no hay duda de there is no doubt **3.1**
¡No me diga(s)! You don't say!
No me gustan nada. I don't like them at all. **1.2**
no muy bien not very well **1.1**
No quiero. I don't want to. **1.4**
No sé. I don't know.
No te preocupes. (*fam.*) Don't worry. **2.1**
no tener razón to be wrong **1.3**
noche *f.* night **1.1**
nombre *m.* name **1.1**
norte *m.* north **3.2**
norteamericano/a *adj.* (North) American **1.3**
nos *pl., d.o. pron.* us **1.5**; *pl., i.o. pron.* to/for us **1.6**
Nos vemos. See you. **1.1**
nosotros/as *sub. pron.* we **1.1**; *obj. pron.* us
noticia *f.* news **2.5**
noticias *f., pl.* news **3.6**
noticiero *m.* newscast **3.6**
novecientos/as nine hundred **1.2**
noveno/a *adj.* ninth **1.5**
noventa ninety **1.2**
noviembre *m.* November **1.5**
novio/a *m., f.* boyfriend/ girlfriend **1.3**
nube *f.* cloud **3.1**
nublado/a *adj.* cloudy **1.5**
Está (muy) nublado. It's very cloudy. **1.5**
nuclear *adj. m. f.* nuclear **3.1**
nuera *f.* daughter-in-law **1.3**
nuestro(s)/a(s) *poss. adj.* our **1.3**; our, (of) ours **2.5**
nueve nine **1.1**
nuevo/a *adj.* new **1.6**
número *m.* number **1.1**; (shoe) size **1.6**
nunca *adv.* never; not ever **2.1**
nutrición *f.* nutrition **3.3**
nutricionista *m., f.* nutritionist **3.3**

O

o or **2.1**
o... o; either... or **2.1**
obedecer *v.* to obey **3.6**
obra *f.* work (*of art, literature, music, etc.*) **3.5**
obra maestra *f.* masterpiece **3.5**
obtener *v.* to obtain; to get **3.4**
obvio/a *adj.* obvious **3.1**
océano *m.* ocean
ochenta eighty **1.2**
ocho eight **1.1**
ochocientos/as eight hundred **1.2**
octavo/a *adj.* eighth **1.5**
octubre *m.* October **1.5**
ocupación *f.* occupation **3.4**
ocupado/a *adj.* busy **1.5**
ocurrir *v.* to occur; to happen **3.6**
odiar *v.* to hate **2.3**
oeste *m.* west **3.2**
oferta *f.* offer
oficina *f.* office **2.6**
oficio *m.* trade **3.4**
ofrecer *v.* to offer **1.6**
oído *m.* (sense of) hearing; inner ear **2.4**
oído/a *p.p.* heard **3.2**
oír *v.* to hear **1.4**
ojalá (que) *interj.* I hope (that); I wish (that) **3.1**
ojo *m.* eye **2.4**
olvidar *v.* to forget **2.4**
once eleven **1.1**
ópera *f.* opera **3.5**
operación *f.* operation **2.4**
ordenado/a *adj.* orderly **1.5**
ordinal *adj.* ordinal (*number*)
oreja *f.* (outer) ear **2.4**
organizarse *v.* to organize oneself **2.6**
orquesta *f.* orchestra **3.5**
ortografía *f.* spelling
ortográfico/a *adj.* spelling
os *fam., pl. d.o. pron.* you **1.5**; *fam., pl. i.o. pron.* to/for you **1.6**
otoño *m.* autumn **1.5**
otro/a *adj.* other; another **1.6**
otra vez again

P

paciente *m., f.* patient **2.4**
padrastro *m.* stepfather **1.3**
padre *m.* father **1.3**
padres *m., pl.* parents **1.3**
pagar *v.* to pay **1.6**
pagar a plazos to pay in installments **3.2**
pagar al contado to pay in cash **3.2**
pagar en efectivo to pay in cash **3.2**
pagar la cuenta to pay the bill
página *f.* page **2.5**
página principal *f.* home page **2.5**
país *m.* country **1.1**
paisaje *m.* landscape **1.5**
pájaro *m.* bird **3.1**
palabra *f.* word **1.1**
paleta helada *f.* popsicle **1.4**
pálido/a *adj.* pale **3.2**
pan *m.* bread **2.2**
pan tostado *m.* toasted bread **2.2**
panadería *f.* bakery **3.2**
pantalla *f.* screen **2.5**
pantalla táctil *f.* touch screen
pantalones *m., pl.* pants **1.6**
pantalones cortos *m., pl.* shorts **1.6**
pantuflas *f.* slippers **2.1**
papa *f.* potato **2.2**
papas fritas *f., pl.* fried potatoes; French fries **2.2**
papá *m.* dad
papás *m., pl.* parents
papel *m.* paper **1.2**; role **3.5**
papelera *f.* wastebasket **1.2**
paquete *m.* package **3.2**
par *m.* pair **1.6**
par de zapatos pair of shoes **1.6**
para *prep.* for; in order to; by; used for; considering **2.5**
para que *conj.* so that **3.1**
parabrisas *m., sing.* windshield **2.5**
parar *v.* to stop **2.5**
parecer *v.* to seem **1.6**
pared *f.* wall **2.6**
pareja *f.* (married) couple; partner **2.3**
parientes *m., pl.* relatives **1.3**
parque *m.* park **1.4**
párrafo *m.* paragraph
parte: de parte de on behalf of **2.5**
partido *m.* game; match (*sports*) **1.4**
pasado/a *adj.* last; past **1.6**
pasado *p.p.* passed
pasaje *m.* ticket **1.5**
pasaje de ida y vuelta *m.* roundtrip ticket **1.5**
pasajero/a *m., f.* passenger **1.1**
pasaporte *m.* passport **1.5**
pasar *v.* to go through
pasar la aspiradora to vacuum **2.6**
pasar por la aduana to go through customs
pasar tiempo to spend time
pasarlo bien/mal to have a good/bad time **2.3**
pasatiempo *m.* pastime; hobby **1.4**
pasear *v.* to take a walk; to stroll **1.4**
pasear en bicicleta to ride a bicycle **1.4**
pasear por to walk around
pasillo *m.* hallway **2.6**

pasta *f.* **de dientes** toothpaste 2.1
pastel *m.* cake; pie 2.3
pastel de chocolate *m.* chocolate cake 2.3
pastel de cumpleaños *m.* birthday cake
pastelería *f.* pastry shop 3.2
pastilla *f.* pill; tablet 2.4
patata *f.* potato 2.2
patatas fritas *f., pl.* fried potatoes; French fries 2.2
patinar (en línea) *v.* to (inline) skate 1.4
patineta *f.* skateboard 1.4
patio *m.* patio; yard 2.6
pavo *m.* turkey 2.2
paz *f.* peace 3.6
pedir (e:i) *v.* to ask for; to request 1.4; to order (*food*) 2.2
pedir prestado *v.* to borrow 3.2
pedir un préstamo *v.* to apply for a loan 3.2
Todos me dijeron que te pidiera una disculpa de su parte. They all told me to ask you to excuse them/forgive them. 3.6
peinarse *v.* to comb one's hair 2.1
película *f.* movie 1.4
peligro *m.* danger 3.1
peligroso/a *adj.* dangerous 3.6
pelirrojo/a *adj.* red-haired 1.3
pelo *m.* hair 2.1
pelota *f.* ball 1.4
peluquería *f.* beauty salon 3.2
peluquero/a *m., f.* hairdresser 3.4
penicilina *f.* penicillin
pensar (e:ie) *v.* to think 1.4
pensar (+ *inf.*) *v.* to intend to; to plan to (*do something*) 1.4
pensar en *v.* to think about 1.4
pensión *f.* boardinghouse
peor *adj.* worse 2.2
el/la peor *adj.* the worst 2.2
pequeño/a *adj.* small 1.3
pera *f.* pear 2.2
perder (e:ie) *v.* to lose; to miss 1.4
perdido/a *adj.* lost 3.1, 3.2
Perdón. Pardon me.; Excuse me. 1.1
perezoso/a *adj.* lazy
perfecto/a *adj.* perfect 1.5
periódico *m.* newspaper 1.4
periodismo *m.* journalism 1.2
periodista *m., f.* journalist 1.3
permiso *m.* permission
pero *conj.* but 1.2
perro *m.* dog 3.1
persona *f.* person 1.3
personaje *m.* character 3.5
personaje principal *m.* main character 3.5
pesas *f. pl.* weights 3.3
pesca *f.* fishing
pescadería *f.* fish market 3.2
pescado *m.* fish (*cooked*) 2.2
pescar *v.* to fish 1.5
peso *m.* weight 3.3
pez *m., sing.* (**peces** *pl.*) fish (*live*) 3.1
pie *m.* foot 2.4
piedra *f.* stone 3.1
pierna *f.* leg 2.4
pimienta *f.* black pepper 2.2
pintar *v.* to paint 3.5
pintor(a) *m., f.* painter 3.4
pintura *f.* painting; picture 2.6, 3.5
piña *f.* pineapple
piscina *f.* swimming pool 1.4
piso *m.* floor (*of a building*) 1.5
pizarra *f.* blackboard 1.2
placer *m.* pleasure
planchar la ropa *v.* to iron the clothes 2.6
planes *m., pl.* plans
planta *f.* plant 3.1
planta baja *f.* ground floor 1.5
plástico *m.* plastic 3.1
plato *m.* dish (*in a meal*) 2.2; *m.* plate 2.6
plato principal *m.* main dish 2.2
playa *f.* beach 1.5
plaza *f.* city or town square 1.4
plazos *m., pl.* periods; time 3.2
pluma *f.* pen 1.2
plumero *m.* duster 2.6
población *f.* population 3.1
pobre *adj. m., f.* poor 1.6
pobrecito/a *adj.* poor thing 1.3
pobreza *f.* poverty
poco *adv.* little 1.5, 2.4
poder (o:ue) *v.* to be able to; can 1.4
¿Podría pedirte algo? Could I ask you something? 3.5
¿Puedo dejar un recado? May I leave a message? 2.5
poema *m.* poem 3.5
poesía *f.* poetry 3.5
poeta *m., f.* poet 3.5
policía *f.* police (force) 2.5
política *f.* politics 3.6
político/a *m., f.* politician 3.4; *adj.* political 3.6
pollo *m.* chicken 2.2
pollo asado *m.* roast chicken 2.2
poner *v.* to put; to place 1.4; to turn on (*electrical appliances*) 2.5
poner la mesa to set the table 2.6
poner una inyección to give an injection 2.4
ponerle el nombre to name someone/something 2.3
ponerse (+ *adj.*) *v.* to become (+ *adj.*) 2.1; to put on 2.1
por *prep.* in exchange for; for; by; in; through; around; along; during; because of; on account of; on behalf of; in search of; by way of; by means of 2.5
por aquí around here 2.5
por ejemplo for example 2.5
por eso that's why; therefore 2.5
por favor please 1.1
por fin finally 2.5
por la mañana in the morning 2.1
por la noche at night 2.1
por la tarde in the afternoon 2.1
por lo menos *adv.* at least 2.4
¿por qué? why? 1.2
Por supuesto. Of course.
por teléfono by phone; on the phone
por último finally 2.1
porque *conj.* because 1.2
portátil *adj.* portable 2.5
portero/a *m., f.* doorman/doorwoman 1.1
porvenir *m.* future 3.4
por el porvenir for/to the future 3.4
posesivo/a *adj.* possessive
posible *adj.* possible 3.1
es posible it's possible 3.1
no es posible it's not possible 3.1
postal *f.* postcard
postre *m.* dessert 2.3
practicar *v.* to practice 1.2
practicar deportes *m., pl.* to play sports 1.4
precio (fijo) *m.* (fixed; set) price 1.6
preferir (e:ie) *v.* to prefer 1.4
pregunta *f.* question
preguntar *v.* to ask (*a question*) 1.2
premio *m.* prize; award 3.5
prender *v.* to turn on 2.5
prensa *f.* press 3.6
preocupado/a (por) *adj.* worried (about) 1.5
preocuparse (por) *v.* to worry (about) 2.1
preparar *v.* to prepare 1.2
preposición *f.* preposition
presentación *f.* introduction
presentar *v.* to introduce; to present 3.5; to put on (*a performance*) 3.5
Le presento a... I would like to introduce you to (name). (*form.*) 1.1
Te presento a... I would like to introduce you to (name). (*fam.*) 1.1
presiones *f., pl.* pressures 3.3
prestado/a *adj.* borrowed
préstamo *m.* loan 3.2
prestar *v.* to lend; to loan 1.6
primavera *f.* spring 1.5
primer, primero/a *adj.* first 1.5
primero *adv.* first 1.2
primo/a *m., f.* cousin 1.3
principal *adj. m., f.* main 2.2

prisa *f.* haste
darse prisa *v.* to hurry; to rush 3.3
probable *adj. m., f.* probable 3.1
es probable it's probable 3.1
no es probable it's not probable 3.1
probar (o:ue) *v.* to taste; to try 2.2
probarse (o:ue) *v.* to try on 2.1
problema *m.* problem 1.1
profesión *f.* profession 1.3; 3.4
profesor(a) *m., f.* teacher 1.1, 1.2
programa *m.* program 1.1
programa de computación *m.* software 2.5
programa de entrevistas *m.* talk show 3.5
programa de realidad *m.* reality show 3.5
programador(a) *m., f.* computer programmer 1.3
prohibir *v.* to prohibit 2.4; to forbid
pronombre *m.* pronoun
pronto *adv.* soon 2.4
propina *f.* tip 2.2
propio/a *adj.* own
proteger *v.* to protect 3.1
proteína *f.* protein 3.3
próximo/a *adj.* next 1.3, 3.4
proyecto *m.* project 2.5
prueba *f.* test; quiz 1.2
psicología *f.* psychology 1.2
psicólogo/a *m., f.* psychologist 3.4
publicar *v.* to publish 3.5
público *m.* audience 3.5
pueblo *m.* town
puerta *f.* door 1.2
puertorriqueño/a *adj.* Puerto Rican 1.3
pues *conj.* well
puesto *m.* position; job 3.4
puesto/a *p.p.* put 3.2
puro/a *adj.* pure 3.1

Q

que *pron.* that; which; who 2.6
¿En qué...? In which...?
¡Qué...! How...!
¡Qué dolor! What pain!
¡Qué ropa más bonita! What pretty clothes! 1.6
¡Qué sorpresa! What a surprise!
¿qué? what? 1.1, 1.2
¿Qué día es hoy? What day is it? 1.2
¿Qué hay de nuevo? What's new? 1.1
¿Qué hora es? What time is it? 1.1
¿Qué les parece? What do you (*pl.*) think?
¿Qué onda? What's up? 3.2
¿Qué pasa? What's happening? What's going on? 1.1
¿Qué pasó? What happened?
¿Qué precio tiene? What is the price?
¿Qué tal...? How are you?; How is it going? 1.1
¿Qué talla lleva/usa? What size do you wear? 1.6
¿Qué tiempo hace? How's the weather? 1.5
quedar *v.* to be left over; to fit (*clothing*) 2.1; to be located 3.2
quedarse *v.* to stay; to remain 2.1
quehaceres domésticos *m., pl.* household chores 2.6
quemar (un CD/DVD) *v.* to burn (a CD/DVD)
querer (e:ie) *v.* to want; to love 1.4
queso *m.* cheese 2.2
quien(es) *pron.* who; whom; that 2.6
¿quién(es)? who?; whom? 1.1, 1.2
¿Quién es...? Who is...? 1.1
¿Quién habla? Who is speaking/calling? (*telephone*) 2.5
química *f.* chemistry 1.2
quince fifteen 1.1
menos quince quarter to (time) 1.1
y quince quarter after (time) 1.1
quinceañera *f.* young woman celebrating her fifteenth birthday 2.3
quinientos/as five hundred 1.2
quinto/a *adj.* fifth 1.5
quisiera *v.* I would like
quitar el polvo *v.* to dust 2.6
quitar la mesa *v.* to clear the table 2.6
quitarse *v.* to take off 2.1
quizás *adv.* maybe 1.5

R

racismo *m.* racism 3.6
radio *f.* radio (*medium*) 1.2; *m.* radio (set) 2.5
radiografía *f.* X-ray 2.4
rápido *adv.* quickly 2.4
ratón *m.* mouse 2.5
ratos libres *m., pl.* spare (free) time 1.4
raya *f.* stripe
razón *f.* reason
rebaja *f.* sale 1.6
receta *f.* prescription 2.4
recetar *v.* to prescribe 2.4
recibir *v.* to receive 1.3
reciclaje *m.* recycling 3.1
reciclar *v.* to recycle 3.1
recién casado/a *m., f.* newlywed 2.3
recoger *v.* to pick up 3.1
recomendar (e:ie) *v.* to recommend 2.2, 2.6
recordar (o:ue) *v.* to remember 1.4
recorrer *v.* to tour an area
recorrido *m.* tour 3.1
recuperar *v.* to recover 2.5
recurso *m.* resource 3.1
recurso natural *m.* natural resource 3.1
red *f.* network; Web 2.5
reducir *v.* to reduce 3.1
refresco *m.* soft drink 2.2
refrigerador *m.* refrigerator 2.6
regalar *v.* to give (a gift) 2.3
regalo *m.* gift 1.6
regatear *v.* to bargain 1.6
región *f.* region; area
regresar *v.* to return 1.2
regular *adv.* so-so; OK 1.1
reído *p.p.* laughed 3.2
reírse (e:i) *v.* to laugh 2.3
relaciones *f., pl.* relationships
relajarse *v.* to relax 2.3
reloj *m.* clock; watch 1.2
renovable *adj.* renewable 3.1
renunciar (a) *v.* to resign (from) 3.4
repetir (e:i) *v.* to repeat 1.4
reportaje *m.* report 3.6
reportero/a *m., f.* reporter 3.4
representante *m., f.* representative 3.6
reproductor de CD *m.* CD player 2.5
reproductor de DVD *m.* DVD player 2.5
reproductor de MP3 *m.* MP3 player 2.5
resfriado *m.* cold (*illness*) 2.4
residencia estudiantil *f.* dormitory 1.2
resolver (o:ue) *v.* to resolve; to solve 3.1
respirar *v.* to breathe 3.1
responsable *adj.* responsible 2.2
respuesta *f.* answer
restaurante *m.* restaurant 1.4
resuelto/a *p.p.* resolved 3.2
reunión *f.* meeting 3.4
revisar *v.* to check 2.5
revisar el aceite *v.* to check the oil 2.5
revista *f.* magazine 1.4
rico/a *adj.* rich 1.6; *adj.* tasty; delicious 2.2
ridículo/a *adj.* ridiculous 3.1
río *m.* river 3.1
rodilla *f.* knee 2.4
rogar (o:ue) *v.* to beg; to plead 2.6
rojo/a *adj.* red 1.6
romántico/a *adj.* romantic 3.5
romper *v.* to break 2.4
romperse la pierna *v.* to break one's leg 2.4
romper (con) *v.* to break up (with) 2.3
ropa *f.* clothing; clothes 1.6

ropa interior *f.* underwear 1.6
rosado/a *adj.* pink 1.6
roto/a *adj.* broken 3.2
rubio/a *adj.* blond(e) 1.3
ruso/a *adj.* Russian 1.3
rutina *f.* routine 2.1
rutina diaria *f.* daily routine 2.1

S

sábado *m.* Saturday 1.2
saber *v.* to know; to know how 1.6
saber a to taste like 2.2
sabrosísimo/a *adj.* extremely delicious 2.2
sabroso/a *adj.* tasty; delicious 2.2
sacar *v.* to take out
sacar buenas notas to get good grades 1.2
sacar fotos to take photos 1.5
sacar la basura to take out the trash 2.6
sacar(se) un diente to have a tooth removed 2.4
sacudir *v.* to dust 2.6
sacudir los muebles to dust the furniture 2.6
sal *f.* salt 2.2
sala *f.* living room 2.6; room
sala de emergencia(s) emergency room 2.4
salario *m.* salary 3.4
salchicha *f.* sausage 2.2
salida *f.* departure; exit 1.5
salir *v.* to leave 1.4; to go out
salir con to go out with; to date 1.4, 2.3
salir de to leave from 1.4
salir para to leave for (*a place*) 1.4
salmón *m.* salmon 2.2
salón de belleza *m.* beauty salon 3.2
salud *f.* health 2.4
saludable *adj.* healthy 2.4
saludar(se) *v.* to greet (each other) 2.5
saludo *m.* greeting 1.1
saludos a... greetings to... 1.1
sandalia *f.* sandal 1.6
sandía *f.* watermelon
sándwich *m.* sandwich 2.2
sano/a *adj.* healthy 2.4
se *ref. pron.* himself, herself, itself, *form.* yourself, themselves, yourselves 2.1
se *impersonal* one 2.4
Se hizo... He/she/it became...
secadora *f.* clothes dryer 2.6
secarse *v.* to dry (oneself) 2.1
sección de (no) fumar *f.* (non) smoking section 2.2
secretario/a *m., f.* secretary 3.4
secuencia *f.* sequence
sed *f.* thirst
seda *f.* silk 1.6
sedentario/a *adj.* sedentary; related to sitting 3.3
seguir (e:i) *v.* to follow; to continue 1.4
según according to
segundo/a *adj.* second 1.5
seguro/a *adj.* sure; safe; confident 1.5
seis six 1.1
seiscientos/as six hundred 1.2
sello *m.* stamp 3.2
selva *f.* jungle 3.1
semáforo *m.* traffic light 3.2
semana *f.* week 1.2
fin *m.* **de semana** weekend 1.4
semana *f.* **pasada** last week 1.6
semestre *m.* semester 1.2
sendero *m.* trail; path 3.1
sentarse (e:ie) *v.* to sit down 2.1
sentir (e:ie) *v.* to be sorry; to regret 3.1
sentirse (e:ie) *v.* to feel 2.1
señor (Sr.); don *m.* Mr.; sir 1.1
señora (Sra.); doña *f.* Mrs.; ma'am 1.1
señorita (Srta.) *f.* Miss 1.1
separado/a *adj.* separated 2.3
separarse (de) *v.* to separate (from) 2.3
septiembre *m.* September 1.5
séptimo/a *adj.* seventh 1.5
ser *v.* to be 1.1
ser aficionado/a (a) to be a fan (of)
ser alérgico/a (a) to be allergic (to) 2.4
ser gratis to be free of charge 3.2
serio/a *adj.* serious
servicio *m.* service 3.3
servilleta *f.* napkin 2.6
servir (e:i) *v.* to serve 2.2; to help 1.5
sesenta sixty 1.2
setecientos/as seven hundred 1.2
setenta seventy 1.2
sexismo *m.* sexism 3.6
sexto/a *adj.* sixth 1.5
sí *adv.* yes 1.1
si *conj.* if 1.4
SIDA *m.* AIDS 3.6
siempre *adv.* always 2.1
siete seven 1.1**silla** *f.* seat 1.2
sillón *m.* armchair 2.6
similar *adj. m., f.* similar
simpático/a *adj.* nice; likeable 1.3
sin *prep.* without 3.1
sin duda without a doubt
sin embargo however
sin que *conj.* without 3.1
sino but (rather) 2.1
síntoma *m.* symptom 2.4
sitio *m.* place 1.3
sitio *m.* **web** website 2.5
situado/a *p.p.* located
sobre *m.* envelope 3.2; *prep.* on; over 1.2
sobre todo above all 3.1
(sobre)población *f.* (over)population 3.1
sobrino/a *m., f.* nephew/niece 1.3
sociología *f.* sociology 1.2
sofá *m.* couch; sofa 2.6
sol *m.* sun 3.1
solar *adj. m., f.* solar 3.1
soldado *m., f.* soldier 3.6
soleado/a *adj.* sunny
solicitar *v.* to apply (*for a job*) 3.4
solicitud (de trabajo) *f.* (job) application 3.4
sólo *adv.* only 1.6
solo/a *adj.* alone
soltero/a *adj.* single 2.3
solución *f.* solution 3.1
sombrero *m.* hat 1.6
Son las dos. It's two o'clock. 1.1
sonar (o:ue) *v.* to ring 2.5
sonreído *p.p.* smiled 3.2
sonreír (e:i) *v.* to smile 2.3
sopa *f.* soup 2.2
sorprender *v.* to surprise 2.3
sorpresa *f.* surprise 2.3
sótano *m.* basement; cellar 2.6
soy I am 1.1
Soy de... I'm from... 1.1
su(s) *poss. adj.* his; her; its; *form.* your; their 1.3
subir(se) a *v.* to get on/into (*a vehicle*) 2.5
sucio/a *adj.* dirty 1.5
sudar *v.* to sweat 3.3
suegro/a *m., f.* father-in-law/ mother-in-law 1.3
sueldo *m.* salary 3.4
suelo *m.* floor 2.6
sueño *m.* sleep
suerte *f.* luck
suéter *m.* sweater 1.6
sufrir *v.* to suffer 2.4
sufrir muchas presiones to be under a lot of pressure 3.3
sufrir una enfermedad to suffer an illness 2.4
sugerir (e:ie) *v.* to suggest 2.6
supermercado *m.* supermarket 3.2
suponer *v.* to suppose 1.4
sur *m.* south 3.2
sustantivo *m.* noun
suyo(s)/a(s) *poss.* (of) his/her; (of) hers; its; *form.* your, (of) yours, (of) theirs, their 2.5

T

tabla de (wind)surf *f.* surf board/sailboard 1.5
tal vez *adv.* maybe 1.5
talentoso/a *adj.* talented 3.5
talla *f.* size 1.6
talla grande *f.* large

taller *m.* **mecánico** garage; mechanic's repair shop **2.5**
también *adv.* also; too **1.2; 2.1**
tampoco *adv.* neither; not either **2.1**
tan *adv.* so **1.5**
tan... como as... as **2.2**
tan pronto como *conj.* as soon as **3.1**
tanque *m.* tank **2.5**
tanto *adv.* so much
tanto... como as much... as **2.2**
tantos/as... como as many... as **2.2**
tarde *adv.* late **2.1**; *f.* afternoon; evening; P.M. **1.1**
tarea *f.* homework **1.2**
tarjeta *f.* (post) card
tarjeta de crédito *f.* credit card **1.6**
tarjeta postal *f.* postcard
taxi *m.* taxi **1.5**
taza *f.* cup **2.6**
te *sing., fam., d.o. pron.* you **1.5**; *sing., fam., i.o. pron.* to/for you **1.6**
Te presento a... *fam.* I would like to introduce you to (name). **1.1**
¿Te gustaría? Would you like to?
¿Te gusta(n)...? Do you like...? **1.2**
té *m.* tea **2.2**
té helado *m.* iced tea **2.2**
teatro *m.* theater **3.5**
teclado *m.* keyboard **2.5**
técnico/a *m., f.* technician **3.4**
tejido *m.* weaving **3.5**
teleadicto/a *m., f.* couch potato **3.3**
(teléfono) celular *m.* (cell) phone **2.5**
telenovela *f.* soap opera **3.5**
teletrabajo *m.* telecommuting **3.4**
televisión *f.* television **1.2**
televisión por cable *f.* cable television
televisor *m.* television set **2.5**
temer *v.* to fear; to be afraid **3.1**
temperatura *f.* temperature **2.4**
temporada *f.* period of time **1.5**
temprano *adv.* early **2.1**
tenedor *m.* fork **2.6**
tener *v.* to have **1.3**
tener... años to be... years old **1.3**
tener (mucho) calor to be (very) hot **1.3**
tener (mucho) cuidado to be (very) careful **1.3**
tener dolor to have pain **2.4**
tener éxito to be successful **3.4**
tener fiebre to have a fever **2.4**
tener (mucho) frío to be (very) cold **1.3**
tener ganas de (+ *inf.*) to feel like (*doing something*) **1.3**
tener (mucha) hambre *f.* to be (very) hungry **1.3**
tener (mucho) miedo (de) to be (very) afraid (of); to be (very) scared (of) **1.3**
tener miedo (de) que to be afraid that
tener planes *m., pl.* to have plans
tener (mucha) prisa to be in a (big) hurry **1.3**
tener que (+ *inf.*) *v.* to have to (*do something*) **1.3**
tener razón *f.* to be right **1.3**
tener (mucha) sed *f.* to be (very) thirsty **1.3**
tener (mucho) sueño to be (very) sleepy **1.3**
tener (mucha) suerte to be (very) lucky **1.3**
tener tiempo to have time **3.2**
tener una cita to have a date; to have an appointment **2.3**
tenis *m.* tennis **1.4**
tensión *f.* tension **3.3**
tercer, tercero/a *adj.* third **1.5**
terco/a *adj.* stubborn **2.4**
terminar *v.* to end; to finish **1.2**
terminar de (+ *inf.*) *v.* to finish (*doing something*)
terremoto *m.* earthquake **3.6**
terrible *adj. m., f.* terrible **3.1**
ti *obj. of prep., fam.* you **2.3**
tiempo *m.* time **3.2**; weather **1.5**
tiempo libre free time
tienda *f.* store **1.6**
tierra *f.* land; soil **3.1**
tío/a *m., f.* uncle/aunt **1.3**
tíos *m., pl.* aunts and uncles **1.3**
título *m.* title **3.4**
tiza *f.* chalk **1.2**
toalla *f.* towel **2.1**
tobillo *m.* ankle **2.4**
tocar *v.* to play (*a musical instrument*) **3.5**; to touch **3.5**
todavía *adv.* yet; still **1.3, 1.5**
todo *m.* everything **1.5**
todo(s)/a(s) *adj.* all
todos *m., pl.* all of us; *m., pl.* everybody; everyone
todos los días *adv.* every day **2.4**
tomar *v.* to take; to drink **1.2**
tomar clases *f., pl.* to take classes **1.2**
tomar el sol to sunbathe **1.4**
tomar en cuenta to take into account
tomar fotos *f., pl.* to take photos **1.5**
tomar la temperatura to take someone's temperature **2.4**
tomar una decisión to make a decision **3.3**
tomate *m.* tomato **2.2**
tonto/a *adj.* foolish **1.3**
torcerse (o:ue) (el tobillo) *v.* to sprain (one's ankle) **2.4**
tormenta *f.* storm **3.6**
tornado *m.* tornado **3.6**
tortuga (marina) *f.* (sea) turtle **3.1**
tos *f., sing.* cough **2.4**
toser *v.* to cough **2.4**
tostado/a *adj.* toasted **2.2**
tostadora *f.* toaster **2.6**
trabajador(a) *adj.* hard-working **1.3**
trabajar *v.* to work **1.2**
trabajo *m.* job; work **3.4**
traducir *v.* to translate **1.6**
traer *v.* to bring **1.4**
tráfico *m.* traffic **2.5**
tragedia *f.* tragedy **3.5**
traído/a *p.p.* brought **3.2**
traje *m.* suit **1.6**
traje de baño *m.* bathing suit **1.6**
trajinera *f.* type of barge **1.3**
tranquilo/a *adj.* calm; quiet **3.3**
Tranquilo/a. Relax. **2.1**
Tranquilo/a, cariño. Relax, sweetie. **2.5**
transmitir *v.* to broadcast **3.6**
tratar de (+ *inf.*) *v.* to try (*to do something*) **3.3**
trece thirteen **1.1**
treinta thirty **1.1, 1.2**
y treinta thirty minutes past the hour (time) **1.1**
tren *m.* train **1.5**
tres three **1.1**
trescientos/as three hundred **1.2**
trimestre *m.* trimester; quarter **1.2**
triste *adj.* sad **1.5**
tú *fam. sub. pron.* you **1.1**
tu(s) *fam. poss. adj.* your **1.3**
turismo *m.* tourism
turista *m., f.* tourist **1.1**
turístico/a *adj.* touristic
tuyo(s)/a(s) *fam. poss. pron.* your; (of) yours **2.5**

U

Ud. *form. sing.* you **1.1**
Uds. *pl.* you **1.1**
último/a *adj.* last **2.1**
la última vez the last time **2.1**
un, uno/a *indef. art.* a; one **1.1**
a la una at one o'clock **1.1**
una vez once **1.6**
una vez más one more time
uno one **1.1**
único/a *adj.* only **1.3**; unique **2.3**
universidad *f.* university; college **1.2**
unos/as *m., f., pl. indef. art.* some **1.1**
urgente *adj.* urgent **2.6**
usar *v.* to wear; to use **1.6**

usted (Ud.) *form. sing.* you 1.1
ustedes (Uds.) *pl.* you 1.1
útil *adj.* useful
uva *f.* grape 2.2

V

vaca *f.* cow 3.1
vacaciones *f. pl.* vacation 1.5
valle *m.* valley 3.1
vamos let's go 1.4
vaquero *m.* cowboy 3.5
  de vaqueros *m., pl.* western (genre) 3.5
varios/as *adj. m. f., pl.* various; several
vaso *m.* glass 2.6
veces *f., pl.* times 1.6
vecino/a *m., f.* neighbor 2.6
veinte twenty 1.1
veinticinco twenty-five 1.1
veinticuatro twenty-four 1.1
veintidós twenty-two 1.1
veintinueve twenty-nine 1.1
veintiocho twenty-eight 1.1
veintiséis twenty-six 1.1
veintisiete twenty-seven 1.1
veintitrés twenty-three 1.1
veintiún, veintiuno/a *adj.* twenty-one 1.1
veintiuno twenty-one 1.1
vejez *f.* old age 2.3
velocidad *f.* speed 2.5
  velocidad máxima *f.* speed limit 2.5
vencer *v.* to expire 3.2
vendedor(a) *m., f.* salesperson 1.6
vender *v.* to sell 1.6
venir *v.* to come 1.3
ventana *f.* window 1.2
ver *v.* to see 1.4
  a ver *v.* let's see
  ver películas *f., pl.* to see movies 1.4
verano *m.* summer 1.5
verbo *m.* verb
verdad *f.* truth 1.4
  (no) es verdad it's (not) true 3.1
  ¿verdad? right? 1.1
verde *adj., m. f.* green 1.6
verduras *pl., f.* vegetables 2.2
vestido *m.* dress 1.6
vestirse (e:i) *v.* to get dressed 2.1
vez *f.* time 1.6
viajar *v.* to travel 1.2
viaje *m.* trip 1.5
viajero/a *m., f.* traveler 1.5
vida *f.* life 2.3
video *m.* video 1.1
videoconferencia *f.* videoconference 3.4
videojuego *m.* video game 1.4
vidrio *m.* glass 3.1
viejo/a *adj.* old 1.3
viento *m.* wind
viernes *m., sing.* Friday 1.2
vinagre *m.* vinegar 2.2
violencia *f.* violence 3.6
visitar *v.* to visit 1.4
  visitar monumentos *m., pl.* to visit monuments 1.4
visto/a *p.p.* seen 3.2
vitamina *f.* vitamin 3.3
viudo/a *adj.* widower/widow 2.3
vivienda *f.* housing 2.6
vivir *v.* to live 1.3
vivo/a *adj.* clever; living
volante *m.* steering wheel 2.5
volcán *m.* volcano 3.1
vóleibol *m.* volleyball 1.4
volver (o:ue) *v.* to return 1.4
volver a ver(te, lo, la) *v.* to see (you, him, her) again
vos *pron.* you
vosotros/as *fam., pl.* you 1.1
votar *v.* to vote 3.6
vuelta *f.* return trip
vuelto/a *p.p.* returned 3.2
vuestro(s)/a(s) *poss. adj.* your 1.3; your, (of) yours *fam., pl.* 2.5

Y

y *conj.* and 1.1
  y cuarto quarter after (time) 1.1
  y media half-past (time) 1.1
  y quince quarter after (time) 1.1
  y treinta thirty (minutes past the hour) 1.1
  ¿Y tú? *fam.* And you? 1.1
  ¿Y usted? *form.* And you? 1.1
ya *adv.* already 1.6
yerno *m.* son-in-law 1.3
yo *sub. pron.* I 1.1
yogur *m.* yogurt 2.2

Z

zanahoria *f.* carrot 2.2
zapatería *f.* shoe store 3.2
zapatos de tenis *m., pl.* tennis shoes, sneakers 1.6

English–Spanish

A

a **un/a** *m., f., sing.; indef. art.* 1.1
@ (*symbol*) **arroba** *f.* 2.5
a.m. **de la mañana** *f.* 1.1
able: be able to **poder (o:ue)** *v.* 1.4
aboard **a bordo**
above all **sobre todo** 3.1
accident **accidente** *m.* 2.4
accompany **acompañar** *v.* 3.2
account **cuenta** *f.* 3.2
on account of **por** *prep.* 2.5
accountant **contador(a)** *m., f.* 3.4
accounting **contabilidad** *f.* 1.2
ache **dolor** *m.* 2.4
acquainted: be acquainted with **conocer** *v.* 1.6
action (genre) **de acción** *f.* 3.5
active **activo/a** *adj.* 3.3
actor **actor** *m.*, **actriz** *f.* 3.4
additional **adicional** *adj.*
address **dirección** *f.* 3.2
adjective **adjetivo** *m.*
adolescence **adolescencia** *f.* 2.3
adventure (genre) **de aventuras** *f.* 3.5
advertise **anunciar** *v.* 3.6
advertisement **anuncio** *m.* 3.4
advice **consejo** *m.*
give advice **dar consejos** 1.6
advise **aconsejar** *v.* 2.6
advisor **consejero/a** *m., f.* 3.4
aerobic **aeróbico/a** *adj.* 3.3
aerobics class **clase de ejercicios aeróbicos** 3.3
to do aerobics **hacer ejercicios aeróbicos** 3.3
affected **afectado/a** *adj.* 3.1
be affected (by) **estar** *v.* **afectado/a (por)** 3.1
affirmative **afirmativo/a** *adj.*
afraid: be (very) afraid (of) **tener (mucho) miedo (de)** 1.3
be afraid that **tener miedo (de) que**
after **después de** *prep.* 2.1; **después de que** *conj.* 3.1
afternoon **tarde** *f.* 1.1
afterward **después** *adv.* 2.1
again **otra vez**
age **edad** *f.* 2.3
agree **concordar** *v.*
agree **estar** *v.* **de acuerdo** 3.5
I agree. **Estoy de acuerdo.** 3.5
I don't agree. **No estoy de acuerdo.** 3.5
agreement **acuerdo** *m.*
AIDS **SIDA** *m.* 3.6
air **aire** *m.* 3.1
air pollution **contaminación del aire** 3.1
airplane **avión** *m.* 1.5
airport **aeropuerto** *m.* 1.5
alarm clock **despertador** *m.* 2.1
all **todo(s)/a(s)** *adj.*
all of us **todos**
allergic **alérgico/a** *adj.* 2.4
be allergic (to) **ser alérgico/a (a)** 2.4
alleviate **aliviar** *v.*
almost **casi** *adv.* 2.4
alone **solo/a** *adj.*
along **por** *prep.* 2.5
already **ya** *adv.* 1.6
also **también** *adv.* 1.2; 2.1
altar **altar** *m.* 2.3
aluminum **aluminio** *m.* 3.1
(made) of aluminum **de aluminio** 3.1
always **siempre** *adv.* 2.1
American (*North*) **norteamericano/a** *adj.* 1.3
among **entre** *prep.* 1.2
amusement **diversión** *f.*
and **y** 1.1, **e** (*before words beginning with* **i** *or* **hi**)
And you? **¿Y tú?** *fam.* 1.1; **¿Y usted?** *form.* 1.1
angel **ángel** *m.* 2.3
angry **enojado/a** *adj.* 1.5
get angry (with) **enojarse** *v.* **(con)** 2.1
animal **animal** *m.* 3.1
ankle **tobillo** *m.* 2.4
anniversary **aniversario** *m.* 2.3
(wedding) anniversary **aniversario** *m.* **(de bodas)** 2.3
announce **anunciar** *v.* 3.6
announcer (*TV/radio*) **locutor(a)** *m., f.* 3.6
annoy **molestar** *v.* 2.1
another **otro/a** *adj.* 1.6
answer **contestar** *v.* 1.2; **respuesta** *f.*
answering machine **contestadora** *f.*
antibiotic **antibiótico** *m.* 2.4
any **algún, alguno/a(s)** *adj.* 2.1
anyone **alguien** *pron.* 2.1
anything **algo** *pron.* 2.1
apartment **apartamento** *m.* 2.6
apartment building **edificio de apartamentos** 2.6
app **aplicación** *f.* 2.5
appear **parecer** *v.*
appetizers **entremeses** *m., pl.* 2.2
applaud **aplaudir** *v.* 3.5
apple **manzana** *f.* 2.2
appliance (electric) **electrodoméstico** *m.* 2.6
applicant **aspirante** *m., f.* 3.4
application **solicitud** *f.* 3.4
job application **solicitud de trabajo** 3.4
apply (*for a job*) **solicitar** *v.* 3.4
apply for a loan **pedir (e:i)** *v.* **un préstamo** 3.2
appointment **cita** *f.* 2.3
have an appointment **tener** *v.* **una cita** 2.3
appreciate **apreciar** *v.* 3.5
April **abril** *m.* 1.5
archeologist **arqueólogo/a** *m., f.* 3.4
archeology **arqueología** *f.* 1.2
architect **arquitecto/a** *m., f.* 3.4
area **región** *f.*
Argentine **argentino/a** *adj.* 1.3
arm **brazo** *m.* 2.4
armchair **sillón** *m.* 2.6
army **ejército** *m.* 3.6
around **por** *prep.* 2.5
around here **por aquí** 2.5
arrange **arreglar** *v.* 2.5
arrival **llegada** *f.* 1.5
arrive **llegar** *v.* 1.2
art **arte** *m.* 1.2
(fine) arts **bellas artes** *f., pl.* 3.5
article **artículo** *m.* 3.6
artist **artista** *m., f.* 1.3
artistic **artístico/a** *adj.* 3.5
arts **artes** *f., pl.* 3.5
as **como** 2.2
as a child **de niño/a** 2.4
as... as **tan... como** 2.2
as many... as **tantos/as... como** 2.2
as much... as **tanto... como** 2.2
as soon as **en cuanto** *conj.* 3.1; **tan pronto como** *conj.* 3.1
ask (*a question*) **preguntar** *v.* 1.2
ask for **pedir (e:i)** *v.* 1.4
asparagus **espárragos** *m., pl.* 2.2
aspirin **aspirina** *f.* 2.4
at **a** *prep.* 1.1; **en** *prep.* 1.2
at + *time* **a la(s)** + *time* 1.1
at home **en casa**
at least **por lo menos** 2.4
at night **por la noche** 2.1
At what time...? **¿A qué hora...?** 1.1
At your service. **A sus órdenes.**
ATM **cajero automático** *m.* 3.2
attempt **intento** *m.* 2.5
attend **asistir (a)** *v.* 1.3
attic **altillo** *m.* 2.6
audience **público** *m.* 3.5
August **agosto** *m.* 1.5
aunt **tía** *f.* 1.3
aunts and uncles **tíos** *m., pl.* 1.3
automobile **automóvil** *m.* 1.5; **carro** *m.*; **coche** *m.* 2.5
autumn **otoño** *m.* 1.5
avenue **avenida** *f.*
avoid **evitar** *v.* 3.1
award **premio** *m.* 3.5

B

backpack **mochila** *f.* 1.2
bad **mal, malo/a** *adj.* 1.3
It's bad that... **Es malo que...** 2.6
It's not bad at all. **No está nada mal.** 1.5
bag **bolsa** *f.* 1.6
bakery **panadería** *f.* 3.2
balanced **equilibrado/a** *adj.* 3.3
to eat a balanced diet **comer una dieta equilibrada** 3.3
balcony **balcón** *m.* 2.6
ball **pelota** *f.* 1.4
banana **banana** *f.* 2.2

band **banda** *f.* 3.5
bank **banco** *m.* 3.2
bargain **ganga** *f.* 1.6; **regatear** *v.* 1.6
baseball (*game*) **béisbol** *m.* 1.4
basement **sótano** *m.* 2.6
basketball (*game*) **baloncesto** *m.* 1.4
bathe **bañarse** *v.* 2.1
bathing suit **traje** *m.* **de baño** 1.6
bathroom **baño** *m.* 2.1; **cuarto de baño** *m.* 2.1
be **ser** *v.* 1.1; **estar** *v.* 1.2
  be... years old **tener... años** 1.3
  be sick of... **estar harto/a de...** 3.6
beach **playa** *f.* 1.5
beans **frijoles** *m., pl.* 2.2
beautiful **hermoso/a** *adj.* 1.6
beauty **belleza** *f.* 3.2
  beauty salon **peluquería** *f.* 3.2; **salón** *m.* **de belleza** 3.2
because **porque** *conj.* 1.2
  because of **por** *prep.* 2.5
become (+ *adj.*) **ponerse (+ *adj.*)** 2.1; **convertirse** *v.*
bed **cama** *f.* 1.5
  go to bed **acostarse (o:ue)** *v.* 2.1
bedroom **alcoba** *f.*, **recámara** *f.*; **dormitorio** *m.* 2.6
beef **carne de res** *f.* 2.2
before **antes** *adv.* 2.1; **antes de** *prep.* 2.1; **antes (de) que** *conj.* 3.1
beg **rogar (o:ue)** *v.* 2.6
begin **comenzar (e:ie)** *v.* 1.4; **empezar (e:ie)** *v.* 1.4
behalf: on behalf of **de parte de** 2.5
behind **detrás de** *prep.* 1.2
believe (in) **creer** *v.* **(en)** 1.3; **creer** *v.* 3.1
  not to believe **no creer** 3.1
believed **creído/a** *p.p.* 3.2
bellhop **botones** *m., f. sing.* 1.5
below **debajo de** *prep.* 1.2
belt **cinturón** *m.* 1.6
benefit **beneficio** *m.* 3.4
beside **al lado de** *prep.* 1.2
besides **además (de)** *adv.* 2.4
best **mejor** *adj.*
  the best **el/la mejor** *m., f.* 2.2 **lo mejor** *neuter*
better **mejor** *adj.* 2.2
  It's better that... **Es mejor que...** 2.6
between **entre** *prep.* 1.2
beverage **bebida** *f.* 2.2
bicycle **bicicleta** *f.* 1.4
big **grande** *adj.* 1.3
bill **cuenta** *f.* 2.2
billion **mil millones**
biology **biología** *f.* 1.2
bird **ave** *f.* 3.1; **pájaro** *m.* 3.1
birth **nacimiento** *m.* 2.3
birthday **cumpleaños** *m., sing.* 2.3
  have a birthday **cumplir** *v.* **años**
black **negro/a** *adj.* 1.6
blackboard **pizarra** *f.* 1.2
blanket **manta** *f.* 2.6
block (city) **cuadra** *f.* 3.2
blog **blog** *m.* 2.5
blond(e) **rubio/a** *adj.* 1.3
blouse **blusa** *f.* 1.6
blue **azul** *adj. m., f.* 1.6
boarding house **pensión** *f.*
boat **barco** *m.* 1.5
body **cuerpo** *m.* 2.4
bone **hueso** *m.* 2.4
book **libro** *m.* 1.2
bookcase **estante** *m.* 2.6
bookshelves **estante** *m.* 2.6
bookstore **librería** *f.* 1.2
boot **bota** *f.* 1.6
bore **aburrir** *v.* 2.1
bored **aburrido/a** *adj.* 1.5
  be bored **estar** *v.* **aburrido/a** 1.5
  get bored **aburrirse** *v.* 3.5
boring **aburrido/a** *adj.* 1.5
born: be born **nacer** *v.* 2.3
borrow **pedir (e:i)** *v.* **prestado** 3.2
borrowed **prestado/a** *adj.*
boss **jefe** *m.*, **jefa** *f.* 3.4
bother **molestar** *v.* 2.1
bottle **botella** *f.* 2.3
bottom **fondo** *m.*
boulevard **bulevar** *m.*
boy **chico** *m.* 1.1; **muchacho** *m.* 1.3
boyfriend **novio** *m.* 1.3
brakes **frenos** *m., pl.*
bread **pan** *m.* 2.2
break **romper** *v.* 2.4
  break (one's leg) **romperse (la pierna)** 2.4
  break down **dañar** *v.* 2.4
  break up (with) **romper** *v.* **(con)** 2.3
breakfast **desayuno** *m.* 2.2
  have breakfast **desayunar** *v.* 1.2
breathe **respirar** *v.* 3.1
bring **traer** *v.* 1.4
broadcast **transmitir** *v.* 3.6; **emitir** *v.* 3.6
brochure **folleto** *m.*
broken **roto/a** *adj.* 3.2
  be broken **estar roto/a**
brother **hermano** *m.* 1.3
brother-in-law **cuñado** *m.* 1.3
brothers and sisters **hermanos** *m., pl.* 1.3
brought **traído/a** *p.p.* 3.2
brown **café** *adj.* 1.6; **marrón** *adj.* 1.6
browser **buscador** *m.* 2.5
brunet(te) **moreno/a** *adj.* 1.3
brush **cepillar(se)** *v.* 2.1
  brush one's hair **cepillarse el pelo** 2.1
  brush one's teeth **cepillarse los dientes** 2.1
bucket **balde** *m.* 1.5
build **construir** *v.*
building **edificio** *m.* 2.6
bump into (*something accidentally*) **darse con** 2.4; (*someone*) **encontrarse** *v.* 2.5
burn (a CD/DVD) **quemar** *v.* **(un CD/DVD)**
bus **autobús** *m.* 1.1
  bus station **estación** *f.* **de autobuses** 1.5
business **negocios** *m. pl.* 3.4
  business administration **administración** *f.* **de empresas** 1.2
  business-related **comercial** *adj.* 3.4
businessperson **hombre** *m.* / **mujer** *f.* **de negocios** 3.4
busy **ocupado/a** *adj.* 1.5
but **pero** *conj.* 1.2; (rather) **sino** *conj.* (*in negative sentences*) 2.1
butcher shop **carnicería** *f.* 3.2
butter **mantequilla** *f.* 2.2
buy **comprar** *v.* 1.2
by **por** *prep.* 2.5; **para** *prep.* 2.5
  by means of **por** *prep.* 2.5
  by phone **por teléfono**
  by plane **en avión** 1.5
  by way of **por** *prep.* 2.5
bye **chau** *interj. fam.* 1.1

C

cable television **televisión** *f.* **por cable** *m.*
café **café** *m.* 1.4
cafeteria **cafetería** *f.* 1.2
caffeine **cafeína** *f.* 3.3
cake **pastel** *m.* 2.3
  chocolate cake **pastel de chocolate** *m.* 2.3
calculator **calculadora** *f.* 1.2
call **llamar** *v.* 2.5
  be called **llamarse** *v.* 2.1
  call on the phone **llamar por teléfono**
calm **tranquilo/a** *adj.* 3.3
calorie **caloría** *f.* 3.3
camera **cámara** *f.* 2.5
camp **acampar** *v.* 1.5
can (*tin*) **lata** *f.* 3.1
can **poder (o:ue)** *v.* 1.4
  Could I ask you something? **¿Podría pedirte algo?** 3.5
Canadian **canadiense** *adj.* 1.3
candidate **aspirante** *m., f.* 3.4; **candidato/a** *m., f.* 3.6
candy **dulces** *m., pl.* 2.3
capital city **capital** *f.*
car **coche** *m.* 2.5; **carro** *m.* 2.5; **auto(móvil)** *m.* 1.5
caramel **caramelo** *m.* 2.3
card **tarjeta** *f.*; (*playing*) **carta** *f.* 1.5

care **cuidado** *m.*
take care of **cuidar** *v.* 3.1
career **carrera** *f.* 3.4
careful: be (very) careful **tener** *v.* **(mucho) cuidado** 1.3
caretaker **ama** *m., f.* **de casa** 2.6
carpenter **carpintero/a** *m., f.* 3.4
carpet **alfombra** *f.* 2.6
carrot **zanahoria** *f.* 2.2
carry **llevar** *v.* 1.2
cartoons **dibujos** *m, pl.* **animados** 3.5
case: in case (that) **en caso (de) que** 3.1
cash (a check) **cobrar** *v.* 3.2;
cash **(en) efectivo** 1.6
cash register **caja** *f.* 1.6
pay in cash **pagar** *v.* **al contado** 3.2; **pagar en efectivo** 3.2
cashier **cajero/a** *m., f.*
cat **gato** *m.* 3.1
CD **disco compacto** *m.* 2.5
CD player **reproductor de CD** *m.* 2.5
CD-ROM **cederrón** *m.*
celebrate **celebrar** *v.* 2.3
celebration **celebración** *f.*
cellar **sótano** *m.* 2.6
(cell) phone **(teléfono) celular** *m.* 2.5
cemetery **cementerio** *m.* 2.3
cereal **cereales** *m., pl.* 2.2
certain **cierto/a** *adj.*; **seguro/a** *adj.* 3.1
it's (not) certain **(no) es cierto/seguro** 3.1
chalk **tiza** *f.* 1.2
change **cambiar** *v.* **(de)** 2.3
change: in change **de cambio** 1.2
channel (*TV*) **canal** *m.* 2.5; 3.5
character (*fictional*) **personaje** *m.* 3.5
(main) character *m.* **personaje (principal)** 3.5
charger **cargador** *m.* 2.5
chat **conversar** *v.* 1.2; **chatear** *v.* 2.5
cheap **barato/a** *adj.* 1.6
check **comprobar (o:ue)** *v.*; **revisar** *v.* 2.5; (*bank*) **cheque** *m.* 3.2
check the oil **revisar el aceite** 2.5
checking account **cuenta** *f.* **corriente** 3.2
cheese **queso** *m.* 2.2
chef **cocinero/a** *m., f.* 3.4
chemistry **química** *f.* 1.2
chest of drawers **cómoda** *f.* 2.6
chicken **pollo** *m.* 2.2
child **niño/a** *m., f.* 1.3
childhood **niñez** *f.* 2.3
children **hijos** *m., pl.* 1.3
Chinese **chino/a** *adj.* 1.3
chocolate **chocolate** *m.* 2.3
chocolate cake **pastel** *m.* **de chocolate** 2.3
cholesterol **colesterol** *m.* 3.3
choose **escoger** *v.* 2.2
chop (*food*) **chuleta** *f.* 2.2
Christmas **Navidad** *f.* 2.3
church **iglesia** *f.* 1.4
cinnamon **canela** *f.* 2.4
citizen **ciudadano/a** *m., f.* 3.6
city **ciudad** *f.*
class **clase** *f.* 1.2
take classes **tomar clases** 1.2
classical **clásico/a** *adj.* 3.5
classmate **compañero/a** *m., f.* **de clase** 1.2
clean **limpio/a** *adj.* 1.5; **limpiar** *v.* 2.6
clean the house *v.* **limpiar la casa** 2.6
clear (*weather*) **despejado/a** *adj.*
clear the table **quitar la mesa** 2.6
It's (very) clear. (*weather*) **Está (muy) despejado.**
clerk **dependiente/a** *m., f.* 1.6
climate change **cambio climático** *m.* 3.1
climb **escalar** *v.* 1.4
climb mountains **escalar montañas** 1.4
clinic **clínica** *f.* 2.4
clock **reloj** *m.* 1.2
close **cerrar (e:ie)** *v.* 1.4
closed **cerrado/a** *adj.* 1.5
closet **armario** *m.* 2.6
clothes **ropa** *f.* 1.6
clothes dryer **secadora** *f.* 2.6
clothing **ropa** *f.* 1.6
cloud **nube** *f.* 3.1
cloudy **nublado/a** *adj.* 1.5
It's (very) cloudy. **Está (muy) nublado.** 1.5
coat **abrigo** *m.* 1.6
coffee **café** *m.* 2.2
coffee maker **cafetera** *f.* 2.6
cold **frío** *m.* 1.5;
(*illness*) **resfriado** *m.* 2.4
be (*feel*) (very) cold **tener (mucho) frío** 1.3
It's (very) cold. (*weather*) **Hace (mucho) frío.** 1.5
college **universidad** *f.* 1.2
collision **choque** *m.* 3.6
color **color** *m.* 1.6
comb one's hair **peinarse** *v.* 2.1
come **venir** *v.* 1.3
come on **ándale** *interj.* 3.2
comedy **comedia** *f.* 3.5
comfortable **cómodo/a** *adj.* 1.5
commerce **negocios** *m., pl.* 3.4
commercial **comercial** *adj.* 3.4
communicate (with) **comunicarse** *v.* **(con)** 3.6
communication **comunicación** *f.* 3.6
means of communication **medios** *m. pl.* **de comunicación** 3.6
community **comunidad** *f.* 1.1
company **compañía** *f.* 3.4; **empresa** *f.* 3.4
comparison **comparación** *f.*
composer **compositor(a)** *m., f.* 3.5
computer **computadora** *f.* 1.1
computer disc **disco** *m.*
computer monitor **monitor** *m.* 2.5
computer programmer **programador(a)** *m., f.* 1.3
computer science **computación** *f.* 1.2
concert **concierto** *m.* 3.5
conductor (*musical*) **director(a)** *m., f.* 3.5
confident **seguro/a** *adj.* 1.5
confirm **confirmar** *v.* 1.5
confirm a reservation **confirmar una reservación** 1.5
confused **confundido/a** *adj.* 1.5
congested **congestionado/a** *adj.* 2.4
Congratulations! **¡Felicidades!; ¡Felicitaciones!** *f., pl.* 2.3
conservation **conservación** *f.* 3.1
conserve **conservar** *v.* 3.1
considering **para** *prep.* 2.5
consume **consumir** *v.* 3.3
container **envase** *m.* 3.1
contamination **contaminación** *f.*
content **contento/a** *adj.* 1.5
contest **concurso** *m.* 3.5
continue **seguir (e:i)** *v.* 1.4
control **control** *m.*; **controlar** *v.* 3.1
conversation **conversación** *f.* 1.1
converse **conversar** *v.* 1.2
cook **cocinar** *v.* 2.6; **cocinero/a** *m., f.* 3.4
cookie **galleta** *f.* 2.3
cool **fresco/a** *adj.* 1.5
It's cool. (*weather*) **Hace fresco.** 1.5
corn **maíz** *m.* 2.2
corner **esquina** *f.* 3.2
cost **costar (o:ue)** *v.* 1.6
Costa Rican **costarricense** *adj.* 1.3
costume **disfraz** *m.* 2.3
cotton **algodón** *f.* 1.6
(made of) cotton **de algodón** 1.6
couch **sofá** *m.* 2.6
couch potato **teleadicto/a** *m., f.* 3.3
cough **tos** *f.* 2.4; **toser** *v.* 2.4
counselor **consejero/a** *m., f.* 3.4
count **contar (o:ue)** *v.* 1.4
country (*nation*) **país** *m.* 1.1
countryside **campo** *m.* 1.5
(married) couple **pareja** *f.* 2.3
course **curso** *m.* 1.2; **materia** *f.* 1.2
courtesy **cortesía** *f.*
cousin **primo/a** *m., f.* 1.3
cover **cubrir** *v.*
covered **cubierto/a** *p.p.*
cow **vaca** *f.* 3.1
crafts **artesanía** *f.* 3.5
craftsmanship **artesanía** *f.* 3.5
crater **cráter** *m.* 3.1
crazy **loco/a** *adj.* 1.6
create **crear** *v.*
credit **crédito** *m.* 1.6
credit card **tarjeta** *f.* **de crédito** 1.6
crime **crimen** *m.* 3.6
cross **cruzar** *v.* 3.2

cry **llorar** *v.* 3.3
Cuban **cubano/a** *adj.* 1.3
culture **cultura** *f.* 1.2, 3.5
cup **taza** *f.* 2.6
currency exchange **cambio** *m.* **de moneda**
current events **actualidades** *f., pl.* 3.6
curtains **cortinas** *f., pl.* 2.6
custard (*baked*) **flan** *m.* 2.3
custom **costumbre** *f.*
customer **cliente/a** *m., f.* 1.6
customs **aduana** *f.*
  customs inspector **inspector(a)** *m., f.* **de aduanas** 1.5
cybercafé **cibercafé** *m.* 2.5
cycling **ciclismo** *m.* 1.4

D

dad **papá** *m.*
daily **diario/a** *adj.* 2.1
  daily routine **rutina** *f.* **diaria** 2.1
damage **dañar** *v.* 2.4
dance **bailar** *v.* 1.2; **danza** *f.* 3.5; **baile** *m.* 3.5
dancer **bailarín/bailarina** *m., f.* 3.5
danger **peligro** *m.* 3.1
dangerous **peligroso/a** *adj.* 3.6
date (*appointment*) **cita** *f.* 2.3; (*calendar*) **fecha** *f.* 1.5; (*someone*) **salir** *v.* **con (alguien)** 2.3
  have a date **tener una cita** 2.3
daughter **hija** *f.* 1.3
daughter-in-law **nuera** *f.* 1.3
day **día** *m.* 1.1
  day before yesterday **anteayer** *adv.* 1.6
death **muerte** *f.* 2.3
decaffeinated **descafeinado/a** *adj.* 3.3
December **diciembre** *m.* 1.5
decide **decidir** *v.* **(+ *inf.*)** 1.3
declare **declarar** *v.* 3.6
deforestation **deforestación** *f.* 3.1
delicious **delicioso/a** *adj.* 2.2; **rico/a** *adj.* 2.2; **sabroso/a** *adj.* 2.2
delighted **encantado/a** *adj.* 1.1
dentist **dentista** *m., f.* 2.4
deny **negar (e:ie)** *v.* 3.1
  not to deny **no negar** 3.1
department store **almacén** *m.* 1.6
departure **salida** *f.* 1.5
deposit **depositar** *v.* 3.2
describe **describir** *v.* 1.3
described **descrito/a** *p.p.* 3.2
desert **desierto** *m.* 3.1
design **diseño** *m.*
designer **diseñador(a)** *m., f.* 3.4
desire **desear** *v.* 1.2
desk **escritorio** *m.* 1.2
dessert **postre** *m.* 2.3
destroy **destruir** *v.* 3.1
develop **desarrollar** *v.* 3.1
diary **diario** *m.* 1.1
dictatorship **dictadura** *f.* 3.6
dictionary **diccionario** *m.* 1.1
die **morir (o:ue)** *v.* 2.2
died **muerto/a** *p.p.* 3.2
diet **dieta** *f.* 3.3; **alimentación**
  balanced diet **dieta equilibrada** 3.3
  be on a diet **estar a dieta** 3.3
difficult **difícil** *adj. m., f.* 1.3
digital camera **cámara** *f.* **digital** 2.5
dining room **comedor** *m.* 2.6
dinner **cena** *f.* 2.2
  have dinner **cenar** *v.* 1.2
direct **dirigir** *v.* 3.5
director **director(a)** *m., f.* 3.5
dirty **ensuciar** *v.*; **sucio/a** *adj.* 1.5
  get (something) dirty **ensuciar** *v.* 2.6
disagree **no estar de acuerdo**
disaster **desastre** *m.* 3.6
discover **descubrir** *v.* 3.1
discovered **descubierto/a** *p.p.* 3.2
discrimination **discriminación** *f.* 3.6
dish **plato** *m.* 2.2, 2.6
  main dish *m.* **plato principal** 2.2
dishwasher **lavaplatos** *m., sing.* 2.6
disk **disco** *m.*
disorderly **desordenado/a** *adj.* 1.5
divorce **divorcio** *m.* 2.3
divorced **divorciado/a** *adj.* 2.3
  get divorced (from) **divorciarse** *v.* **(de)** 2.3
dizzy **mareado/a** *adj.* 2.4
do **hacer** *v.* 1.4
  do aerobics **hacer ejercicios aeróbicos** 3.3
  do household chores **hacer quehaceres domésticos** 2.6
  do stretching exercises **hacer ejercicios de estiramiento** 3.3
  (I) don't want to. **No quiero.** 1.4
doctor **doctor(a)** *m., f.* 1.3; 2.4; **médico/a** *m., f.* 1.3
documentary (*film*) **documental** *m.* 3.5
dog **perro** *m.* 3.1
domestic **doméstico/a** *adj.*
  domestic appliance **electrodoméstico** *m.*
done **hecho/a** *p.p.* 3.2
door **puerta** *f.* 1.2
doorman/doorwoman **portero/a** *m., f.* 1.1
dormitory **residencia** *f.* **estudiantil** 1.2
double **doble** *adj.* 1.5
  double room **habitación** *f.* **doble** 1.5
doubt **duda** *f.* 3.1; **dudar** *v.* 3.1
  not to doubt **no dudar** 3.1
  there is no doubt that **no cabe duda de** 3.1; **no hay duda de** 3.1
download **descargar** *v.* 2.5
downtown **centro** *m.* 1.4
drama **drama** *m.* 3.5
dramatic **dramático/a** *adj.* 3.5
draw **dibujar** *v.* 1.2
drawing **dibujo** *m.*
dress **vestido** *m.* 1.6
  get dressed **vestirse (e:i)** *v.* 2.1
drink **beber** *v.* 1.3; **bebida** *f.* 2.2; **tomar** *v.* 1.2
drive **conducir** *v.* 1.6; **manejar** *v.* 2.5
driver **conductor(a)** *m., f.* 1.1
dry (oneself) **secarse** *v.* 2.1
during **durante** *prep.* 2.1; **por** *prep.* 2.5
dust **sacudir** *v.* 2.6; **quitar** *v.* **el polvo** 2.6
dust the furniture **sacudir los muebles** 2.6
duster **plumero** *m.* 2.6
DVD player **reproductor** *m.* **de DVD** 2.5

E

each **cada** *adj.* 1.6
ear (outer) **oreja** *f.* 2.4
early **temprano** *adv.* 2.1
earn **ganar** *v.* 3.4
earring **arete** *m.* 1.6
earthquake **terremoto** *m.* 3.6
ease **aliviar** *v.*
east **este** *m.* 3.2
  to the east **al este** 3.2
easy **fácil** *adj. m., f.* 1.3
eat **comer** *v.* 1.3
ecological **ecológico/a** *adj.* 3.1
ecologist **ecologista** *m., f.* 3.1
ecology **ecología** *f.* 3.1
economics **economía** *f.* 1.2
ecotourism **ecoturismo** *m.* 3.1
Ecuadorian **ecuatoriano/a** *adj.* 1.3
effective **eficaz** *adj. m., f.*
egg **huevo** *m.* 2.2
eight **ocho** 1.1
eight hundred **ochocientos/as** 1.2
eighteen **dieciocho** 1.1
eighth **octavo/a** 1.5
eighty **ochenta** 1.2
either... or **o... o** *conj.* 2.1
elect **elegir (e:i)** *v.* 3.6
election **elecciones** *f. pl.* 3.6
electric appliance **electrodoméstico** *m.* 2.6
electrician **electricista** *m., f.* 3.4
electricity **luz** *f.* 2.6
elegant **elegante** *adj. m., f.* 1.6
elevator **ascensor** *m.* 1.5
eleven **once** 1.1
e-mail **correo** *m.* **electrónico** 1.4
  e-mail address **dirección** *f.* **electrónica** 2.5
  e-mail message **mensaje** *m.* **electrónico** 1.4
  read e-mail **leer** *v.* **el correo electrónico** 1.4
embarrassed **avergonzado/a** *adj.* 1.5
embrace (each other) **abrazar(se)** *v.* 2.5

emergency **emergencia** *f.* 2.4
emergency room **sala** *f.* **de emergencia(s)** 2.4
employee **empleado/a** *m., f.* 1.5
employment **empleo** *m.* 3.4
end **fin** *m.* 1.4; **terminar** *v.* 1.2
end table **mesita** *f.* 2.6
endure **aguantar** *v.* 3.2
energy **energía** *f.* 3.1
engaged: get engaged (to) **comprometerse** *v.* **(con)** 2.3
engineer **ingeniero/a** *m., f.* 1.3
English (*language*) **inglés** *m.* 1.2; **inglés, inglesa** *adj.* 1.3
enjoy **disfrutar** *v.* **(de)** 3.3
enough **bastante** *adv.* 2.4
entertainment **diversión** *f.* 1.4
entrance **entrada** *f.* 2.6
envelope **sobre** *m.* 3.2
environment **medio ambiente** *m.* 3.1
environmental science **ciencias ambientales** 1.2
equality **igualdad** *f.* 3.6
erase **borrar** *v.* 2.5
eraser **borrador** *m.* 1.2
errand **diligencia** *f.* 3.2
essay **ensayo** *m.* 1.3
establish **establecer** *v.* 3.4
evening **tarde** *f.* 1.1
event **acontecimiento** *m.* 3.6
every day **todos los días** 2.4
everything **todo** *m.* 1.5
exactly **en punto** 1.1
exam **examen** *m.* 1.2
excellent **excelente** *adj.* 1.5
excess **exceso** *m.* 3.3
in excess **en exceso** 3.3
exchange **intercambiar** *v.*
in exchange for **por** 2.5
exciting **emocionante** *adj. m., f.*
excursion **excursión** *f.*
excuse **disculpar** *v.*
Excuse me. (*May I?*) **Con permiso.** 1.1; (*I beg your pardon.*) **Perdón.** 1.1
exercise **ejercicio** *m.* 3.3; **hacer** *v.* **ejercicio** 3.3; (a degree/profession) **ejercer** *v.* 3.4
exit **salida** *f.* 1.5
expensive **caro/a** *adj.* 1.6
experience **experiencia** *f.*
expire **vencer** *v.* 3.2
explain **explicar** *v.* 1.2
explore **explorar** *v.*
expression **expresión** *f.*
extinction **extinción** *f.* 3.1
eye **ojo** *m.* 2.4

F

fabulous **fabuloso/a** *adj.* 1.5
face **cara** *f.* 2.1
facing **enfrente de** *prep.* 3.2
fact: in fact **de hecho**
factory **fábrica** *f.* 3.1
fall (down) **caerse** *v.* 2.4
fall asleep **dormirse (o:ue)** *v.* 2.1
fall in love (with) **enamorarse** *v.* **(de)** 2.3
fall (season) **otoño** *m.* 1.5
fallen **caído/a** *p.p.* 3.2
family **familia** *f.* 1.3
famous **famoso/a** *adj.*
fan **aficionado/a** *m., f.* 1.4
be a fan (of) **ser aficionado/a (a)**
far from **lejos de** *prep.* 1.2
farewell **despedida** *f.*
fascinate **fascinar** *v.* 2.1
fashion **moda** *f.* 1.6
be in fashion **estar de moda** 1.6
fast **rápido/a** *adj.*
fat **gordo/a** *adj.* 1.3; **grasa** *f.* 3.3
father **padre** *m.* 1.3
father-in-law **suegro** *m.* 1.3
favorite **favorito/a** *adj.* 1.4
fax (machine) ***fax*** *m.*
fear **miedo** *m.*; **temer** *v.* 3.1
February **febrero** *m.* 1.5
feel **sentir(se) (e:ie)** *v.* 2.1
feel like (*doing something*) **tener ganas de (+ *inf.*)** 1.3
festival **festival** *m.* 3.5
fever **fiebre** *f.* 2.4
have a fever **tener** *v.* **fiebre** 2.4
few **pocos/as** *adj. pl.*
fewer than **menos de** (+ *number*) 2.2
field: major field of study **especialización** *f.*
fifteen **quince** 1.1
fifteen-year-old girl celebrating her birthday **quinceañera** *f.*
fifth **quinto/a** 1.5
fifty **cincuenta** 1.2
fight (for/against) **luchar** *v.* **(por/contra)** 3.6
figure (*number*) **cifra** *f.*
file **archivo** *m.* 2.5
fill **llenar** *v.* 2.5
fill out (a form) **llenar (un formulario)** 3.2
fill the tank **llenar el tanque** 2.5
finally **finalmente** *adv.*; **por último** 2.1; **por fin** 2.5
find **encontrar (o:ue)** *v.* 1.4
find (each other) **encontrar(se)**
find out **enterarse** *v.* 3.4
fine **multa** *f.*
That's fine. **Está bien.**
(fine) arts **bellas artes** *f., pl.* 3.5
finger **dedo** *m.* 2.4
finish **terminar** *v.* 1.2
finish (*doing something*) **terminar** *v.* **de (+ *inf.*)**
fire **incendio** *m.* 3.6; **despedir (e:i)** *v.* 3.4
firefighter **bombero/a** *m., f.* 3.4
firm **compañía** *f.* 3.4; **empresa** *f.* 3.4
first **primer, primero/a** 1.2, 1.5
fish (*food*) **pescado** *m.* 2.2; **pescar** *v.* 1.5; (*live*) **pez** *m., sing.* (**peces** *pl.*) 3.1
fish market **pescadería** *f.* 3.2
fishing **pesca** *f.*
fit (*clothing*) **quedar** *v.* 2.1
five **cinco** 1.1
five hundred **quinientos/as** 1.2
fix (*put in working order*) **arreglar** *v.* 2.5; (*clothes, hair, etc. to go out*) **arreglarse** *v.* 2.1
fixed **fijo/a** *adj.* 1.6
flag **bandera** *f.*
flexible **flexible** *adj.* 3.3
flood **inundación** *f.* 3.6
floor (*of a building*) **piso** *m.* 1.5; **suelo** *m.* 2.6
ground floor **planta baja** *f.* 1.5
top floor **planta** *f.* **alta**
flower **flor** *f.* 3.1
flu **gripe** *f.* 2.4
fog **niebla** *f.*
folk **folclórico/a** *adj.* 3.5
follow **seguir (e:i)** *v.* 1.4
food **comida** *f.* 1.4, 2.2
foolish **tonto/a** *adj.* 1.3
foot **pie** *m.* 2.4
football **fútbol** *m.* **americano** 1.4
for **para** *prep.* 2.5; **por** *prep.* 2.5
for example **por ejemplo** 2.5
for me **para mí** 2.2
forbid **prohibir** *v.*
foreign **extranjero/a** *adj.* 3.5
foreign languages **lenguas** *f., pl.* **extranjeras** 1.2
forest **bosque** *m.* 3.1
forget **olvidar** *v.* 2.4
fork **tenedor** *m.* 2.6
form **formulario** *m.* 3.2
forty **cuarenta** 1.2
four **cuatro** 1.1
four hundred **cuatrocientos/as** 1.2
fourteen **catorce** 1.1
fourth **cuarto/a** *m., f.* 1.5
free **libre** *adj. m., f.* 1.4
be free (of charge) **ser gratis** 3.2
free time **tiempo libre**; spare (free) time **ratos libres** 1.4
freedom **libertad** *f.* 3.6
freezer **congelador** *m.* 2.6
French **francés, francesa** *adj.* 1.3
French fries **papas** *f., pl.* **fritas** 2.2; **patatas** *f., pl.* **fritas** 2.2
frequently **frecuentemente** *adv.*; **con frecuencia** *adv.* 2.4
Friday **viernes** *m., sing.* 1.2
fried **frito/a** *adj.* 2.2
fried potatoes **papas** *f., pl.* **fritas** 2.2; **patatas** *f., pl.* **fritas** 2.2
friend **amigo/a** *m., f.* 1.3
friendly **amable** *adj. m., f.* 1.5

friendship **amistad** *f.* 2.3
from **de** *prep.* 1.1; **desde** *prep.* 1.6
from the United States **estadounidense** *m., f. adj.* 1.3
from time to time **de vez en cuando** 2.4
I'm from... **Soy de...** 1.1
front: (cold) front **frente (frío)** *m.* 1.5
fruit **fruta** *f.* 2.2
fruit juice **jugo** *m.* **de fruta** 2.2
fruit store **frutería** *f.* 3.2
full **lleno/a** *adj.* 2.5
fun **divertido/a** *adj.*
fun activity **diversión** *f.* 1.4
have fun **divertirse (e:ie)** *v.* 2.3
function **funcionar** *v.*
furniture **muebles** *m., pl.* 2.6
furthermore **además (de)** *adv.* 2.4
future **porvenir** *m.* 3.4
for/to the future **por el porvenir** 3.4
in the future **en el futuro**

G

gain weight **aumentar** *v.* **de peso** 3.3; **engordar** *v.* 3.3
game **juego** *m.*; (*match*) **partido** *m.* 1.4
game show **concurso** *m.* 3.5
garage (*in a house*) **garaje** *m.* 2.6; **garaje** *m.* 2.5; **taller (mecánico)** 2.5
garden **jardín** *m.* 2.6
garlic **ajo** *m.* 2.2
gas station **gasolinera** *f.* 2.5
gasoline **gasolina** *f.* 2.5
gentleman **caballero** *m.* 2.2
geography **geografía** *f.* 1.2
German **alemán, alemana** *adj.* 1.3
get **conseguir(e:i)** *v.* 1.4; **obtener** *v.* 3.4
get along well/badly (with) **llevarse bien/mal (con)** 2.3
get bigger **aumentar** *v.* 3.1
get bored **aburrirse** *v.* 3.5
get good grades **sacar buenas notas** 1.2
get into trouble **meterse en problemas** *v.* 3.1
get off of (a vehicle) **bajar(se)** *v.* **de** 2.5
get on/into (a vehicle) **subir(se)** *v.* **a** 2.5
get out of (a vehicle) **bajar(se)** *v.* **de** 2.5
get ready **arreglarse** *v.* 2.1
get up **levantarse** *v.* 2.1
gift **regalo** *m.* 1.6
ginger **jengibre** *m.* 2.4
girl **chica** *f.* 1.1; **muchacha** *f.* 1.3
girlfriend **novia** *f.* 1.3
give **dar** *v.* 1.6; (*as a gift*) **regalar** 2.3
give directions **indicar cómo llegar** 3.2
glass (*drinking*) **vaso** *m.* 2.6; **vidrio** *m.* 3.1
(made) of glass **de vidrio** 3.1
glasses **gafas** *f., pl.* 1.6
sunglasses **gafas** *f., pl.* **de sol** 1.6
global warming **calentamiento global** *m.* 3.1
gloves **guantes** *m., pl.* 1.6
go **ir** *v.* 1.4
go away **irse** 2.1
go by boat **ir en barco** 1.5
go by bus **ir en autobús** 1.5
go by car **ir en auto(móvil)** 1.5
go by motorcycle **ir en moto(cicleta)** 1.5
go by plane **ir en avión** 1.5
go by taxi **ir en taxi** 1.5
go down **bajar(se)** *v.*
go on a hike **ir de excursión** 1.4
go out (with) **salir** *v.* **(con)** 2.3
go up **subir** *v.*
Let's go. **Vamos.** 1.4
goblet **copa** *f.* 2.6
going to: be going to (*do something*) **ir a (+ *inf.*)** 1.4
golf **golf** *m.* 1.4
good **buen, bueno/a** *adj.* 1.3, 1.6
Good afternoon. **Buenas tardes.** 1.1
Good evening. **Buenas noches.** 1.1
Good morning. **Buenos días.** 1.1
Good night. **Buenas noches.** 1.1
It's good that... **Es bueno que...** 2.6
goodbye **adiós** *m.* 1.1
say goodbye (to) **despedirse** *v.* **(de) (e:i)** 3.6
good-looking **guapo/a** *adj.* 1.3
government **gobierno** *m.* 3.1
GPS **navegador GPS** *m.* 2.5
graduate (from/in) **graduarse** *v.* **(de/en)** 2.3
grains **cereales** *m., pl.* 2.2
granddaughter **nieta** *f.* 1.3
grandfather **abuelo** *m.* 1.3
grandmother **abuela** *f.* 1.3
grandparents **abuelos** *m., pl.* 1.3
grandson **nieto** *m.* 1.3
grape **uva** *f.* 2.2
grass **hierba** *f.* 3.1
grave **grave** *adj.* 2.4
gray **gris** *adj. m., f.* 1.6
great **fenomenal** *adj. m., f.* 1.5; **genial** *adj.* 3.4
great-grandfather **bisabuelo** *m.* 1.3
great-grandmother **bisabuela** *f.* 1.3
green **verde** *adj. m., f.* 1.6
greet (each other) **saludar(se)** *v.* 2.5
greeting **saludo** *m.* 1.1
Greetings to... **Saludos a...** 1.1
grilled **a la plancha** 2.2
ground floor **planta baja** *f.* 1.5
grow **aumentar** *v.* 3.1
guest (*at a house/hotel*) **huésped** *m., f.* 1.5 (*invited to a function*) **invitado/a** *m., f.* 2.3
guide **guía** *m., f.*
gymnasium **gimnasio** *m.* 1.4

H

hair **pelo** *m.* 2.1
hairdresser **peluquero/a** *m., f.* 3.4
half **medio/a** *adj.* 1.3
half-brother **medio hermano** *m.* 1.3
half-past... (*time*) **...y media** 1.1
half-sister **media hermana** *f.* 1.3
hallway **pasillo** *m.* 2.6
ham **jamón** *m.* 2.2
hamburger **hamburguesa** *f.* 2.2
hand **mano** *f.* 1.1
hand in **entregar** *v.* 2.5
handsome **guapo/a** *adj.* 1.3
happen **ocurrir** *v.* 3.6
happiness **alegría** *v.* 2.3
Happy birthday! **¡Feliz cumpleaños!** 2.3
happy **alegre** *adj.* 1.5; **contento/a** *adj.* 1.5; **feliz** *adj. m., f.* 1.5
be happy **alegrarse** *v.* **(de)** 3.1
hard **difícil** *adj. m., f.* 1.3
hard-working **trabajador(a)** *adj.* 1.3
hardly **apenas** *adv.* 2.4
hat **sombrero** *m.* 1.6
hate **odiar** *v.* 2.3
have **tener** *v.* 1.3
have time **tener tiempo** 3.2
have to (*do something*) **tener que (+ *inf.*)** 1.3
have a tooth removed **sacar(se) un diente** 2.4
he **él** 1.1
head **cabeza** *f.* 2.4
headache **dolor** *m.* **de cabeza** 2.4
health **salud** *f.* 2.4
healthy **saludable** *adj. m., f.* 2.4; **sano/a** *adj.* 2.4
lead a healthy lifestyle **llevar** *v.* **una vida sana** 3.3
hear **oír** *v.* 1.4
heard **oído/a** *p.p.* 3.2
hearing: sense of hearing **oído** *m.* 2.4
heart **corazón** *m.* 2.4
heat **calor** *m.*
Hello. **Hola.** 1.1; (*on the telephone*) **Aló.** 2.5; **Bueno.** 2.5; **Diga.** 2.5
help **ayudar** *v.*; **servir (e:i)** *v.* 1.5
help each other **ayudarse** *v.* 2.5
her **su(s)** *poss. adj.* 1.3; (of) hers **suyo(s)/a(s)** *poss.* 2.5
her **la** *f., sing., d.o. pron.* 1.5
to/for her **le** *f., sing., i.o. pron.* 1.6

here **aquí** *adv.* 1.1
Here is/are... **Aquí está(n)...** 1.5
Hi. **Hola.** 1.1
highway **autopista** *f.* 2.5; **carretera** *f.* 2.5
hike **excursión** *f.* 1.4
go on a hike **ir de excursión** 1.4
hiker **excursionista** *m., f.*
hiking **de excursión** 1.4
him *m., sing., d.o. pron.* **lo** 1.5; to/for him **le** *m., sing., i.o. pron.* 1.6
hire **contratar** *v.* 3.4
his **su(s)** *poss. adj.* 1.3; (of) his **suyo(s)/a(s)** *poss. pron.* 2.5
history **historia** *f.* 1.2; 3.5
hobby **pasatiempo** *m.* 1.4
hockey **hockey** *m.* 1.4
hold up **aguantar** *v.* 3.2
hole **hueco** *m.* 1.4
holiday **día** *m.* **de fiesta** 2.3
home **casa** *f.* 1.2
home page **página** *f.* **principal** 2.5
homework **tarea** *f.* 1.2
honey **miel** *f.* 2.4
hood **capó** *m.* 2.5; **cofre** *m.* 2.5
hope **esperar** *v.* **(+ *inf.*)** 1.2; **esperar** *v.* 3.1
I hope (that) **ojalá (que)** 3.1
horror (genre) **de horror** *m.* 3.5
hors d'oeuvres **entremeses** *m., pl.* 2.2
horse **caballo** *m.* 1.5
hospital **hospital** *m.* 2.4
hot: be (*feel*) (very) hot **tener (mucho) calor** 1.3
It's (very) hot. **Hace (mucho) calor.** 1.5
hotel **hotel** *m.* 1.5
hour **hora** *f.* 1.1
house **casa** *f.* 1.2
household chores **quehaceres** *m. pl.* **domésticos** 2.6
housekeeper **ama** *m., f.* **de casa** 2.6
housing **vivienda** *f.* 2.6
How...! **¡Qué...!**
how **¿cómo?** *adv.* 1.1, 1.2
How are you? **¿Qué tal?** 1.1
How are you?**¿Cómo estás?** *fam.* 1.1
How are you?**¿Cómo está usted?** *form.* 1.1
How can I help you? **¿En qué puedo servirles?** 1.5
How is it going? **¿Qué tal?** 1.1
How is the weather? **¿Qué tiempo hace?** 1.5
How much/many? **¿Cuánto(s)/a(s)?** 1.1
How much does... cost? **¿Cuánto cuesta...?** 1.6
How old are you? **¿Cuántos años tienes?** *fam.*
however **sin embargo**
hug (each other) **abrazar(se)** *v.* 2.5
humanities **humanidades** *f., pl.* 1.2
hundred **cien, ciento** 1.2
hunger **hambre** *f.*
hungry: be (very) hungry **tener** *v.* **(mucha) hambre** 1.3
hunt **cazar** *v.* 3.1
hurricane **huracán** *m.* 3.6
hurry **apurarse** *v.* 3.3; **darse prisa** *v.* 3.3
be in a (big) hurry **tener** *v.* **(mucha) prisa** 1.3
hurt **doler (o:ue)** *v.* 2.4
husband **esposo** *m.* 1.3

I

I **yo** 1.1
I hope (that) **Ojalá (que)** *interj.* 3.1
I wish (that) **Ojalá (que)** *interj.* 3.1
ice cream **helado** *m.* 2.3
ice cream shop **heladería** *f.* 3.2
iced **helado/a** *adj.* 2.2
iced tea **té** *m.* **helado** 2.2
idea **idea** *f.* 3.6
if **si** *conj.* 1.4
illness **enfermedad** *f.* 2.4
important **importante** *adj.* 1.3
be important to **importar** *v.* 2.1
It's important that... **Es importante que...** 2.6
impossible **imposible** *adj.* 3.1
it's impossible **es imposible** 3.1
improbable **improbable** *adj.* 3.1
it's improbable **es improbable** 3.1
improve **mejorar** *v.* 3.1
in **en** *prep.* 1.2; **por** *prep.* 2.5
in the afternoon **de la tarde** 1.1; **por la tarde** 2.1
in a bad mood **de mal humor** 1.5
in the direction of **para** *prep.* 2.5
in the early evening **de la tarde** 1.1
in the evening **de la noche** 1.1; **por la tarde** 2.1
in a good mood **de buen humor** 1.5
in the morning **de la mañana** 1.1; **por la mañana** 2.1
in love (with) **enamorado/a (de)** 1.5
in search of **por** *prep.* 2.5
in front of **delante de** *prep.* 1.2
increase **aumento** *m.*
incredible **increíble** *adj.* 1.5
inequality **desigualdad** *f.* 3.6
infection **infección** *f.* 2.4
inform **informar** *v.* 3.6
injection **inyección** *f.* 2.4
give an injection *v.* **poner una inyección** 2.4
injure (oneself) **lastimarse** 2.4
injure (one's foot) **lastimarse** *v.* **(el pie)** 2.4
inner ear **oído** *m.* 2.4
inside **dentro** *adv.*
insist (on) **insistir** *v.* **(en)** 2.6
installments: pay in installments **pagar** *v.* **a plazos** 3.2
intelligent **inteligente** *adj.* 1.3
intend to **pensar** *v.* **(+ *inf.*)** 1.4
interest **interesar** *v.* 2.1
interesting **interesante** *adj.* 1.3
be interesting to **interesar** *v.* 2.1
international **internacional** *adj. m., f.* 3.6
Internet **Internet** 2.5
interview **entrevista** *f.* 3.4; interview **entrevistar** *v.* 3.4
interviewer **entrevistador(a)** *m., f.* 3.4
introduction **presentación** *f.*
I would like to introduce you to (name). **Le presento a...** *form.* 1.1; **Te presento a...** *fam.* 1.1
invest **invertir (e:ie)** *v.* 3.4
invite **invitar** *v.* 2.3
iron (clothes) **planchar** *v.* **la ropa** 2.6
it **lo/la** *sing., d.o., pron.* 1.5
Italian **italiano/a** *adj.* 1.3
its **su(s)** *poss. adj.* 1.3; **suyo(s)/a(s)** *poss. pron.* 2.5
it's the same **es igual** 1.5

J

jacket **chaqueta** *f.* 1.6
January **enero** *m.* 1.5
Japanese **japonés, japonesa** *adj.* 1.3
jeans **(blue)jeans** *m., pl.* 1.6
jewelry store **joyería** *f.* 3.2
job **empleo** *m.* 3.4; **puesto** *m.* 3.4; **trabajo** *m.* 3.4
job application **solicitud** *f.* **de trabajo** 3.4
jog **correr** *v.*
journalism **periodismo** *m.* 1.2
journalist **periodista** *m., f.* 1.3
joy **alegría** *f.* 2.3
juice **jugo** *m.* 2.2
July **julio** *m.* 1.5
June **junio** *m.* 1.5
jungle **selva, jungla** *f.* 3.1
just **apenas** *adv.*
have just done something **acabar de (+ *inf.*)** 1.6

K

key **llave** *f.* 1.5
keyboard **teclado** *m.* 2.5
kilometer **kilómetro** *m.* 2.5

kiss **beso** *m.* 2.3
kiss each other **besarse** *v.* 2.5
kitchen **cocina** *f.* 2.3, 2.6
knee **rodilla** *f.* 2.4
knife **cuchillo** *m.* 2.6
know **saber** *v.* 1.6; **conocer** *v.* 1.6
know how **saber** *v.* 1.6

L

laboratory **laboratorio** *m.* 1.2
lack **faltar** *v.* 2.1
lake **lago** *m.* 3.1
lamp **lámpara** *f.* 2.6
land **tierra** *f.* 3.1
landscape **paisaje** *m.* 1.5
language **lengua** *f.* 1.2
laptop (computer) **computadora** *f.* **portátil** 2.5
large **grande** *adj.* 1.3
large (*clothing size*) **talla grande**
last **durar** *v.* 3.6; **pasado/a** *adj.* 1.6; **último/a** *adj.* 2.1
last name **apellido** *m.* 1.3
last night **anoche** *adv.* 1.6
last week **semana** *f.* **pasada** 1.6
last year **año** *m.* **pasado** 1.6
the last time **la última vez** 2.1
late **tarde** *adv.* 2.1
later (on) **más tarde** 2.1
See you later. **Hasta la vista.** 1.1; **Hasta luego.** 1.1
laugh **reírse (e:i)** *v.* 2.3
laughed **reído** *p.p.* 3.2
laundromat **lavandería** *f.* 3.2
law **ley** *f.* 3.1
lawyer **abogado/a** *m., f.* 3.4
lazy **perezoso/a** *adj.*
learn **aprender** *v.* **(a +** *inf.***)** 1.3
least, at **por lo menos** *adv.* 2.4
leave **salir** *v.* 1.4; **irse** *v.* 2.1
leave a tip **dejar una propina**
leave behind **dejar** *v.* 3.4
leave for (*a place*) **salir para**
leave from **salir de**
left **izquierda** *f.* 1.2
be left over **quedar** *v.* 2.1
to the left of **a la izquierda de** 1.2
leg **pierna** *f.* 2.4
lemon **limón** *m.* 2.2
lend **prestar** *v.* 1.6
less **menos** *adv.* 2.4
less... than **menos... que** 2.2
less than **menos de** (+ *number*)
lesson **lección** *f.* 1.1
let **dejar** *v.*
let's see **a ver**
letter **carta** *f.* 1.4, 3.2
lettuce **lechuga** *f.* 2.2
liberty **libertad** *f.* 3.6
library **biblioteca** *f.* 1.2
license (*driver's*) **licencia** *f.* **de conducir** 2.5
lie **mentira** *f.* 1.4
life **vida** *f.* 2.3
lifestyle: lead a healthy lifestyle **llevar una vida sana** 3.3
lift **levantar** *v.* 3.3
lift weights **levantar pesas** 3.3
light **luz** *f.* 2.6
like **como** *prep.* 2.2; **gustar** *v.* 1.2
I like... **Me gusta(n)...** 1.2
like this **así** *adv.* 2.4
like very much **encantar** *v.*; **fascinar** *v.* 2.1
Do you like...? **¿Te gusta(n)...?** 1.2
likeable **simpático/a** *adj.* 1.3
likewise **igualmente** *adv.* 1.1
line **línea** *f.* 1.4; **cola** (*queue*) *f.* 3.2
listen (to) **escuchar** *v.* 1.2
listen to music **escuchar música** 1.2
listen to the radio **escuchar la radio** 1.2
literature **literatura** *f.* 1.2
little (*quantity*) **poco** *adv.* 2.4
live **vivir** *v.* 1.3; **en vivo** *adj.* 2.1
living room **sala** *f.* 2.6
loan **préstamo** *m.* 3.2; **prestar** *v.* 1.6, 3.2
lobster **langosta** *f.* 2.2
located **situado/a** *adj.*
be located **quedar** *v.* 3.2
long **largo/a** *adj.* 1.6
look (at) **mirar** *v.* 1.2
look for **buscar** *v.* 1.2
lose **perder (e:ie)** *v.* 1.4
lose weight **adelgazar** *v.* 3.3
lost **perdido/a** *adj.* 3.1, 3.2
be lost **estar perdido/a** 3.2
lot, a **muchas veces** *adv.* 2.4
lot of, a **mucho/a** *adj.* 1.3; **un montón de** 1.4
love (*another person*) **querer (e:ie)** *v.* 1.4; (*inanimate objects*) **encantar** *v.* 2.1; **amor** *m.* 2.3
in love **enamorado/a** *adj.* 1.5
love at first sight **amor a primera vista** 2.3
luck **suerte** *f.*
lucky: be (very) lucky **tener (mucha) suerte** 1.3
luggage **equipaje** *m.* 1.5
lunch **almuerzo** *m.* 1.4, 2.2
have lunch **almorzar (o:ue)** *v.* 1.4

M

ma'am **señora (Sra.)**; **doña** *f.* 1.1
mad **enojado/a** *adj.* 1.5
magazine **revista** *f.* 1.4
magnificent **magnífico/a** *adj.* 1.5
mail **correo** *m.* 3.2; **enviar** *v.*, **mandar** *v.* 3.2; **echar (una carta) al buzón** 3.2
mail carrier **cartero** *m.* 3.2
mailbox **buzón** *m.* 3.2
main **principal** *adj. m., f.* 2.2
maintain **mantener** *v.* 3.3
major **especialización** *f.* 1.2
make **hacer** *v.* 1.4
make a decision **tomar una decisión** 3.3
make the bed **hacer la cama** 2.6
makeup **maquillaje** *m.* 2.1
put on makeup **maquillarse** *v.* 2.1
man **hombre** *m.* 1.1
manager **gerente** *m., f.* 2.2, 3.4
many **mucho/a** *adj.* 1.3
many times **muchas veces** 2.4
map **mapa** *m.* 1.1, 1.2
March **marzo** *m.* 1.5
margarine **margarina** *f.* 2.2
marinated fish **ceviche** *m.* 2.2
lemon-marinated shrimp **ceviche** *m.* **de camarón** 2.2
marital status **estado** *m.* **civil** 2.3
market **mercado** *m.* 1.6
open-air market **mercado al aire libre** 1.6
marriage **matrimonio** *m.* 2.3
married **casado/a** *adj.* 2.3
get married (to) **casarse** *v.* **(con)** 2.3
I'll marry you! **¡Acepto casarme contigo!** 3.5
marvelous **maravilloso/a** *adj.* 1.5
massage **masaje** *m.* 3.3
masterpiece **obra maestra** *f.* 3.5
match (*sports*) **partido** *m.* 1.4
match (with) **hacer** *v.* **juego (con)** 1.6
mathematics **matemáticas** *f., pl.* 1.2
matter **importar** *v.* 2.1
maturity **madurez** *f.* 2.3
maximum **máximo/a** *adj.* 2.5
May **mayo** *m.* 1.5
May I leave a message? **¿Puedo dejar un recado?** 2.5
maybe **tal vez** 1.5; **quizás** 1.5
mayonnaise **mayonesa** *f.* 2.2
me **me** *sing., d.o. pron.* 1.5
to/for me **me** *sing., i.o. pron.* 1.6
meal **comida** *f.* 2.2
means of communication **medios** *m., pl.* **de comunicación** 3.6
meat **carne** *f.* 2.2
mechanic **mecánico/a** *m., f.* 2.5
mechanic's repair shop **taller mecánico** 2.5
media **medios** *m., pl.* **de comunicación** 3.6
medical **médico/a** *adj.* 2.4
medication **medicamento** *m.* 2.4
medicine **medicina** *f.* 2.4
medium **mediano/a** *adj.*
meet (each other) **encontrar(se)** *v.* 2.5; **conocer(se)** *v.* 2.2
meet up with **encontrarse con** 2.1
meeting **reunión** *f.* 3.4
menu **menú** *m.* 2.2

message **mensaje** *m.*
Mexican **mexicano/a** *adj.* 1.3
microwave **microonda** *f.* 2.6
microwave oven **horno** *m.* **de microondas** 2.6
middle age **madurez** *f.* 2.3
midnight **medianoche** *f.* 1.1
mile **milla** *f.*
milk **leche** *f.* 2.2
million **millón** *m.* 1.2
million of **millón de** 1.2
mine **mío(s)/a(s)** *poss.* 2.5
mineral **mineral** *m.* 3.3
mineral water **agua** *f.* **mineral** 2.2
minute **minuto** *m.*
mirror **espejo** *m.* 2.1
Miss **señorita (Srta.)** *f.* 1.1
miss **perder (e:ie)** *v.* 1.4; **extrañar** *v.* 3.4
mistaken **equivocado/a** *adj.*
modern **moderno/a** *adj.* 3.5
mom **mamá** *f.*
Monday **lunes** *m., sing.* 1.2
money **dinero** *m.* 1.6
monitor **monitor** *m.* 2.5
monkey **mono** *m.* 3.1
month **mes** *m.* 1.5
monument **monumento** *m.* 1.4
moon **luna** *f.* 3.1
more **más** 1.2
more... than **más... que** 2.2
more than **más de (+ *number*)** 2.2
morning **mañana** *f.* 1.1
mother **madre** *f.* 1.3
mother-in-law **suegra** *f.* 1.3
motor **motor** *m.*
motorcycle **moto(cicleta)** *f.* 1.5
mountain **montaña** *f.* 1.4
mouse **ratón** *m.* 2.5
mouth **boca** *f.* 2.4
move (*from one house to another*) **mudarse** *v.* 2.6
movie **película** *f.* 1.4
movie star **estrella** *f.* **de cine** 3.5
movie theater **cine** *m.* 1.4
MP3 player **reproductor** *m.* **de MP3** 2.5
Mr. **señor (Sr.)**; **don** *m.* 1.1
Mrs. **señora (Sra.)**; **doña** *f.* 1.1
much **mucho/a** *adj.* 1.3
mud **lodo** *m.*
murder **crimen** *m.* 3.6
muscle **músculo** *m.* 3.3
museum **museo** *m.* 1.4
mushroom **champiñón** *m.* 2.2
music **música** *f.* 1.2, 3.5
musical **musical** *adj., m., f.* 3.5
musician **músico/a** *m., f.* 3.5
must **deber** *v.* **(+ *inf.*)** 1.3
my **mi(s)** *poss. adj.* 1.3; **mío(s)/a(s)** *poss. pron.* 2.5

N

name **nombre** *m.* 1.1
be named **llamarse** *v.* 2.1
in the name of **a nombre de** 1.5
last name **apellido** *m.* 1.3
My name is... **Me llamo...** 1.1
name someone/something **ponerle el nombre** 2.3
napkin **servilleta** *f.* 2.6
national **nacional** *adj. m., f.* 3.6
nationality **nacionalidad** *f.* 1.1
natural **natural** *adj. m., f.* 3.1
natural disaster **desastre** *m.* **natural** 3.6
natural resource **recurso** *m.* **natural** 3.1
nature **naturaleza** *f.* 3.1
nauseated **mareado/a** *adj.* 2.4
near **cerca de** *prep.* 1.2
neaten **arreglar** *v.* 2.6
necessary **necesario/a** *adj.* 2.6
It is necessary that... **Es necesario que...** 2.6
neck **cuello** *m.* 2.4
need **faltar** *v.* 2.1; **necesitar** *v.* **(+ *inf.*)** 1.2
neighbor **vecino/a** *m., f.* 2.6
neighborhood **barrio** *m.* 2.6
neither **tampoco** *adv.* 2.1
neither... nor **ni... ni** *conj.* 2.1
nephew **sobrino** *m.* 1.3
nervous **nervioso/a** *adj.* 1.5
network **red** *f.* 2.5
never **nunca** *adj.* 2.1; **jamás** 2.1
new **nuevo/a** *adj.* 1.6
newlywed **recién casado/a** *m., f.* 2.3
news **noticias** *f., pl.* 3.6; **actualidades** *f., pl.* 3.6; **noticia** *f.* 2.5
newscast **noticiero** *m.* 3.6
newspaper **periódico** 1.4; **diario** *m.* 3.6
next **próximo/a** *adj.* 1.3, 3.4
next to **al lado de** *prep.* 1.2
nice **simpático/a** *adj.* 1.3; **amable** *adj.* 1.5
niece **sobrina** *f.* 1.3
night **noche** *f.* 1.1
night stand **mesita** *f.* **de noche** 2.6
nine **nueve** 1.1
nine hundred **novecientos/as** 1.2
nineteen **diecinueve** 1.1
ninety **noventa** 1.2
ninth **noveno/a** 1.5
no **no** 1.1; **ningún, ninguno/a(s)** *adj.* 2.1
no one **nadie** *pron.* 2.1
nobody **nadie** 2.1
none **ningún, ninguno/a(s)** *adj.* 2.1
noon **mediodía** *m.* 1.1
nor **ni** *conj.* 2.1
north **norte** *m.* 3.2
to the north **al norte** 3.2
nose **nariz** *f.* 2.4
not **no** 1.1
not any **ningún, ninguno/a(s)** *adj.* 2.1
not anyone **nadie** *pron.* 2.1
not anything **nada** *pron.* 2.1
not bad at all **nada mal** 1.5
not either **tampoco** *adv.* 2.1
not ever **nunca** *adv.* 2.1; **jamás** *adv.* 2.1
not very well **no muy bien** 1.1
not working **descompuesto/a** *adj.* 2.5
notebook **cuaderno** *m.* 1.1
nothing **nada** 1.1; 2.1
noun **sustantivo** *m.*
November **noviembre** *m.* 1.5
now **ahora** *adv.* 1.2
nowadays **hoy día** *adv.*
nuclear **nuclear** *adj. m., f.* 3.1
nuclear energy **energía nuclear** 3.1
number **número** *m.* 1.1
nurse **enfermero/a** *m., f.* 2.4
nutrition **nutrición** *f.* 3.3
nutritionist **nutricionista** *m., f.* 3.3

O

o'clock: It's... o'clock **Son las...** 1.1
It's one o'clock. **Es la una.** 1.1
obey **obedecer** *v.* 3.6
obligation **deber** *m.* 3.6
obtain **conseguir (e:i)** *v.* 1.4; **obtener** *v.* 3.4
obvious **obvio/a** *adj.* 3.1
it's obvious **es obvio** 3.1
occupation **ocupación** *f.* 3.4
occur **ocurrir** *v.* 3.6
October **octubre** *m.* 1.5
of **de** *prep.* 1.1
Of course. **Claro que sí.; Por supuesto.**
offer **oferta** *f.*; **ofrecer (c:zc)** *v.* 1.6
office **oficina** *f.* 2.6
doctor's office **consultorio** *m.* 2.4
often **a menudo** *adv.* 2.4
Oh! **¡Ay!**
oil **aceite** *m.* 2.2
OK **regular** *adj.* 1.1
It's okay. **Está bien.**
old **viejo/a** *adj.* 1.3
old age **vejez** *f.* 2.3
older **mayor** *adj. m., f.* 1.3
older brother, sister **hermano/a mayor** *m., f.* 1.3
oldest **el/la mayor** 2.2
on **en** *prep.* 1.2; **sobre** *prep.* 1.2

on behalf of **por** *prep.* 2.5
on the dot **en punto** 1.1
on time **a tiempo** 2.4
on top of **encima de** 1.2
once **una vez** 1.6
one **uno** 1.1
one hundred **cien(to)** 1.2
one million **un millón** *m.* 1.2
one more time **una vez más**
one thousand **mil** 1.2
one time **una vez** 1.6
onion **cebolla** *f.* 2.2
only **sólo** *adv.* 1.6; **único/a** *adj.* 1.3
only child **hijo/a único/a** *m., f.* 1.3
open **abierto/a** *adj.* 1.5, 3.2; **abrir** *v.* 1.3
open-air **al aire libre** 1.6
opera **ópera** *f.* 3.5
operation **operación** *f.* 2.4
opposite **enfrente de** *prep.* 3.2
or **o** *conj.* 2.1
orange **anaranjado/a** *adj.* 1.6; **naranja** *f.* 2.2
orchestra **orquesta** *f.* 3.5
order **mandar** 2.6; (*food*) **pedir (e:i)** *v.* 2.2
in order to **para** *prep.* 2.5
orderly **ordenado/a** *adj.* 1.5
ordinal (*numbers*) **ordinal** *adj.*
organize oneself **organizarse** *v.* 2.6
other **otro/a** *adj.* 1.6
ought to **deber** *v.* **(+ *inf.*)** *adj.* 1.3
our **nuestro(s)/a(s)** *poss. adj.* 1.3; *poss. pron.* 2.5
out of order **descompuesto/a** *adj.* 2.5
outside **afuera** *adv.* 1.5
outskirts **afueras** *f., pl.* 2.6
oven **horno** *m.* 2.6
over **sobre** *prep.* 1.2
(over)population **(sobre)población** *f.* 3.1
over there **allá** *adv.* 1.2
own **propio/a** *adj.*
owner **dueño/a** *m., f.* 2.2

P

p.m. **de la tarde, de la noche** *f.* 1.1
pack (one's suitcases) **hacer** *v.* **las maletas** 1.5
package **paquete** *m.* 3.2
page **página** *f.* 2.5
pain **dolor** *m.* 2.4
have pain **tener** *v.* **dolor** 2.4
paint **pintar** *v.* 3.5
painter **pintor(a)** *m., f.* 3.4
painting **pintura** *f.* 2.6, 3.5
pair **par** *m.* 1.6
pair of shoes **par** *m.* **de zapatos** 1.6
pale **pálido/a** *adj.* 3.2
pants **pantalones** *m., pl.* 1.6
pantyhose **medias** *f., pl.* 1.6
paper **papel** *m.* 1.2; (*report*) **informe** *m.* 3.6
Pardon me. (*May I?*) **Con permiso.** 1.1; (*Excuse me.*) Pardon me. **Perdón.** 1.1
parents **padres** *m., pl.* 1.3; **papás** *m., pl.*
park **estacionar** *v.* 2.5; **parque** *m.* 1.4
parking lot **estacionamiento** *m.* 3.2
partner (*one of a married couple*) **pareja** *f.* 2.3
party **fiesta** *f.* 2.3
passed **pasado/a** *p.p.*
passenger **pasajero/a** *m., f.* 1.1
passport **pasaporte** *m.* 1.5
past **pasado/a** *adj.* 1.6
pastime **pasatiempo** *m.* 1.4
pastry shop **pastelería** *f.* 3.2
path **sendero** *m.* 3.1
patient **paciente** *m., f.* 2.4
patio **patio** *m.* 2.6
pay **pagar** *v.* 1.6
pay in cash **pagar** *v.* **al contado; pagar en efectivo** 3.2
pay in installments **pagar** *v.* **a plazos** 3.2
pay the bill **pagar la cuenta**
pea **arveja** *m.* 2.2
peace **paz** *f.* 3.6
peach **melocotón** *m.* 2.2
peak **cima** *f.* 3.3
pear **pera** *f.* 2.2
pen **pluma** *f.* 1.2
pencil **lápiz** *m.* 1.1
penicillin **penicilina** *f.*
people **gente** *f.* 1.3
pepper (*black*) **pimienta** *f.* 2.2
per **por** *prep.* 2.5
perfect **perfecto/a** *adj.* 1.5
period of time **temporada** *f.* 1.5
person **persona** *f.* 1.3
pharmacy **farmacia** *f.* 2.4
phenomenal **fenomenal** *adj.* 1.5
photograph **foto(grafía)** *f.* 1.1
physical (exam) **examen** *m.* **médico** 2.4
physician **doctor(a), médico/a** *m., f.* 1.3
physics **física** *f. sing.* 1.2
pick up **recoger** *v.* 3.1
picture **cuadro** *m.* 2.6; **pintura** *f.* 2.6
pie **pastel** *m.* 2.3
pill (tablet) **pastilla** *f.* 2.4
pillow **almohada** *f.* 2.6
pineapple **piña** *f.*
pink **rosado/a** *adj.* 1.6
place **lugar** *m.* 1.2, 1.4; **sitio** *m.* 1.3; **poner** *v.* 1.4
plaid **de cuadros** 1.6
plans **planes** *m., pl.*
have plans **tener planes**
plant **planta** *f.* 3.1
plastic **plástico** *m.* 3.1
(made) of plastic **de plástico** 3.1
plate **plato** *m.* 2.6
play **drama** *m.* 3.5; **comedia** *f.* 3.5 **jugar (u:ue)** *v.* 1.4; (*a musical instrument*) **tocar** *v.* 3.5; (*a role*) **hacer el papel de** 3.5; (*cards*) **jugar a (las cartas)** 1.5; (*sports*) **practicar deportes** 1.4
player **jugador(a)** *m., f.* 1.4
playwright **dramaturgo/a** *m., f.* 3.5
plead **rogar (o:ue)** *v.* 2.6
pleasant **agradable** *adj.*
please **por favor** 1.1
Pleased to meet you. **Mucho gusto.** 1.1; **Encantado/a.** *adj.* 1.1
pleasing: be pleasing to **gustar** *v.* 2.1
pleasure **gusto** *m.* 1.1; **placer** *m.*
The pleasure is mine. **El gusto es mío.** 1.1
poem **poema** *m.* 3.5
poet **poeta** *m., f.* 3.5
poetry **poesía** *f.* 3.5
police (force) **policía** *f.* 2.5
political **político/a** *adj.* 3.6
politician **político/a** *m., f.* 3.4
politics **política** *f.* 3.6
polka-dotted **de lunares** 1.6
poll **encuesta** *f.* 3.6
pollute **contaminar** *v.* 3.1
polluted **contaminado/a** *m., f.* 3.1
be polluted **estar contaminado/a** 3.1
pollution **contaminación** *f.* 3.1
pool **piscina** *f.* 1.4
poor **pobre** *adj., m., f.* 1.6
poor thing **pobrecito/a** *adj.* 1.3
popsicle **paleta helada** *f.* 1.4
population **población** *f.* 3.1
pork **cerdo** *m.* 2.2
pork chop **chuleta** *f.* **de cerdo** 2.2
portable **portátil** *adj.* 2.5
portable computer **computadora** *f.* **portátil** 2.5
position **puesto** *m.* 3.4
possessive **posesivo/a** *adj.*
possible **posible** *adj.* 3.1
it's (not) possible **(no) es posible** 3.1
post office **correo** *m.* 3.2
postcard **postal** *f.*
poster **cartel** *m.* 2.6
potato **papa** *f.* 2.2; **patata** *f.* 2.2
pottery **cerámica** *f.* 3.5
practice **entrenarse** *v.* 3.3; **practicar** *v.* 1.2; (a degree/profession) **ejercer** *v.* 3.4
prefer **preferir (e:ie)** *v.* 1.4
pregnant **embarazada** *adj. f.* 2.4
prepare **preparar** *v.* 1.2
preposition **preposición** *f.*
prescribe (*medicine*) **recetar** *v.* 2.4
prescription **receta** *f.* 2.4
present **regalo** *m.*; **presentar** *v.* 3.5

press **prensa** *f.* 3.6
pressure **presión** *f.*
be under a lot of pressure **sufrir muchas presiones** 3.3
pretty **bonito/a** *adj.* 1.3
price **precio** *m.* 1.6
(fixed, set) price **precio** *m.* **fijo** 1.6
print **imprimir** *v.* 2.5
printer **impresora** *f.* 2.5
prize **premio** *m.* 3.5
probable **probable** *adj.* 3.1
it's (not) probable **(no) es probable** 3.1
problem **problema** *m.* 1.1
profession **profesión** *f.* 1.3; 3.4
professor **profesor(a)** *m., f.*
program **programa** *m.* 1.1
programmer **programador(a)** *m., f.* 1.3
prohibit **prohibir** *v.* 2.4
project **proyecto** *m.* 2.5
promotion (*career*) **ascenso** *m.* 3.4
pronoun **pronombre** *m.*
protect **proteger** *v.* 3.1
protein **proteína** *f.* 3.3
provided (that) **con tal (de) que** *conj.* 3.1
psychologist **psicólogo/a** *m., f.* 3.4
psychology **psicología** *f.* 1.2
publish **publicar** *v.* 3.5
Puerto Rican **puertorriqueño/a** *adj.* 1.3
purchases **compras** *f., pl.*
pure **puro/a** *adj.* 3.1
purple **morado/a** *adj.* 1.6
purse **bolsa** *f.* 1.6
put **poner** *v.* 1.4; **puesto/a** *p.p.* 3.2
put (a letter) in the mailbox **echar (una carta) al buzón** 3.2
put on (*a performance*) **presentar** *v.* 3.5
put on (*clothing*) **ponerse** *v.* 2.1
put on makeup **maquillarse** *v.* 2.1

Q

quality **calidad** *f.* 1.6
quarter (*academic*) **trimestre** *m.* 1.2
quarter after (*time*) **y cuarto** 1.1; **y quince** 1.1
quarter to (*time*) **menos cuarto** 1.1; **menos quince** 1.1
question **pregunta** *f.*
quickly **rápido** *adv.* 2.4
quiet **tranquilo/a** *adj.* 3.3
quit **dejar** *v.* 3.4
quiz **prueba** *f.* 1.2

R

racism **racismo** *m.* 3.6
radio (*medium*) **radio** *f.* 1.2
radio (set) **radio** *m.* 2.5
rain **llover (o:ue)** *v.* 1.5; **lluvia** *f.*
It's raining. **Llueve.** 1.5; **Está lloviendo.** 1.5
raincoat **impermeable** *m.* 1.6
rain forest **bosque** *m.* **tropical** 3.1
raise (*salary*) **aumento de sueldo** 3.4
rather **bastante** *adv.* 2.4
read **leer** *v.* 1.3; **leído/a** *p.p.* 3.2
read e-mail **leer el correo electrónico** 1.4
read a magazine **leer una revista** 1.4
read a newspaper **leer un periódico** 1.4
ready **listo/a** *adj.* 1.5
reality show **programa de realidad** *m.* 3.5
reap the benefits (of) *v.* **disfrutar** *v.* **(de)** 3.3
receive **recibir** *v.* 1.3
recommend **recomendar (e:ie)** *v.* 2.2; 2.6
record **grabar** *v.* 2.5
recover **recuperar** *v.* 2.5
recreation **diversión** *f.* 1.4
recycle **reciclar** *v.* 3.1
recycling **reciclaje** *m.* 3.1
red **rojo/a** *adj.* 1.6
red-haired **pelirrojo/a** *adj.* 1.3
reduce **reducir** *v.* 3.1; **disminuir** *v.* 3.4
reduce stress/tension **aliviar el estrés/la tensión** 3.3
refrigerator **refrigerador** *m.* 2.6
region **región** *f.*
regret **sentir (e:ie)** *v.* 3.1
relatives **parientes** *m., pl.* 1.3
relax **relajarse** *v.* 2.3
Relax. **Tranquilo/a.** 2.1
Relax, sweetie. **Tranquilo/a, cariño.** 2.5
remain **quedarse** *v.* 2.1
remember **acordarse (o:ue)** *v.* **(de)** 2.1; **recordar (o:ue)** *v.* 1.4
remote control **control remoto** *m.* 2.5
renewable **renovable** *adj.* 3.1
rent **alquilar** *v.* 2.6; (payment) **alquiler** *m.* 2.6
repeat **repetir (e:i)** *v.* 1.4
report **informe** *m.* 3.6; **reportaje** *m.* 3.6
reporter **reportero/a** *m., f.* 3.4
representative **representante** *m., f.* 3.6
request **pedir (e:i)** *v.* 1.4
reservation **reservación** *f.* 1.5
resign (from) **renunciar (a)** *v.* 3.4
resolve **resolver (o:ue)** *v.* 3.1
resolved **resuelto/a** *p.p.* 3.2
resource **recurso** *m.* 3.1
responsibility **deber** *m.* 3.6; **responsabilidad** *f.*
responsible **responsable** *adj.* 2.2
rest **descansar** *v.* 1.2
restaurant **restaurante** *m.* 1.4
résumé **currículum** *m.* 3.4
retire (from work) **jubilarse** *v.* 2.3
return **regresar** *v.* 1.2; **volver (o:ue)** *v.* 1.4
returned **vuelto/a** *p.p.* 3.2
rice **arroz** *m.* 2.2
rich **rico/a** *adj.* 1.6
ride a bicycle **pasear** *v.* **en bicicleta** 1.4
ride a horse **montar** *v.* **a caballo** 1.5
ridiculous **ridículo/a** *adj.* 3.1
it's ridiculous **es ridículo** 3.1
right **derecha** *f.* 1.2
be right **tener razón** 1.3
right? (*question tag*) **¿no?** 1.1; **¿verdad?** 1.1
right away **enseguida** *adv.*
right now **ahora mismo** 1.5
to the right of **a la derecha de** 1.2
rights **derechos** *m.* 3.6
ring **anillo** *m.* 3.5
ring (*a doorbell*) **sonar (o:ue)** *v.* 2.5
river **río** *m.* 3.1
road **carretera** f. 2.5; **camino** *m.*
roast **asado/a** *adj.* 2.2
roast chicken **pollo** *m.* **asado** 2.2
rollerblade **patinar en línea** *v.*
romantic **romántico/a** *adj.* 3.5
room **habitación** *f.* 1.5; **cuarto** *m.* 1.2; 2.1
living room **sala** *f.* 2.6
roommate **compañero/a** *m., f.* **de cuarto** 1.2
roundtrip **de ida y vuelta** 1.5
roundtrip ticket **pasaje** *m.* **de ida y vuelta** 1.5
routine **rutina** *f.* 2.1
rug **alfombra** *f.* 2.6
run **correr** *v.* 1.3
run errands **hacer diligencias** 3.2
run into (*have an accident*) **chocar (con)** *v.*; (*meet accidentally*) **encontrar(se) (o:ue)** *v.* 2.5; (*run into something*) **darse (con)** 2.4
run into (each other) **encontrar(se) (o:ue)** *v.* 2.5
rush **apurarse, darse prisa** *v.* 3.3
Russian **ruso/a** *adj.* 1.3

S

sad **triste** *adj.* 1.5; 3.1
it's sad **es triste** 3.1
safe **seguro/a** *adj.* 1.5
said **dicho/a** *p.p.* 3.2
sailboard **tabla de windsurf** *f.* 1.5
salad **ensalada** *f.* 2.2
salary **salario** *m.* 3.4; **sueldo** *m.* 3.4
sale **rebaja** *f.* 1.6
salesperson **vendedor(a)** *m., f.* 1.6
salmon **salmón** *m.* 2.2
salt **sal** *f.* 2.2
same **mismo/a** *adj.* 1.3
sandal **sandalia** *f.* 1.6
sandwich **sándwich** *m.* 2.2
Saturday **sábado** *m.* 1.2
sausage **salchicha** *f.* 2.2
save (*on a computer*) **guardar** *v.* 2.5; save (money) **ahorrar** *v.* 3.2
savings **ahorros** *m.* 3.2
savings account **cuenta** *f.* **de ahorros** 3.2
say **decir** *v.* 1.4; **declarar** *v.* 3.6
say (that) **decir (que)** *v.* 1.4
say the answer **decir la respuesta** 1.4
scan **escanear** *v.* 2.5
scarcely **apenas** *adv.* 2.4
scared: be (very) scared (of) **tener (mucho) miedo (de)** 1.3
schedule **horario** *m.* 1.2
school **escuela** *f.* 1.1
sciences *f., pl.* **ciencias** 1.2
science fiction (genre) **de ciencia ficción** *f.* 3.5
scientist **científico/a** *m., f.* 3.4
scream **grito** *m.* 1.5; **gritar** *v.*
screen **pantalla** *f.* 2.5
scuba dive **bucear** *v.* 1.4
sculpt **esculpir** *v.* 3.5
sculptor **escultor(a)** *m., f.* 3.5
sculpture **escultura** *f.* 3.5
sea **mar** *m.* 1.5
(sea) turtle **tortuga (marina)** *f.* 3.1
season **estación** *f.* 1.5
seat **silla** *f.* 1.2
second **segundo/a** 1.5
secretary **secretario/a** *m., f.* 3.4
sedentary **sedentario/a** *adj.* 3.3
see **ver** *v.* 1.4
see (you, him, her) again **volver a ver(te, lo, la)**
see movies **ver películas** 1.4
See you. **Nos vemos.** 1.1
See you later. **Hasta la vista.** 1.1; **Hasta luego.** 1.1
See you soon. **Hasta pronto.** 1.1
See you tomorrow. **Hasta mañana.** 1.1
seem **parecer** *v.* 1.6
seen **visto/a** *p.p.* 3.2
sell **vender** *v.* 1.6
semester **semestre** *m.* 1.2
send **enviar; mandar** *v.* 3.2
separate (from) **separarse** *v.* **(de)** 2.3
separated **separado/a** *adj.* 2.3
September **septiembre** *m.* 1.5
sequence **secuencia** *f.*
serious **grave** *adj.* 2.4
serve **servir (e:i)** *v.* 2.2
service **servicio** *m.* 3.3
set (*fixed*) **fijo/a** *adj.* 1.6
set the table **poner la mesa** 2.6
seven **siete** 1.1
seven hundred **setecientos/as** 1.2
seventeen **diecisiete** 1.1
seventh **séptimo/a** 1.5
seventy **setenta** 1.2
several **varios/as** *adj. pl.*
sexism **sexismo** *m.* 3.6
shame **lástima** *f.* 3.1
it's a shame **es una lástima** 3.1
shampoo **champú** *m.* 2.1
shape **forma** *f.* 3.3
be in good shape **estar en buena forma** 3.3
stay in shape **mantenerse en forma** 3.3
share **compartir** *v.* 1.3
sharp (*time*) **en punto** 1.1
shave **afeitarse** *v.* 2.1
shaving cream **crema** *f.* **de afeitar** 1.5, 2.1
she **ella** 1.1
shellfish **mariscos** *m., pl.* 2.2
ship **barco** *m.*
shirt **camisa** *f.* 1.6
shoe **zapato** *m.* 1.6
shoe size **número** *m.* 1.6
shoe store **zapatería** *f.* 3.2
tennis shoes **zapatos** *m., pl.* **de tenis** 1.6
shop **tienda** *f.* 1.6
shopping, to go **ir de compras** 1.5
shopping mall **centro comercial** *m.* 1.6
short (*in height*) **bajo/a** *adj.* 1.3; (*in length*) **corto/a** *adj.* 1.6
short story **cuento** *m.* 3.5
shorts **pantalones cortos** *m., pl.* 1.6
should (*do something*) **deber** *v.* **(+ *inf.*)** 1.3
shout **gritar** *v.*
show **espectáculo** *m.* 3.5; **mostrar (o:ue)** *v.* 1.4
game show **concurso** *m.* 3.5
shower **ducha** *f.* 2.1; **ducharse** *v.* 2.1
shrimp **camarón** *m.* 2.2
siblings **hermanos/as** *pl.* 1.3
sick **enfermo/a** *adj.* 2.4
be sick **estar enfermo/a** 2.4
get sick **enfermarse** *v.* 2.4
sign **firmar** *v.* 3.2; **letrero** *m.* 3.2
silk **seda** *f.* 1.6
(made of) silk **de seda** 1.6
since **desde** *prep.*
sing **cantar** *v.* 1.2
singer **cantante** *m., f.* 3.5
single **soltero/a** *adj.* 2.3
single room **habitación** *f.* **individual** 1.5
sink **lavabo** *m.* 2.1
sir **señor (Sr.), don** *m.* 1.1; **caballero** *m.* 2.2
sister **hermana** *f.* 1.3
sister-in-law **cuñada** *f.* 1.3
sit down **sentarse (e:ie)** *v.* 2.1
six **seis** 1.1
six hundred **seiscientos/as** 1.2
sixteen **dieciséis** 1.1
sixth **sexto/a** 1.5
sixty **sesenta** 1.2
size **talla** *f.* 1.6
shoe size *m.* **número** 1.6
(in-line) skate **patinar (en línea)** 1.4
skateboard **andar en patineta** *v.* 1.4
ski **esquiar** *v.* 1.4
skiing **esquí** *m.* 1.4
water-skiing **esquí** *m.* **acuático** 1.4
skirt **falda** *f.* 1.6
skull made out of sugar **calavera de azúcar** *f.* 2.3
sky **cielo** *m.* 3.1
sleep **dormir (o:ue)** *v.* 1.4; **sueño** *m.*
go to sleep **dormirse (o:ue)** *v.* 2.1
sleepy: be (very) sleepy **tener (mucho) sueño** 1.3
slender **delgado/a** *adj.* 1.3
slim down **adelgazar** *v.* 3.3
slippers **pantuflas** *f.* 2.1
slow **lento/a** *adj.* 2.5
slowly **despacio** *adv.* 2.4
small **pequeño/a** *adj.* 1.3
smart **listo/a** *adj.* 1.5
smile **sonreír (e:i)** *v.* 2.3
smiled **sonreído** *p.p.* 3.2
smoggy: It's (very) smoggy. **Hay (mucha) contaminación.**
smoke **fumar** *v.* 3.3
(not) to smoke **(no) fumar** 3.3
smoking section **sección** *f.* **de fumar** 2.2
(non) smoking section *f.* **sección de (no) fumar** 2.2
snack **merendar (e:ie)** *v.* 2.2
afternoon snack **merienda** *f.* 3.3
have a snack **merendar** *v.* 2.2
sneakers **los zapatos de tenis** 1.6
sneeze **estornudar** *v.* 2.4
snow **nevar (e:ie)** *v.* 1.5; **nieve** *f.*
snowing: It's snowing. **Nieva.** 1.5; **Está nevando.** 1.5
so (*in such a way*) **así** *adv.* 2.4; **tan** *adv.* 1.5
so much **tanto** *adv.*
so-so **regular** 1.1
so that **para que** *conj.* 3.1
soap **jabón** *m.* 2.1
soap opera **telenovela** *f.* 3.5
soccer **fútbol** *m.* 1.4
sociology **sociología** *f.* 1.2
sock(s) **calcetín (calcetines)** *m.* 1.6
sofa **sofá** *m.* 2.6
soft drink **refresco** *m.* 2.2
software **programa** *m.* **de computación** 2.5
soil **tierra** *f.* 3.1
solar **solar** *adj., m., f.* 3.1
solar energy **energía solar** 3.1

soldier **soldado** *m., f.* 3.6
solution **solución** *f.* 3.1
solve **resolver (o:ue)** *v.* 3.1
some **algún, alguno/a(s)** *adj.* 2.1; **unos/as** *indef. art.* 1.1
somebody **alguien** *pron.* 2.1
someone **alguien** *pron.* 2.1
something **algo** *pron.* 2.1
sometimes **a veces** *adv.* 2.4
son **hijo** *m.* 1.3
song **canción** *f.* 3.5
son-in-law **yerno** *m.* 1.3
soon **pronto** *adv.* 2.4
See you soon. **Hasta pronto.** 1.1
sorry: be sorry **sentir (e:ie)** *v.* 3.1
I'm sorry. **Lo siento.** 1.1
soul **alma** *f.* 2.3
soup **sopa** *f.* 2.2
south **sur** *m.* 3.2
to the south **al sur** 3.2
Spain **España** *f.*
Spanish (*language*) **español** *m.* 1.2; **español(a)** *adj.* 1.3
spare (free) time **ratos libres** 1.4
speak **hablar** *v.* 1.2
Speaking. (*on the telephone*) **Con él/ella habla.** 2.5
special: today's specials **las especialidades del día** 2.2
spectacular **espectacular** *adj. m., f.*
speech **discurso** *m.* 3.6
speed **velocidad** *f.* 2.5
speed limit **velocidad** *f.* **máxima** 2.5
spelling **ortografía** *f.*, **ortográfico/a** *adj.*
spend (*money*) **gastar** *v.* 1.6
spoon (*table or large*) **cuchara** *f.* 2.6
sport **deporte** *m.* 1.4
sports-related **deportivo/a** *adj.* 1.4
spouse **esposo/a** *m., f.* 1.3
sprain (one's ankle) **torcerse (o:ue)** *v.* **(el tobillo)** 2.4
spring **primavera** *f.* 1.5
(city or town) square **plaza** *f.* 1.4
stadium **estadio** *m.* 1.2
stage **etapa** *f.* 2.3
stairs **escalera** *f.* 2.6
stairway **escalera** *f.* 2.6
stamp **estampilla** *f.* 3.2; **sello** *m.* 3.2
stand in line **hacer** *v.* **cola** 3.2
star **estrella** *f.* 3.1
start (*a vehicle*) **arrancar** *v.* 2.5
station **estación** *f.* 1.5
statue **estatua** *f.* 3.5
status: marital status **estado** *m.* **civil** 2.3
stay **quedarse** *v.* 2.1
stay in shape **mantenerse en forma** 3.3
steak **bistec** *m.* 2.2
steering wheel **volante** *m.* 2.5
step **escalón** *m.* 3.3
stepbrother **hermanastro** *m.* 1.3
stepdaughter **hijastra** *f.* 1.3
stepfather **padrastro** *m.* 1.3
stepmother **madrastra** *f.* 1.3
stepsister **hermanastra** *f.* 1.3
stepson **hijastro** *m.* 1.3
stereo **estéreo** *m.* 2.5
still **todavía** *adv.* 1.5
stockbroker **corredor(a)** *m., f.* **de bolsa** 3.4
stockings **medias** *f., pl.* 1.6
stomach **estómago** *m.* 2.4
stone **piedra** *f.* 3.1
stop **parar** *v.* 2.5
stop (*doing something*) **dejar de (+ *inf.*)** 3.1
store **tienda** *f.* 1.6
storm **tormenta** *f.* 3.6
story **cuento** *m.* 3.5; **historia** *f.* 3.5
stove **cocina, estufa** *f.* 2.6
straight **derecho** *adv.* 3.2
straight (ahead) **derecho** 3.2
straighten up **arreglar** *v.* 2.6
strange **extraño/a** *adj.* 3.1
it's strange **es extraño** 3.1
street **calle** *f.* 2.5
stress **estrés** *m.* 3.3
stretching **estiramiento** *m.* 3.3
do stretching exercises **hacer ejercicios** *m. pl.* **de estiramiento** 3.3
strike (*labor*) **huelga** *f.* 3.6
striped **de rayas** 1.6
stroll **pasear** *v.* 1.4
strong **fuerte** *adj. m., f.* 3.3
struggle (for/against) **luchar** *v.* **(por/contra)** 3.6
student **estudiante** *m., f.* 1.1; 1.2; **estudiantil** *adj.* 1.2
study **estudiar** *v.* 1.2
stupendous **estupendo/a** *adj.* 1.5
style **estilo** *m.*
suburbs **afueras** *f., pl.* 2.6
subway **metro** *m.* 1.5
subway station **estación** *f.* **del metro** 1.5
success **éxito** *m.*
successful: be successful **tener éxito** 3.4
such as **tales como**
suddenly **de repente** *adv.* 1.6
suffer **sufrir** *v.* 2.4
suffer an illness **sufrir una enfermedad** 2.4
sugar **azúcar** *m.* 2.2
suggest **sugerir (e:ie)** *v.* 2.6
suit **traje** *m.* 1.6
suitcase **maleta** *f.* 1.1
summer **verano** *m.* 1.5
sun **sol** *m.* 3.1
sunbathe **tomar** *v.* **el sol** 1.4
Sunday **domingo** *m.* 1.2
(sun)glasses **gafas** *f., pl.* **(de sol)** 1.6
sunny: It's (very) sunny. **Hace (mucho) sol.** 1.5
supermarket **supermercado** *m.* 3.2
suppose **suponer** *v.* 1.4
sure **seguro/a** *adj.* 1.5
be sure **estar seguro/a** 1.5
surf **hacer** *v.* **surf** 1.5; (*the Internet*) **navegar** *v.* **(en Internet)** 2.5
surfboard **tabla de surf** *f.* 1.5
surprise **sorprender** *v.* 2.3; **sorpresa** *f.* 2.3
survey **encuesta** *f.* 3.6
sweat **sudar** *v.* 3.3
sweater **suéter** *m.* 1.6
sweep the floor **barrer el suelo** 2.6
sweets **dulces** *m., pl.* 2.3
swim **nadar** *v.* 1.4
swimming **natación** *f.* 1.4
swimming pool **piscina** *f.* 1.4
symptom **síntoma** *m.* 2.4

T

table **mesa** *f.* 1.2
tablespoon **cuchara** *f.* 2.6
tablet (*pill*) **pastilla** *f.* 2.4
take **tomar** *v.* 1.2; **llevar** *v.* 1.6
take care of **cuidar** *v.* 3.1
take someone's temperature **tomar** *v.* **la temperatura** 2.4
take (*wear*) a shoe size **calzar** *v.* 1.6
take a bath **bañarse** *v.* 2.1
take a shower **ducharse** *v.* 2.1
take off **quitarse** *v.* 2.1
take out the trash *v.* **sacar la basura** 2.6
take photos **tomar** *v.* **fotos** 1.5; **sacar** *v.* **fotos** 1.5
talented **talentoso/a** *adj.* 3.5
talk **hablar** *v.* 1.2
talk show **programa** *m.* **de entrevistas** 3.5
tall **alto/a** *adj.* 1.3
tank **tanque** *m.* 2.5
taste **probar (o:ue)** *v.* 2.2
taste like **saber a** 2.2
tasty **rico/a** *adj.* 2.2; **sabroso/a** *adj.* 2.2
tax **impuesto** *m.* 3.6
taxi **taxi** *m.* 1.5
tea **té** *m.* 2.2
teach **enseñar** *v.* 1.2
teacher **profesor(a)** *m., f.* 1.1, 1.2; **maestro/a** *m., f.* 3.4
team **equipo** *m.* 1.4
technician **técnico/a** *m., f.* 3.4
telecommuting **teletrabajo** *m.* 3.4
telephone **teléfono** 2.5
television **televisión** *f.* 1.2
television set **televisor** *m.* 2.5
tell **contar** *v.* 1.4; **decir** *v.* 1.4
tell (that) **decir** *v.* **(que)** 1.4
tell lies **decir mentiras** 1.4
tell the truth **decir la verdad** 1.4
temperature **temperatura** *f.* 2.4
ten **diez** 1.1
tennis **tenis** *m.* 1.4

tennis shoes **zapatos** *m., pl.* **de tenis** 1.6
tension **tensión** *f.* 3.3
tent **tienda** *f.* **de campaña**
tenth **décimo/a** 1.5
terrible **terrible** *adj. m., f.* 3.1
it's terrible **es terrible** 3.1
terrific **chévere** *adj.*
test **prueba** *f.* 1.2; **examen** *m.* 1.2
text message **mensaje** *m.* **de texto** 2.5
Thank you. **Gracias.** *f., pl.* 1.1
Thank you (very much). **(Muchas) gracias.** 1.1
Thanks (a lot). **(Muchas) gracias.** 1.1
Thanks for inviting me. **Gracias por invitarme.** 2.3
that **que, quien(es)** *pron.* 2.6
that (one) **ése, ésa, eso** *pron.* 1.6; **ese, esa,** *adj.* 1.6
that (*over there*) **aquél, aquélla, aquello** *pron.* 1.6; **aquel, aquella** *adj.* 1.6
that which **lo que** 2.6
that's why **por eso** 2.5
the **el** *m.*, **la** *f. sing.*, **los** *m.*, **las** *f., pl.* 1.1
theater **teatro** *m.* 3.5
their **su(s)** *poss. adj.* 1.3; **suyo(s)/a(s)** *poss. pron.* 2.5
them **los/las** *pl., d.o. pron.* 1.5
to/for them **les** *pl., i.o. pron.* 1.6
then (*afterward*) **después** *adv.* 2.1; (*as a result*) **entonces** *adv.* 1.5, 2.1; (*next*) **luego** *adv.* 2.1
there **allí** *adv.* 1.2
There is/are... **Hay...** 1.1
There is/are not... **No hay...** 1.1
therefore **por eso** 2.5
these **éstos, éstas** *pron.* 1.6; **estos, estas** *adj.* 1.6
they **ellos** *m.*, **ellas** *f. pron.* 1.1
They all told me to ask you to excuse them/forgive them. **Todos me dijeron que te pidiera una disculpa de su parte.** 3.6
thin **delgado/a** *adj.* 1.3
thing **cosa** *f.* 1.1
think **pensar (e:ie)** *v.* 1.4; (believe) **creer** *v.*
think about **pensar en** *v.* 1.4
third **tercero/a** 1.5
thirst **sed** *f.*
thirsty: be (very) thirsty **tener (mucha) sed** 1.3
thirteen **trece** 1.1
thirty **treinta** 1.1; thirty (*minutes past the hour*) **y treinta; y media** 1.1
this **este, esta** *adj.*; **éste, ésta, esto** *pron.* 1.6
those **ésos, ésas** *pron.* 1.6; **esos, esas** *adj.* 1.6
those (over there) **aquéllos, aquéllas** *pron.* 1.6; **aquellos, aquellas** *adj.* 1.6
thousand **mil** *m.* 1.2
three **tres** 1.1
three hundred **trescientos/as** 1.2
throat **garganta** *f.* 2.4
through **por** *prep.* 2.5
Thursday **jueves** *m., sing.* 1.2
thus (*in such a way*) **así** *adv.*
ticket **boleto** *m.* 1.2, 3.5; **pasaje** *m.* 1.5
tie **corbata** *f.* 1.6
time **vez** *f.* 1.6; **tiempo** *m.* 3.2
have a good/bad time **pasarlo bien/mal** 2.3
I've had a fantastic time. **Lo he pasado de película.** 3.6
What time is it? **¿Qué hora es?** 1.1
(At) What time...? **¿A qué hora...?** 1.1
times **veces** *f., pl.* 1.6
many times **muchas veces** 2.4
two times **dos veces** 1.6
tip **propina** *f.* 2.2
tire **llanta** *f.* 2.5
tired **cansado/a** *adj.* 1.5
be tired **estar cansado/a** 1.5
title **título** *m.* 3.4
to **a** *prep.* 1.1
toast (*drink*) **brindar** *v.* 2.3
toast **pan** *m.* **tostado** 2.2
toasted **tostado/a** *adj.* 2.2
toasted bread **pan tostado** *m.* 2.2
toaster **tostadora** *f.* 2.6
today **hoy** *adv.* 1.2
Today is... **Hoy es...** 1.2
toe **dedo** *m.* **del pie** 2.4
together **juntos/as** *adj.* 2.3
toilet **inodoro** *m.* 2.1
tomato **tomate** *m.* 2.2
tomorrow **mañana** *f.* 1.1
See you tomorrow. **Hasta mañana.** 1.1
tonight **esta noche** *adv.*
too **también** *adv.* 1.2; 2.1
too much **demasiado** *adv.* 1.6; **en exceso** 3.3
tooth **diente** *m.* 2.1
toothpaste **pasta** *f.* **de dientes** 2.1
top **cima** *f.* 3.3
tornado **tornado** *m.* 3.6
touch **tocar** *v.* 3.5
touch screen **pantalla táctil** *f.*
tour **excursión** *f.* 1.4; **recorrido** *m.* 3.1
tour an area **recorrer** *v.*
tourism **turismo** *m.*
tourist **turista** *m., f.* 1.1; **turístico/a** *adj.*
toward **hacia** *prep.* 3.2; **para** *prep.* 2.5
towel **toalla** *f.* 2.1
town **pueblo** *m.*
trade **oficio** *m.* 3.4
traffic **circulación** *f.* 2.5; **tráfico** *m.* 2.5
traffic light **semáforo** *m.* 3.2
tragedy **tragedia** *f.* 3.5
trail **sendero** *m.* 3.1
train **entrenarse** *v.* 3.3; **tren** *m.* 1.5
train station **estación** *f.* **de tren** *m.* 1.5
trainer **entrenador(a)** *m., f.* 3.3
translate **traducir** *v.* 1.6
trash **basura** *f.* 2.6
travel **viajar** *v.* 1.2
travel agency **agencia** f. **de viajes** 1.5
travel agent **agente** *m., f.* **de viajes** 1.5
traveler **viajero/a** *m., f.* 1.5
(traveler's) check **cheque (de viajero)** 3.2
treadmill **cinta caminadora** *f.* 3.3
tree **árbol** *m.* 3.1
trillion **billón** *m.*
trimester **trimestre** *m.* 1.2
trip **viaje** *m.* 1.5
take a trip **hacer un viaje** 1.5
tropical forest **bosque** *m.* **tropical** 3.1
true: it's (not) true **(no) es verdad** 3.1
trunk **baúl** *m.* 2.5
truth **verdad** *f.* 1.4
try **intentar** *v.*; **probar (o:ue)** *v.* 2.2
try (*to do something*) **tratar de (+ *inf.*)** 3.3
try on **probarse (o:ue)** *v.* 2.1
t-shirt **camiseta** *f.* 1.6
Tuesday **martes** *m., sing.* 1.2
tuna **atún** *m.* 2.2
turkey **pavo** *m.* 2.2
turn **doblar** *v.* 3.2
turn off (*electricity/appliance*) **apagar** *v.* 2.5
turn on (*electricity/appliance*) **poner** *v.* 2.5; **prender** *v.* 2.5
twelve **doce** 1.1
twenty **veinte** 1.1
twenty-eight **veintiocho** 1.1
twenty-five **veinticinco** 1.1
twenty-four **veinticuatro** 1.1
twenty-nine **veintinueve** 1.1
twenty-one **veintiuno** 1.1; **veintiún, veintiuno/a** *adj.* 1.1
twenty-seven **veintisiete** 1.1
twenty-six **veintiséis** 1.1
twenty-three **veintitrés** 1.1
twenty-two **veintidós** 1.1
twice **dos veces** 1.6
twin **gemelo/a** *m., f.* 1.3
two **dos** 1.1
two hundred **doscientos/as** 1.2
two times **dos veces** 1.6

U

ugly **feo/a** *adj.* 1.3
uncle **tío** *m.* 1.3
under **debajo de** *prep.* 1.2
understand **comprender** *v.* 1.3; **entender (e:ie)** *v.* 1.4
underwear **ropa interior** 1.6
unemployment **desempleo** *m.* 3.6

unique **único/a** *adj.* 2.3
United States **Estados Unidos (EE.UU.)** *m. pl.*
university **universidad** *f.* 1.2
unless **a menos que** *conj.* 3.1
unmarried **soltero/a** *adj.* 2.3
unpleasant **antipático/a** *adj.* 1.3
until **hasta** *prep.* 1.6; **hasta que** *conj.* 3.1
urgent **urgente** *adj.* 2.6
It's urgent that... **Es urgente que...** 2.6
us **nos** *pl., d.o. pron.* 1.5
to/for us **nos** *pl., i.o. pron.* 1.6
use **usar** *v.* 1.6
used for **para** *prep.* 2.5
useful **útil** *adj. m., f.*

V

vacation **vacaciones** *f., pl.* 1.5
be on vacation **estar de vacaciones** 1.5
go on vacation **ir de vacaciones** 1.5
vacuum **pasar** *v.* **la aspiradora** 2.6
vacuum cleaner **aspiradora** *f.* 2.6
valley **valle** *m.* 3.1
various **varios/as** *adj. m., f. pl.*
vegetables **verduras** *pl., f.* 2.2
verb **verbo** *m.*
very **muy** *adv.* 1.1
(Very) well, thank you. **(Muy) bien, gracias.** 1.1
video **video** *m.* 1.1
video camera **cámara** *f.* **de video** 2.5
video game **videojuego** *m.* 1.4
videoconference **videoconferencia** *f.* 3.4
vinegar **vinagre** *m.* 2.2
violence **violencia** *f.* 3.6
visit **visitar** *v.* 1.4
visit monuments **visitar monumentos** 1.4
vitamin **vitamina** *f.* 3.3
voice mail **correo de voz** *m.* 2.5
volcano **volcán** *m.* 3.1
volleyball **vóleibol** *m.* 1.4
vote **votar** *v.* 3.6

W

wait (for) **esperar** *v.* **(+ *inf.*)** 1.2
waiter/waitress **camarero/a** *m., f.* 2.2
wake up **despertarse (e:ie)** *v.* 2.1
walk **caminar** *v.* 1.2
take a walk **pasear** *v.* 1.4
walk around **pasear por** 1.4
wall **pared** *f.* 2.6; **muro** *m.* 3.3
wallet **cartera** *f.* 1.4, 1.6
want **querer (e:ie)** *v.* 1.4
war **guerra** *f.* 3.6
warm up **calentarse (e:ie)** *v.* 3.3
wash **lavar** *v.* 2.6
wash one's face/hands **lavarse la cara/las manos** 2.1
wash (the floor, the dishes) **lavar (el suelo, los platos)** 2.6
wash oneself **lavarse** *v.* 2.1
washing machine **lavadora** *f.* 2.6
wastebasket **papelera** *f.* 1.2
watch **mirar** *v.* 1.2; **reloj** *m.* 1.2
watch television **mirar (la) televisión** 1.2
water **agua** *f.* 2.2
water pollution **contaminación del agua** 3.1
water-skiing **esquí** *m.* **acuático** 1.4
way **manera** *f.*
we **nosotros(as)** *m., f.* 1.1
weak **débil** *adj. m., f.* 3.3
wear **llevar** *v.* 1.6; **usar** *v.* 1.6
weather **tiempo** *m.*
The weather is bad. **Hace mal tiempo.** 1.5
The weather is good. **Hace buen tiempo.** 1.5
weaving **tejido** *m.* 3.5
Web **red** *f.* 2.5
website **sitio** *m.* **web** 2.5
wedding **boda** *f.* 2.3
Wednesday **miércoles** *m., sing.* 1.2
week **semana** *f.* 1.2
weekend **fin** *m.* **de semana** 1.4
weight **peso** *m.* 3.3
lift weights **levantar** *v.* **pesas** *f., pl.* 3.3
welcome **bienvenido(s)/a(s)** *adj.* 1.1
well: (Very) well, thanks. **(Muy) bien, gracias.** 1.1
well-being **bienestar** *m.* 3.3
well organized **ordenado/a** *adj.* 1.5
west **oeste** *m.* 3.2
to the west **al oeste** 3.2
western (*genre*) **de vaqueros** 3.5
whale **ballena** *f.* 3.1
what **lo que** *pron.* 2.6
what? **¿qué?** 1.1
At what time...? **¿A qué hora...?** 1.1
What a pleasure to...! **¡Qué gusto (+ *inf.*)...!** 3.6
What day is it? **¿Qué día es hoy?** 1.2
What do you guys think? **¿Qué les parece?**
What happened? **¿Qué pasó?**
What is today's date? **¿Cuál es la fecha de hoy?** 1.5
What nice clothes! **¡Qué ropa más bonita!** 1.6
What size do you wear? **¿Qué talla lleva (usa)?** 1.6
What time is it? **¿Qué hora es?** 1.1
What's going on? **¿Qué pasa?** 1.1
What's happening? **¿Qué pasa?** 1.1
What's... like? **¿Cómo es...?**
What's new? **¿Qué hay de nuevo?** 1.1
What's the weather like? **¿Qué tiempo hace?** 1.5
What's up? **¿Qué onda?** 3.2
What's wrong? **¿Qué pasó?**
What's your name? **¿Cómo se llama usted?** *form.* 1.1; **¿Cómo te llamas (tú)?** *fam.* 1.1
when **cuando** *conj.* 2.1; 3.1
When? **¿Cuándo?** 1.2
where **donde**
where (to)? (*destination*) **¿adónde?** 1.2; (*location*) **¿dónde?** 1.1, 1.2
Where are you from? **¿De dónde eres (tú)?** (*fam.*) 1.1; **¿De dónde es (usted)?** (*form.*) 1.1
Where is...? **¿Dónde está...?** 1.2
which **que** *pron.*, **lo que** *pron.* 2.6
which? **¿cuál?** 1.2; **¿qué?** 1.2
In which...? **¿En qué...?**
which one(s)? **¿cuál(es)?** 1.2
while **mientras** *conj.* 2.4
who **que** *pron.* 2.6; **quien(es)** *pron.* 2.6
who? **¿quién(es)?** 1.1, 1.2
Who is...? **¿Quién es...?** 1.1
Who is speaking/calling? (*on telephone*) **¿De parte de quién?** 2.5
Who is speaking? (*on telephone*) **¿Quién habla?** 2.5
whole **todo/a** *adj.*
whom **quien(es)** *pron.* 2.6
whose? **¿de quién(es)?** 1.1
why? **¿por qué?** 1.2
widower/widow **viudo/a** *adj.* 2.3
wife **esposa** *f.* 1.3
win **ganar** *v.* 1.4
wind **viento** *m.*
window **ventana** *f.* 1.2
windshield **parabrisas** *m., sing.* 2.5
windsurf **hacer** *v.* **windsurf** 1.5
windy: It's (very) windy. **Hace (mucho) viento.** 1.5
winter **invierno** *m.* 1.5
wireless connection **conexión inalámbrica** *f.* 2.5
wish **desear** *v.* 1.2; **esperar** *v.* 3.1
I wish (that) **ojalá (que)** 3.1
with **con** *prep.* 1.2
with me **conmigo** 1.4; 2.3
with you **contigo** *fam.* 1.5, 2.3
within (ten years) **dentro de (diez años)** *prep.* 3.4
without **sin** *prep.* 1.2; **sin que** *conj.* 3.1
woman **mujer** *f.* 1.1

wool **lana** *f.* 1.6
(made of) wool **de lana** 1.6
word **palabra** *f.* 1.1
work **trabajar** *v.* 1.2; **funcionar** *v.* 2.5; **trabajo** *m.* 3.4
work (*of art, literature, music, etc.*) **obra** *f.* 3.5
work out **hacer gimnasia** 3.3
world **mundo** *m.* 2.2
worldwide **mundial** *adj. m., f.*
worried (about) **preocupado/a (por)** *adj.* 1.5
worry (about) **preocuparse** *v.* **(por)** 2.1
Don't worry. **No te preocupes.** *fam.* 2.1
worse **peor** *adj. m., f.* 2.2
worst **el/la peor** 2.2
Would you like to...? **¿Te gustaría...?** *fam.*
Would you do me the honor of marrying me? **¿Me harías el honor de casarte conmigo?** 3.5
wow **híjole** *interj.* 1.6
wrench **llave** *f.* 2.5
write **escribir** *v.* 1.3
write a letter/an e-mail **escribir una carta/un mensaje electrónico** 1.4
writer **escritor(a)** *m., f* 3.5
written **escrito/a** *p.p.* 3.2
wrong **equivocado/a** *adj.* 1.5
be wrong **no tener razón** 1.3

X

X-ray **radiografía** *f.* 2.4

Y

yard **jardín** *m.* 2.6; **patio** *m.* 2.6
year **año** *m.* 1.5
be... years old **tener... años** 1.3
yellow **amarillo/a** *adj.* 1.6
yes **sí** *interj.* 1.1
yesterday **ayer** *adv.* 1.6
yet **todavía** *adv.* 1.5
yogurt **yogur** *m.* 2.2
you **tú** *fam.* **usted (Ud.)** *form. sing.* **vosotros/as** *m., f. fam. pl.* **ustedes (Uds.)** *pl.* 1.1; (to, for) you *fam. sing.* **te** *pl.* **os** 1.6; *form. sing.* **le** *pl.* **les** 1.6
you **te** *fam., sing.*, **lo/la** *form., sing.*, **os** *fam., pl.*, **los/las** *pl, d.o. pron.* 1.5
You don't say! **¡No me digas!** *fam.;* **¡No me diga!** *form.*
You're welcome. **De nada.** 1.1; **No hay de qué.** 1.1
young **joven** *adj., sing.* (**jóvenes** *pl.*) 1.3
young person **joven** *m., f., sing.* (**jóvenes** *pl.*) 1.1
young woman **señorita (Srta.)** *f.*
younger **menor** *adj. m., f.* 1.3
younger: younger brother, sister *m., f.* **hermano/a menor** 1.3
youngest **el/la menor** *m., f.* 2.2
your **su(s)** *poss. adj. form.* 1.3; **tu(s)** *poss. adj. fam. sing.* 1.3; **vuestro/a(s)** *poss. adj. fam. pl.* 1.3
your(s) *form.* **suyo(s)/a(s)** *poss. pron. form.* 2.5; **tuyo(s)/a(s)** *poss. fam. sing.* 2.5; **vuestro(s) /a(s)** *poss. fam.* 2.5
youth *f.* **juventud** 2.3

Z

zero **cero** *m.* 1.1

MATERIAS	ACADEMIC SUBJECTS
la administración de empresas	business administration
la agronomía	agriculture
el alemán	German
el álgebra	algebra
la antropología	anthropology
la arqueología	archaeology
la arquitectura	architecture
el arte	art
la astronomía	astronomy
la biología	biology
la bioquímica	biochemistry
la botánica	botany
el cálculo	calculus
el chino	Chinese
las ciencias políticas	political science
la computación	computer science
las comunicaciones	communications
la contabilidad	accounting
la danza	dance
el derecho	law
la economía	economics
la educación	education
la educación física	physical education
la enfermería	nursing
el español	Spanish
la filosofía	philosophy
la física	physics
el francés	French
la geografía	geography
la geología	geology
el griego	Greek
el hebreo	Hebrew
la historia	history
la informática	computer science
la ingeniería	engineering
el inglés	English
el italiano	Italian
el japonés	Japanese
el latín	Latin
las lenguas clásicas	classical languages
las lenguas romances	Romance languages
la lingüística	linguistics
la literatura	literature
las matemáticas	mathematics
la medicina	medicine
el mercadeo/ la mercadotecnia	marketing
la música	music
los negocios	business
el periodismo	journalism
el portugués	Portuguese
la psicología	psychology
la química	chemistry
el ruso	Russian
los servicios sociales	social services
la sociología	sociology
el teatro	theater
la trigonometría	trigonometry

LOS ANIMALES	ANIMALS
la abeja	bee
la araña	spider
la ardilla	squirrel
el ave (*f.*), el pájaro	bird
la ballena	whale
el burro	donkey
la cabra	goat
el caimán	alligator
el camello	camel
la cebra	zebra
el ciervo, el venado	deer
el cochino, el cerdo, el puerco	pig
el cocodrilo	crocodile
el conejo	rabbit
el coyote	coyote
la culebra, la serpiente, la víbora	snake
el elefante	elephant
la foca	seal
la gallina	hen
el gallo	rooster
el gato	cat
el gorila	gorilla
el hipopótamo	hippopotamus
la hormiga	ant
el insecto	insect
la jirafa	giraffe
el lagarto	lizard
el león	lion
el lobo	wolf
el loro, la cotorra, el papagayo, el perico	parrot
la mariposa	butterfly
el mono	monkey
la mosca	fly
el mosquito	mosquito
el oso	bear
la oveja	sheep
el pato	duck
el perro	dog
el pez	fish
la rana	frog
el ratón	mouse
el rinoceronte	rhinoceros
el saltamontes, el chapulín	grasshopper
el tiburón	shark
el tigre	tiger
el toro	bull
la tortuga	turtle
la vaca	cow
el zorro	fox

EL CUERPO HUMANO Y LA SALUD — THE HUMAN BODY AND HEALTH

El cuerpo humano — The human body

la barba	beard
el bigote	mustache
la boca	mouth
el brazo	arm
la cabeza	head
la cadera	hip
la ceja	eyebrow
el cerebro	brain
la cintura	waist
el codo	elbow
el corazón	heart
la costilla	rib
el cráneo	skull
el cuello	neck
el dedo	finger
el dedo del pie	toe
la espalda	back
el estómago	stomach
la frente	forehead
la garganta	throat
el hombro	shoulder
el hueso	bone
el labio	lip
la lengua	tongue
la mandíbula	jaw
la mejilla	cheek
el mentón, la barba, la barbilla	chin
la muñeca	wrist
el músculo	muscle
el muslo	thigh
las nalgas, el trasero, las asentaderas	buttocks
la nariz	nose
el nervio	nerve
el oído	(inner) ear
el ojo	eye
el ombligo	navel, belly button
la oreja	(outer) ear
la pantorrilla	calf
el párpado	eyelid
el pecho	chest
la pestaña	eyelash
el pie	foot
la piel	skin
la pierna	leg
el pulgar	thumb
el pulmón	lung
la rodilla	knee
la sangre	blood
el talón	heel
el tobillo	ankle
el tronco	torso, trunk
la uña	fingernail
la uña del dedo del pie	toenail
la vena	vein

Los cinco sentidos — The five senses

el gusto	taste
el oído	hearing
el olfato	smell
el tacto	touch
la vista	sight

La salud — Health

el accidente	accident
alérgico/a	allergic
el antibiótico	antibiotic
la aspirina	aspirin
el ataque cardiaco, el ataque al corazón	heart attack
el cáncer	cancer
la cápsula	capsule
la clínica	clinic
congestionado/a	congested
el consultorio	doctor's office
la curita	adhesive bandage
el/la dentista	dentist
el/la doctor(a), el/la médico/a	doctor
el dolor (de cabeza)	(head)ache, pain
embarazada	pregnant
la enfermedad	illness, disease
el/la enfermero/a	nurse
enfermo/a	ill, sick
la erupción	rash
el examen médico	physical exam
la farmacia	pharmacy
la fiebre	fever
la fractura	fracture
la gripe	flu
la herida	wound
el hospital	hospital
la infección	infection
el insomnio	insomnia
la inyección	injection
el jarabe	(cough) syrup
mareado/a	dizzy, nauseated
el medicamento	medication
la medicina	medicine
las muletas	crutches
la operación	operation
el/la paciente	patient
el/la paramédico/a	paramedic
la pastilla, la píldora	pill, tablet
los primeros auxilios	first aid
la pulmonía	pneumonia
los puntos	stitches
la quemadura	burn
el quirófano	operating room
la radiografía	x-ray
la receta	prescription
el resfriado	cold (illness)
la sala de emergencia(s)	emergency room
saludable	healthy, healthful
sano/a	healthy
el seguro médico	medical insurance
la silla de ruedas	wheelchair
el síntoma	symptom
el termómetro	thermometer
la tos	cough
la transfusión	transfusion

la vacuna	vaccination
la venda	bandage
el virus	virus

cortar(se)	to cut (oneself)
curar	to cure, to treat
desmayar(se)	to faint
enfermarse	to get sick
enyesar	to put in a cast
estornudar	to sneeze
guardar cama	to stay in bed
hinchar(se)	to swell
internar(se) en el hospital	to check into the hospital
lastimarse (el pie)	to hurt (one's foot)
mejorar(se)	to get better; to improve
operar	to operate
quemar(se)	to burn
respirar (hondo)	to breathe (deeply)
romperse (la pierna)	to break (one's leg)
sangrar	to bleed
sufrir	to suffer
tomarle la presión a alguien	to take someone's blood pressure
tomarle el pulso a alguien	to take someone's pulse
torcerse (el tobillo)	to sprain (one's ankle)
vendar	to bandage

EXPRESIONES ÚTILES PARA LA CLASE / USEFUL CLASSROOM EXPRESSIONS

Palabras útiles / Useful words

ausente	absent
el departamento	department
el dictado	dictation
la conversación, las conversaciones	conversation(s)
la expresión, las expresiones	expression(s)
el examen, los exámenes	test(s), exam(s)
la frase	sentence
la hoja de actividades	activity sheet
el horario de clases	class schedule
la oración, las oraciones	sentence(s)
el párrafo	paragraph
la persona	person
presente	present
la prueba	test, quiz
siguiente	following
la tarea	homework

Expresiones útiles / Useful expressions

Abra(n) su(s) libro(s).	Open your book(s).
Cambien de papel.	Change roles.
Cierre(n) su(s) libro(s).	Close your book(s).
¿Cómo se dice ___ en español?	How do you say ___ in Spanish?
¿Cómo se escribe ___ en español?	How do you write ___ in Spanish?
¿Comprende(n)?	Do you understand?
(No) comprendo.	I (don't) understand.
Conteste(n) las preguntas.	Answer the questions.
Continúe(n), por favor.	Continue, please.
Escriba(n) su nombre.	Write your name.
Escuche(n) el audio.	Listen to the audio.
Estudie(n) la Lección tres.	Study Lesson three.
Haga(n) la actividad (el ejercicio) número cuatro.	Do activity (exercise) number four.
Lea(n) la oración en voz alta.	Read the sentence aloud.
Levante(n) la mano.	Raise your hand(s).
Más despacio, por favor.	Slower, please.
No sé.	I don't know.
Páse(n)me los exámenes.	Pass me the tests.
¿Qué significa ___?	What does ___ mean?
Repita(n), por favor.	Repeat, please.
Siénte(n)se, por favor.	Sit down, please.
Siga(n) las instrucciones.	Follow the instructions.
¿Tiene(n) alguna pregunta?	Do you have any questions?
Vaya(n) a la página dos.	Go to page two.

COUNTRIES & NATIONALITIES / PAÍSES Y NACIONALIDADES

North America / Norteamérica

Canada	**Canadá**	***canadiense***
Mexico	**México**	***mexicano/a***
United States	**Estados Unidos**	***estadounidense***

Central America / Centroamérica

Belize	**Belice**	***beliceño/a***
Costa Rica	**Costa Rica**	***costarricense***
El Salvador	**El Salvador**	***salvadoreño/a***
Guatemala	**Guatemala**	***guatemalteco/a***
Honduras	**Honduras**	***hondureño/a***
Nicaragua	**Nicaragua**	***nicaragüense***
Panama	**Panamá**	***panameño/a***

The Caribbean	El Caribe	
Cuba	**Cuba**	*cubano/a*
Dominican Republic	**República Dominicana**	*dominicano/a*
Haiti	**Haití**	*haitiano/a*
Puerto Rico	**Puerto Rico**	*puertorriqueño/a*
South America	**Suramérica**	
Argentina	**Argentina**	*argentino/a*
Bolivia	**Bolivia**	*boliviano/a*
Brazil	**Brasil**	*brasileño/a*
Chile	**Chile**	*chileno/a*
Colombia	**Colombia**	*colombiano/a*
Ecuador	**Ecuador**	*ecuatoriano/a*
Paraguay	**Paraguay**	*paraguayo/a*
Peru	**Perú**	*peruano/a*
Uruguay	**Uruguay**	*uruguayo/a*
Venezuela	**Venezuela**	*venezolano/a*
Europe	**Europa**	
Armenia	**Armenia**	*armenio/a*
Austria	**Austria**	*austríaco/a*
Belgium	**Bélgica**	*belga*
Bosnia	**Bosnia**	*bosnio/a*
Bulgaria	**Bulgaria**	*búlgaro/a*
Croatia	**Croacia**	*croata*
Czech Republic	**República Checa**	*checo/a*
Denmark	**Dinamarca**	*danés, danesa*
England	**Inglaterra**	*inglés, inglesa*
Estonia	**Estonia**	*estonio/a*
Finland	**Finlandia**	*finlandés, finlandesa*
France	**Francia**	*francés, francesa*
Germany	**Alemania**	*alemán, alemana*
Great Britain (United Kingdom)	**Gran Bretaña (Reino Unido)**	*británico/a*
Greece	**Grecia**	*griego/a*
Hungary	**Hungría**	*húngaro/a*
Iceland	**Islandia**	*islandés, islandesa*
Ireland	**Irlanda**	*irlandés, irlandesa*
Italy	**Italia**	*italiano/a*
Latvia	**Letonia**	*letón, letona*
Lithuania	**Lituania**	*lituano/a*
Netherlands (Holland)	**Países Bajos (Holanda)**	*holandés, holandesa*
Norway	**Noruega**	*noruego/a*
Poland	**Polonia**	*polaco/a*
Portugal	**Portugal**	*portugués, portuguesa*
Romania	**Rumania**	*rumano/a*
Russia	**Rusia**	*ruso/a*
Scotland	**Escocia**	*escocés, escocesa*
Serbia	**Serbia**	*serbio/a*
Slovakia	**Eslovaquia**	*eslovaco/a*
Slovenia	**Eslovenia**	*esloveno/a*
Spain	**España**	*español(a)*
Sweden	**Suecia**	*sueco/a*
Switzerland	**Suiza**	*suizo/a*
Ukraine	**Ucrania**	*ucraniano/a*
Wales	**Gales**	*galés, galesa*
Asia	**Asia**	
Bangladesh	**Bangladés**	*bangladesí*
Cambodia	**Camboya**	*camboyano/a*
China	**China**	*chino/a*
India	**India**	*indio/a*
Indonesia	**Indonesia**	*indonesio/a*
Iran	**Irán**	*iraní*
Iraq	**Iraq, Irak**	*iraquí*

Israel	**Israel**	***israelí***
Japan	**Japón**	***japonés, japonesa***
Jordan	**Jordania**	***jordano/a***
Korea	**Corea**	***coreano/a***
Kuwait	**Kuwait**	***kuwaití***
Lebanon	**Líbano**	***libanés, libanesa***
Malaysia	**Malasia**	***malasio/a***
Pakistan	**Pakistán**	***pakistaní***
Russia	**Rusia**	***ruso/a***
Saudi Arabia	**Arabia Saudí**	***saudí***
Singapore	**Singapur**	***singapurés, singapuresa***
Syria	**Siria**	***sirio/a***
Taiwan	**Taiwán**	***taiwanés, taiwanesa***
Thailand	**Tailandia**	***tailandés, tailandesa***
Turkey	**Turquía**	***turco/a***
Vietnam	**Vietnam**	***vietnamita***
Africa	**África**	
Algeria	**Argelia**	***argelino/a***
Angola	**Angola**	***angoleño/a***
Cameroon	**Camerún**	***camerunés, camerunesa***
Congo	**Congo**	***congolés, congolesa***
Egypt	**Egipto**	***egipcio/a***
Equatorial Guinea	**Guinea Ecuatorial**	***ecuatoguineano/a***
Ethiopia	**Etiopía**	***etíope***
Ivory Coast	**Costa de Marfil**	***marfileño/a***
Kenya	**Kenia, Kenya**	***keniano/a, keniata***
Libya	**Libia**	***libio/a***
Mali	**Malí**	***maliense***
Morocco	**Marruecos**	***marroquí***
Mozambique	**Mozambique**	***mozambiqueño/a***
Nigeria	**Nigeria**	***nigeriano/a***
Rwanda	**Ruanda**	***ruandés, ruandesa***
Somalia	**Somalia**	***somalí***
South Africa	**Sudáfrica**	***sudafricano/a***
Sudan	**Sudán**	***sudanés, sudanesa***
Tunisia	**Tunicia, Túnez**	***tunecino/a***
Uganda	**Uganda**	***ugandés, ugandesa***
Zambia	**Zambia**	***zambiano/a***
Zimbabwe	**Zimbabue**	***zimbabuense***
Australia and the Pacific	**Australia y el Pacífico**	
Australia	**Australia**	***australiano/a***
New Zealand	**Nueva Zelanda**	***neozelandés, neozelandesa***
Philippines	**Filipinas**	***filipino/a***

MONEDAS DE LOS PAÍSES HISPANOS
CURRENCIES OF HISPANIC COUNTRIES

País / Country	Moneda / Currency
Argentina	el peso
Bolivia	el boliviano
Chile	el peso
Colombia	el peso
Costa Rica	el colón
Cuba	el peso
Ecuador	el dólar estadounidense
El Salvador	el dólar estadounidense
España	el euro
Guatemala	el quetzal
Guinea Ecuatorial	el franco
Honduras	el lempira
México	el peso
Nicaragua	el córdoba
Panamá	el balboa, el dólar estadounidense
Paraguay	el guaraní
Perú	el nuevo sol
Puerto Rico	el dólar estadounidense
República Dominicana	el peso
Uruguay	el peso
Venezuela	el bolívar

EXPRESIONES Y REFRANES / EXPRESSIONS AND SAYINGS

Expresiones y refranes con partes del cuerpo / Expressions and sayings with parts of the body

Expresiones y refranes con partes del cuerpo	Expressions and sayings with parts of the body
A cara o cruz	Heads or tails
A corazón abierto	Open heart
A ojos vistas	Clearly, visibly
Al dedillo	Like the back of one's hand
¡Choca/Vengan esos cinco!	Put it there!/Give me five!
Codo con codo	Side by side
Con las manos en la masa	Red-handed
Costar un ojo de la cara	To cost an arm and a leg
Darle a la lengua	To chatter/To gab
De rodillas	On one's knees
Duro de oído	Hard of hearing
En cuerpo y alma	In body and soul
En la punta de la lengua	On the tip of one's tongue
En un abrir y cerrar de ojos	In a blink of the eye
Entrar por un oído y salir por otro	In one ear and out the other
Estar con el agua al cuello	To be up to one's neck with/in
Estar para chuparse los dedos	To be delicious/To be finger-licking good
Hablar entre dientes	To mutter/To speak under one's breath
Hablar por los codos	To talk a lot/To be a chatterbox
Hacer la vista gorda	To turn a blind eye on something
Hombro con hombro	Shoulder to shoulder
Llorar a lágrima viva	To sob/To cry one's eyes out
Metérsele (a alguien) algo entre ceja y ceja	To get an idea in your head
No pegar ojo	Not to sleep a wink
No tener corazón	Not to have a heart
No tener dos dedos de frente	Not to have an ounce of common sense
Ojos que no ven, corazón que no siente	Out of sight, out of mind
Perder la cabeza	To lose one's head
Quedarse con la boca abierta	To be thunderstruck
Romper el corazón	To break someone's heart
Tener buen/mal corazón	Have a good/bad heart
Tener un nudo en la garganta	Have a knot in your throat
Tomarse algo a pecho	To take something too seriously
Venir como anillo al dedo	To fit like a charm/To suit perfectly

Expresiones y refranes con animales / Expressions and sayings with animals

Expresiones y refranes con animales	Expressions and sayings with animals
A caballo regalado no le mires el diente.	Don't look a gift horse in the mouth.
Comer como un cerdo	To eat like a pig
Cuando menos se piensa, salta la liebre.	Things happen when you least expect it.
Llevarse como el perro y el gato	To fight like cats and dogs
Perro ladrador, poco mordedor./Perro que ladra no muerde.	His/her bark is worse than his/her bite.
Por la boca muere el pez.	Talking too much can be dangerous.
Poner el cascabel al gato	To stick one's neck out
Ser una tortuga	To be a slowpoke

Expresiones y refranes con alimentos / Expressions and sayings with food

Expresiones y refranes con alimentos	Expressions and sayings with food
Agua que no has de beber, déjala correr.	If you're not interested, don't ruin it for everybody else.
Con pan y vino se anda el camino.	Things never seem as bad after a good meal.
Contigo pan y cebolla.	You are all I need.
Dame pan y dime tonto.	I don't care what you say, as long as I get what I want.
Descubrir el pastel	To let the cat out of the bag
Dulce como la miel	Sweet as honey
Estar como agua para chocolate	To furious/To be at the boiling point
Estar en el ajo	To be in the know
Estar en la higuera	To have one's head in the clouds
Estar más claro que el agua	To be clear as a bell
Ganarse el pan	To earn a living/To earn one's daily bread
Llamar al pan, pan y al vino, vino.	Not to mince words.
No hay miel sin hiel.	Every rose has its thorn./There's always a catch.
No sólo de pan vive el hombre.	Man doesn't live by bread alone.
Pan con pan, comida de tontos.	Variety is the spice of life.
Ser agua pasada	To be water under the bridge
Ser más bueno que el pan	To be kindness itself
Temblar como un flan	To shake/tremble like a leaf

Expresiones y refranes con colores / Expressions and sayings with colors

Expresiones y refranes con colores	Expressions and sayings with colors
Estar verde	To be inexperienced/wet behind the ears
Poner los ojos en blanco	To roll one's eyes
Ponerle a alguien un ojo morado	To give someone a black eye
Ponerse rojo	To turn red/To blush
Ponerse rojo de ira	To turn red with anger
Ponerse verde de envidia	To be green with envy
Quedarse en blanco	To go blank
Verlo todo de color de rosa	To see the world through rose-colored glasses

Refranes	Sayings
A buen entendedor, pocas palabras bastan.	A word to the wise is enough.
Ande o no ande, caballo grande.	Bigger is always better.
A quien madruga, Dios le ayuda.	The early bird catches the worm.
Cuídate, que te cuidaré.	Take care of yourself, and then I'll take care of you.
De tal palo tal astilla.	A chip off the old block.
Del dicho al hecho hay mucho trecho.	Easier said than done.
Dime con quién andas y te diré quién eres.	A man is known by the company he keeps.
El saber no ocupa lugar.	One never knows too much.
Lo que es moda no incomoda.	You have to suffer in the name of fashion.
Más vale maña que fuerza.	Brains are better than brawn.
Más vale prevenir que curar.	Prevention is better than cure.
Más vale solo que mal acompañado.	Better alone than with people you don't like.
Más vale tarde que nunca.	Better late than never.
No es oro todo lo que reluce.	All that glitters is not gold.
Poderoso caballero es don Dinero.	Money talks.

COMMON FALSE FRIENDS

False friends are Spanish words that look similar to English words but have very different meanings. While recognizing the English relatives of unfamiliar Spanish words you encounter is an important way of constructing meaning, there are some Spanish words whose similarity to English words is deceptive. Here is a list of some of the most common Spanish false friends.

actualmente ≠ actually
actualmente = nowadays, currently
actually = **de hecho, en realidad, en efecto**

argumento ≠ argument
argumento = plot
argument = **discusión, pelea**

armada ≠ army
armada = navy
army = **ejército**

balde ≠ bald
balde = pail, bucket
bald = **calvo/a**

batería ≠ battery
batería = drum set
battery = **pila**

bravo ≠ brave
bravo = wild; fierce
brave = **valiente**

cándido/a ≠ candid
cándido/a = innocent
candid = **sincero/a**

carbón ≠ carbon
carbón = coal
carbon = **carbono**

casual ≠ casual
casual = accidental, chance
casual = **informal, despreocupado/a**

casualidad ≠ casualty
casualidad = chance, coincidence
casualty = **víctima**

colegio ≠ college
colegio = school
college = **universidad**

collar ≠ collar (of a shirt)
collar = necklace
collar = **cuello (de camisa)**

comprensivo/a ≠ comprehensive
comprensivo/a = understanding
comprehensive = **completo, extensivo**

constipado ≠ constipated
estar constipado/a = to have a cold
to be constipated = **estar estreñido/a**

crudo/a ≠ crude
crudo/a = raw, undercooked
crude = **burdo/a, grosero/a**

divertir ≠ to divert
divertirse = to enjoy oneself
to divert = **desviar**

educado/a ≠ educated
educado/a = well-mannered
educated = **culto/a, instruido/a**

embarazada ≠ embarrassed
estar embarazada = to be pregnant
to be embarrassed = **estar avergonzado/a; dar/tener vergüenza**

eventualmente ≠ eventually
eventualmente = possibly
eventually = **finalmente, al final**

éxito ≠ exit
éxito = success
exit = **salida**

físico/a ≠ physician
físico/a = physicist
physician = **médico/a**

fútbol ≠ football
fútbol = soccer
football = **fútbol americano**

lectura ≠ lecture
lectura = reading
lecture = **conferencia**

librería ≠ library
librería = bookstore
library = **biblioteca**

máscara ≠ mascara
máscara = mask
mascara = **rímel**

molestar ≠ to molest
molestar = to bother, to annoy
to molest = **abusar**

oficio ≠ office
oficio = trade, occupation
office = **oficina**

rato ≠ rat
rato = while, time
rat = **rata**

realizar ≠ to realize
realizar = to carry out; to fulfill
to realize = **darse cuenta de**

red ≠ red
red = net
red = **rojo/a**

revolver ≠ revolver
revolver = to stir, to rummage through
revolver = **revólver**

sensible ≠ sensible
sensible = sensitive
sensible = **sensato/a, razonable**

suceso ≠ success
suceso = event
success = **éxito**

sujeto ≠ subject (topic)
sujeto = fellow; individual
subject = **tema, asunto**

LOS ALIMENTOS — FOODS

Frutas	Fruits
la aceituna	olive
el aguacate	avocado
el albaricoque, el damasco	apricot
la banana, el plátano	banana
la cereza	cherry
la ciruela	plum
el dátil	date
la frambuesa	raspberry
la fresa, la frutilla	strawberry
el higo	fig
el limón	lemon; lime
el melocotón, el durazno	peach
la mandarina	tangerine
el mango	mango
la manzana	apple
la naranja	orange
la papaya	papaya
la pera	pear
la piña	pineapple
el pomelo, la toronja	grapefruit
la sandía	watermelon
las uvas	grapes

Vegetales	Vegetables
la alcachofa	artichoke
el apio	celery
la arveja, el guisante	pea
la berenjena	eggplant
el brócoli	broccoli
la calabaza	squash; pumpkin
la cebolla	onion
el champiñón, la seta	mushroom
la col, el repollo	cabbage
la coliflor	cauliflower
los espárragos	asparagus
las espinacas	spinach
los frijoles, las habichuelas	beans
las habas	fava beans
las judías verdes, los ejotes	string beans, green beans
la lechuga	lettuce
el maíz, el choclo, el elote	corn
la papa, la patata	potato
el pepino	cucumber
el pimentón	bell pepper
el rábano	radish
la remolacha	beet
el tomate, el jitomate	tomato
la zanahoria	carrot

El pescado y los mariscos	Fish and shellfish
la almeja	clam
el atún	tuna
el bacalao	cod
el calamar	squid
el cangrejo	crab
el camarón, la gamba	shrimp
la langosta	lobster
el langostino	prawn
el lenguado	sole; flounder
el mejillón	mussel
la ostra	oyster
el pulpo	octopus
el salmón	salmon
la sardina	sardine
la vieira	scallop

La carne	Meat
la albóndiga	meatball
el bistec	steak
la carne de res	beef
el chorizo	hard pork sausage
la chuleta de cerdo	pork chop
el cordero	lamb
los fiambres	cold cuts, food served cold
el filete	fillet
la hamburguesa	hamburger
el hígado	liver
el jamón	ham
el lechón	suckling pig, roasted pig
el pavo	turkey
el pollo	chicken
el cerdo	pork
la salchicha	sausage
la ternera	veal
el tocino	bacon

Otras comidas	Other foods
el ajo	garlic
el arroz	rice
el azúcar	sugar
el batido	milkshake
el budín	pudding
el cacahuete, el maní	peanut
el café	coffee
los fideos	noodles, pasta
la harina	flour
el huevo	egg
el jugo, el zumo	juice
la leche	milk
la mermelada	marmalade, jam
la miel	honey
el pan	bread
el queso	cheese
la sal	salt
la sopa	soup
el té	tea
la tortilla	omelet (Spain), tortilla (Mexico)
el yogur	yogurt

Cómo describir la comida	Ways to describe food
a la plancha, a la parrilla	grilled
ácido/a	sour
al horno	baked
amargo/a	bitter
caliente	hot
dulce	sweet
duro/a	tough
frío/a	cold
frito/a	fried
fuerte	strong, heavy
ligero/a	light
picante	spicy
sabroso/a	tasty
salado/a	salty

DÍAS FESTIVOS	HOLIDAYS
enero	**January**
Año Nuevo (1)	New Year's Day
Día de los Reyes Magos (6)	Three Kings Day (Epiphany)
Día de Martin Luther King, Jr.	Martin Luther King, Jr. Day
febrero	**February**
Día de San Blas (Paraguay) (3)	St. Blas Day (Paraguay)
Día de San Valentín, Día de los Enamorados (14)	Valentine's Day
Día de los Presidentes	Presidents' Day
Carnaval	Carnival (Mardi Gras)
marzo	**March**
Día de San Patricio (17)	St. Patrick's Day
Nacimiento de Benito Juárez (México) (21)	Benito Juárez's Birthday (Mexico)
abril	**April**
Semana Santa	Holy Week
Pésaj	Passover
Pascua	Easter
Declaración de la Independencia de Venezuela (19)	Declaration of Independence of Venezuela
Día de la Tierra (22)	Earth Day
mayo	**May**
Día del Trabajo (1)	Labor Day
Cinco de Mayo (5) (México)	Cinco de Mayo (May 5th) (Mexico)
Día de las Madres	Mother's Day
Independencia Patria (Paraguay) (15)	Independence Day (Paraguay)
Día Conmemorativo	Memorial Day
junio	**June**
Día de los Padres	Father's Day
Día de la Bandera (14)	Flag Day
Día del Indio (Perú) (24)	Native People's Day (Peru)
julio	**July**
Día de la Independencia de los Estados Unidos (4)	Independence Day (United States)
Día de la Independencia de Venezuela (5)	Independence Day (Venezuela)
Día de la Independencia de la Argentina (9)	Independence Day (Argentina)
Día de la Independencia de Colombia (20)	Independence Day (Colombia)
Nacimiento de Simón Bolívar (24)	Simón Bolívar's Birthday
Día de la Revolución (Cuba) (26)	Revolution Day (Cuba)
Día de la Independencia del Perú (28)	Independence Day (Peru)
agosto	**August**
Día de la Independencia de Bolivia (6)	Independence Day (Bolivia)
Día de la Independencia del Ecuador (10)	Independence Day (Ecuador)
Día de San Martín (Argentina) (17)	San Martín Day (anniversary of his death) (Argentina)
Día de la Independencia del Uruguay (25)	Independence Day (Uruguay)
septiembre	**September**
Día del Trabajo (EE. UU.)	Labor Day (U.S.)
Día de la Independencia de Costa Rica, El Salvador, Guatemala, Honduras y Nicaragua (15)	Independence Day (Costa Rica, El Salvador, Guatemala, Honduras, Nicaragua)
Día de la Independencia de México (16)	Independence Day (Mexico)
Día de la Independencia de Chile (18)	Independence Day (Chile)
Año Nuevo Judío	Jewish New Year
Día de la Virgen de las Mercedes (Perú) (24)	Day of the Virgin of Mercedes (Peru)
octubre	**October**
Día de la Raza (12)	Columbus Day
Noche de Brujas (31)	Halloween
noviembre	**November**
Día de los Muertos (2)	All Souls Day
Día de los Veteranos (11)	Veterans' Day
Día de la Revolución Mexicana (20)	Mexican Revolution Day
Día de Acción de Gracias	Thanksgiving
Día de la Independencia de Panamá (28)	Independence Day (Panama)
diciembre	**December**
Día de la Virgen (8)	Day of the Virgin
Día de la Virgen de Guadalupe (México) (12)	Day of the Virgin of Guadalupe (Mexico)
Januká	Chanukah
Nochebuena (24)	Christmas Eve
Navidad (25)	Christmas
Año Viejo (31)	New Year's Eve

NOTE: In Spanish, dates are written with the day first, then the month. Christmas Day is **el 25 de diciembre**. In Latin America and in Europe, abbreviated dates also follow this pattern. Halloween, for example, falls on 31/10. You may also see the numbers in dates separated by periods: 27.4.16. When referring to centuries, roman numerals are always used. The 16th century, therefore, is **el siglo XVI**.

PESOS Y MEDIDAS / WEIGHTS AND MEASURES

Longitud / Length

El sistema métrico Metric system	**El equivalente estadounidense** U.S. equivalent
milímetro = 0,001 metro millimeter = 0.001 meter	= 0.039 inch
centímetro = 0,01 metro centimeter = 0.01 meter	= 0.39 inch
decímetro = 0,1 metro decimeter = 0.1 meter	= 3.94 inches
metro meter	= 39.4 inches
decámetro = 10 metros dekameter = 10 meters	= 32.8 feet
hectómetro = 100 metros hectometer = 100 meters	= 328 feet
kilómetro = 1.000 metros kilometer = 1,000 meters	= .62 mile

U.S. system **El sistema estadounidense**	Metric equivalent **El equivalente métrico**
inch **pulgada**	= 2.54 centimeters **= 2,54 centímetros**
foot = 12 inches **pie = 12 pulgadas**	= 30.48 centimeters **= 30,48 centímetros**
yard = 3 feet **yarda = 3 pies**	= 0.914 meter **= 0,914 metro**
mile = 5,280 feet **milla = 5.280 pies**	= 1.609 kilometers **= 1,609 kilómetros**

Superficie / Surface Area

El sistema métrico Metric system	**El equivalente estadounidense** U.S. equivalent
metro cuadrado square meter	= 10.764 square feet
área = 100 metros cuadrados area = 100 square meters	= 0.025 acre
hectárea = 100 áreas hectare = 100 ares	= 2.471 acres

U.S. system **El sistema estadounidense**	Metric equivalent **El equivalente métrico**

yarda cuadrada = 9 pies cuadrados = 0,836 metros cuadrados
square yard = 9 square feet = 0.836 square meters
acre = 4.840 yardas cuadradas = 0,405 hectáreas
acre = 4,840 square yards = 0.405 hectares

Capacidad / Capacity

El sistema métrico Metric system	**El equivalente estadounidense** U.S. equivalent
mililitro = 0,001 litro milliliter = 0.001 liter	= 0.034 ounces
centilitro = 0,01 litro centiliter = 0.01 liter	= 0.34 ounces
decilitro = 0,1 litro deciliter = 0.1 liter	= 3.4 ounces
litro liter	= 1.06 quarts
decalitro = 10 litros dekaliter = 10 liters	= 2.64 gallons
hectolitro = 100 litros hectoliter = 100 liters	= 26.4 gallons
kilolitro = 1.000 litros kiloliter = 1,000 liters	= 264 gallons

U.S. system **El sistema estadounidense**	Metric equivalent **El equivalente métrico**
ounce **onza**	= 29.6 milliliters **= 29,6 mililitros**
cup = 8 ounces **taza = 8 onzas**	= 236 milliliters **= 236 mililitros**
pint = 2 cups **pinta = 2 tazas**	= 0.47 liters **= 0,47 litros**
quart = 2 pints **cuarto = 2 pintas**	= 0.95 liters **= 0,95 litros**
gallon = 4 quarts **galón = 4 cuartos**	= 3.79 liters **= 3,79 litros**

Peso / Weight

El sistema métrico Metric system	**El equivalente estadounidense** U.S. equivalent
miligramo = 0,001 gramo milligram = 0.001 gram	
gramo gram	= 0.035 ounce
decagramo = 10 gramos dekagram = 10 grams	= 0.35 ounces
hectogramo = 100 gramos hectogram = 100 grams	= 3.5 ounces
kilogramo = 1.000 gramos kilogram = 1,000 grams	= 2.2 pounds
tonelada (métrica) = 1.000 kilogramos metric ton = 1,000 kilograms	= 1.1 tons

U.S. system **El sistema estadounidense**	Metric equivalent **El equivalente métrico**
ounce **onza**	= 28.35 grams **= 28,35 gramos**
pound = 16 ounces **libra = 16 onzas**	= 0.45 kilograms **= 0,45 kilogramos**
ton = 2,000 pounds **tonelada = 2.000 libras**	= 0.9 metric tons **= 0,9 toneladas métricas**

Temperatura / Temperature

Grados centígrados Degrees Celsius	**Grados Fahrenheit** Degrees Fahrenheit
To convert from Celsius to Fahrenheit, multiply by $\frac{9}{5}$ and add 32.	To convert from Fahrenheit to Celsius, subtract 32 and multiply by $\frac{5}{9}$.

NÚMEROS / NUMBERS

Números ordinales / Ordinal numbers

Números ordinales		Ordinal numbers	
primer, primero/a	**1º/1ª**	first	1st
segundo/a	**2º/2ª**	second	2nd
tercer, tercero/a	**3º/3ª**	third	3rd
cuarto/a	**4º/4ª**	fourth	4th
quinto/a	**5º/5ª**	fifth	5th
sexto/a	**6º/6ª**	sixth	6th
séptimo/a	**7º/7ª**	seventh	7th
octavo/a	**8º/8ª**	eighth	8th
noveno/a	**9º/9ª**	ninth	9th
décimo/a	**10º/10ª**	tenth	10th

Fracciones / Fractions

Fracciones		Fractions
$\frac{1}{2}$	**un medio, la mitad**	one half
$\frac{1}{3}$	**un tercio**	one third
$\frac{1}{4}$	**un cuarto**	one fourth (quarter)
$\frac{1}{5}$	**un quinto**	one fifth
$\frac{1}{6}$	**un sexto**	one sixth
$\frac{1}{7}$	**un séptimo**	one seventh
$\frac{1}{8}$	**un octavo**	one eighth
$\frac{1}{9}$	**un noveno**	one ninth
$\frac{1}{10}$	**un décimo**	one tenth
$\frac{2}{3}$	**dos tercios**	two thirds
$\frac{3}{4}$	**tres cuartos**	three fourths (quarters)
$\frac{5}{8}$	**cinco octavos**	five eighths

Decimales / Decimals

Decimales		Decimals	
un décimo	**0,1**	one tenth	0.1
un centésimo	**0,01**	one hundredth	0.01
un milésimo	**0,001**	one thousandth	0.001

OCUPACIONES / OCCUPATIONS

OCUPACIONES	OCCUPATIONS
el/la abogado/a	lawyer
el actor, la actriz	actor
el/la administrador(a) de empresas	business administrator
el/la agente de bienes raíces	real estate agent
el/la agente de seguros	insurance agent
el/la agricultor(a)	farmer
el/la arqueólogo/a	archaeologist
el/la arquitecto/a	architect
el/la artesano/a	artisan
el/la auxiliar de vuelo	flight attendant
el/la basurero/a	garbage collector
el/la bibliotecario/a	librarian
el/la bombero/a	firefighter
el/la cajero/a	bank teller, cashier
el/la camionero/a	truck driver
el/la carnicero/a	butcher
el/la carpintero/a	carpenter
el/la científico/a	scientist
el/la cirujano/a	surgeon
el/la cobrador(a)	bill collector
el/la cocinero/a	cook, chef
el/la consejero/a	counselor, advisor
el/la contador(a)	accountant
el/la corredor(a) de bolsa	stockbroker
el/la diplomático/a	diplomat
el/la diseñador(a) (gráfico/a)	(graphic) designer
el/la electricista	electrician
el/la fisioterapeuta	physical therapist
el/la fotógrafo/a	photographer
el hombre/la mujer de negocios	businessperson
el/la ingeniero/a en computación	computer engineer
el/la intérprete	interpreter
el/la juez(a)	judge
el/la maestro/a	elementary school teacher
el/la marinero/a	sailor
el/la obrero/a	manual laborer
el/la optometrista	optometrist
el/la panadero/a	baker
el/la paramédico/a	paramedic
el/la peluquero/a	hairdresser
el/la piloto	pilot
el/la pintor(a)	painter
el/la plomero/a	plumber
el/la político/a	politician
el/la programador(a)	computer programer
el/la psicólogo/a	psychologist
el/la reportero/a	reporter
el/la sastre	tailor
el/la secretario/a	secretary
el/la técnico/a (en computación)	(computer) technician
el/la vendedor(a)	sales representative
el/la veterinario/a	veterinarian

About the Author

José A. Blanco founded Vista Higher Learning in 1998. A native of Barranquilla, Colombia, Mr. Blanco holds degrees in Literature and Hispanic Studies from Brown University and the University of California, Santa Cruz. He has worked as a writer, editor, and translator for Houghton Mifflin and D.C. Heath and Company, and has taught Spanish at the secondary and university levels. Mr. Blanco is also the co-author of several other Vista Higher Learning programs: Vistas, Panorama, Aventuras, and ¡Viva! at the introductory level; Ventanas, Facetas, Enfoques, Imagina, and Sueña at the intermediate level; and Revista at the advanced conversation level.

About the Illustrators

Yayo, an internationally acclaimed illustrator, was born in Colombia. He has illustrated children's books, newspapers, and magazines, and has been exhibited around the world. He currently lives in Montreal, Canada.

Pere Virgili lives and works in Barcelona, Spain. His illustrations have appeared in textbooks, newspapers, and magazines throughout Spain and Europe.

Born in Caracas, Venezuela, **Hermann Mejía** studied illustration at the Instituto de Diseño de Caracas. Hermann currently lives and works in the United States.

Comic Credits

page 54 © Joaquin Salvador Lavado (QUINO) Toda Mafalda - Ediciones de La Flor, 1993.

TV Clip Credits

page 58 Courtesy of Mastercard. WARNER CHAPPELL MUSIC ARGENTINA (SADAIC) All Rights Reserved.
page 96 Courtesy of Cencosud Supermercados.
page 134 Courtesy of Banco Galicia/Mercado McCann.

Photography Credits

Cover: Gary Tognoni/iStockphoto.

Front matter (SE): xii: (l) Bettmann/Getty Images; (r) Florian Biamm/123RF; **xiii:** (l) Lawrence Manning/Corbis; (r) Design Pics Inc/Alamy; **xiv:** Jose Blanco; **xv:** (l) Digital Vision/Getty Images; (r) Andres/Big Stock Photo; **xvi:** Fotolia IV/Fotolia; **xvii:** (l) Goodshoot/Corbis; (r) Tyler Olson/Shutterstock; **xviii:** Shelly Wall/Shutterstock.

Front matter (TE): T4: Teodor Cucu/500PX; **T15:** Asiseeit/iStockphoto; **T27:** Corbis Photography/Veer; (inset) Fancy Photography/Veer; **T48:** Braun S/iStockphoto.

Preliminary Lesson:
1: Brian Pineda/Offset; **2:** (t) Eric Raptosh Photography/Media Bakery; (bl) Paula Diez; (br) Monkey Business/Deposit Photos; **2-3:** GTS/Shutterstock; **6:** (t) Paula Diez; (ml) Paula Diez; (mr) Duel/AGE Fotostock; (bl) Wavebreakmedia/Shutterstock; (br) BST2012/Deposit Photos; **6-7:** Sviat Studio/Shutterstock; **7:** Pixfiction/Shutterstock; **9:** (t) Lev Dolgachov/Alamy; (b) Pixfiction/Shutterstock; **10:** (t) Tomsickova/Fotolia; (m) Martin Bernetti; (bl) Paula Diez; (br) Paula Diez; **10-11:** Milos Vucicevic/Shutterstock; Findeep/Deposit Photos; **12:** (all) Carolina Zapata; **13:** Carolina Zapata; **14:** (l) Media Bakery RF; (r) FatCamera/iStockphoto; **15:** Jeff Malet Photography/Newscom; **16-17:** Jojo Ensslin; (unsure if we will credit him. Please keep in bold); **18:** Deepspacedave/Deposit Photos; Miflippo/Deposit Photos; (t) Bowdenimages/iStockphoto; (m) ImageBroker/AGE Fotostock; (b) Moxie Productions/AGE Fotostock; **18-19:** Logos2012/Deposit Photos; **19:** Hero Images/AGE Fotostock; **20:** (t) Martin Bernetti; (ml) Martin Bernetti; (mr) Jack Frog/Shutterstock; (b) Jose Blanco; Sang Lee/Shutterstock; **20-21:** Dgolbay/Deposit Photos; **22:** Asiseeit/iStockphoto; **23:** (t) Human_306/Deposit Photos; (mtl) Graphicbee/123RF; (mtr) BenchyB/Deposit Photos; (mbl) MadalBK/Shutterstock; (mbr) Natis76/Deposit Photos; (btl) VIPDesignUSA/Deposit Photos; (btr) HappyRoman/Deposit Photos; (bl) Cobalt88/Deposit Photos; (br) Vnstudio/Deposit Photos; **24:** Klaus Vedfelt/Getty Images.

Lesson 1:
25: Paula Díez; **26:** John Henley/Getty Images; **27:** Martín Bernetti; **28:** Paula Díez; **34:** (l) Rachel Distler; (r) Paula Díez; **35:** (t) Hans Georg Roth/Getty Images; (ml) Chris Pizzello/AP Images; (mr) Paola Ríos-Schaaf; **36:** (l) Janet Dracksdorf; (r) Tom Grill/Corbis; **40:** (l) José Girarte/iStockphoto; (r) Blend Images/Alamy; **43:** (l) Buzzshotz/Alamy; (m) Anne Loubet; (r) Shutterstock; **51:** Martín Bernetti; **52:** (all) Martín Bernetti; **55:** (tl) Ana Cabezas Martín; (tml) Martín Bernetti; (tmr) Kadmy/Fotolia; (tr) Vanessa Bertozzi; (bl) Corey Hochachka/Design Pics/Corbis; (bm)Sanek70974/Fotolia; (br) Ramiro Isaza/Fotocolombia; **56:** Carolina Zapata; **57:** Paula Díez; **60:** (t) Robert Holmes/Getty Images; (m) Jon Arnold Images/Alamy; (b) Andres R/Shutterstock; **61:** (t) PhotoLink/Getty Images; (mr) Tony Arruza/Getty Images; (ml) A. Katz/Shutterstock; (b) Torontonian/Alamy.

Lesson 2
63: Pamela Moore/iStockphoto; **66:** Jim Erickson/Media Bakery; **67:** Chris Schmidt/iStockphoto; **72:** (l) Hill Street Studios/AGE Fotostock; (r) David Ashley/Corbis; **73:** Guayo Fuentes/Shutterstock; **81:** Chris Schmidt/iStockphoto; **83:** (l) Paola Rios-Schaaf; (r) Image Source/Corbis; **91:** (l) Rick Gomez/Corbis; (r) Hola Images/Workbook.com; **92:** PigProx/Fotolia; **93:** Andres Benitez/Media Bakery; **94:** (t) Sam Edwards/Media Bakery; (b) Zdyma4/Fotolia; **95:** Kadmy/Fotolia; **98:** (tl) José Blanco; (tr) José Blanco; (m) Jack Q/Shutterstock; (b) Andrew Innerarity/Reuters/Newscom; **99:** (tl) Courtesy of Charles Ommanney; (tr) José Blanco; (ml) José Blanco; (mr) VHL; (b) Iconotec/Fotosearch.

Lesson 3
101: Paul Bradbury/AGE Fotostock; **103:** Martín Bernetti; **104:** (tl) Anne Loubet; (tr) Blend Images/Alamy; (mtl) Ana Cabezas Martín; (mtr) Maskot/Media Bakery; (mbl) Martín Bernetti; (mbr) Martín Bernetti; (bl) Himchenko/Fotolia; (br) Martín Bernetti; **110:** (tl) Minerva Studio/Fotolia; (tr) Mangostock/Shutterstock; (b) John Roman Images/Shutterstock; **111:** (t) Robin Utrecht/Sipa Press/Newscom; (b) DPA Picture Alliance/Alamy; **114:** (l) Martín Bernetti; (r) José Blanco; **116:** Andres Rodriguez/Alamy; **119:** Monkey Business Images/Shutterstock; **121:** (l) Tyler Olson/Fotolia; (r) Michael Puche/Bigstock; **122:** Martín Bernetti; **127:** Fotoluminate/123RF; **130:** (all) Martín Bernetti; **131:** (t) Nora y Susana/Fotocolombia; (m) Monkey Business Images/Fotolia; (b) Martín Bernetti; **132:** Tom & Dee Ann McCarthy/Getty Images; **133:** AGE Fotostock RF; **136:** (t) Martín Bernetti; (ml) Martín Bernetti; (mm) Iván Mejía; (mr) Lauren Krolick; (b) Martín Bernetti; **137:** (tl) Martín Bernetti; (tr) Pablo Corral V/Getty Images; (m) Martín Bernetti; (bl) Martín Bernetti; (br) Gerardo Mora.

O

P

Q

R

S

T

V

W